SALTLEY FIRING DAYS

Volume 2

SALTLEY FIRING DAYS

Volume 2
Through the Links, 1952-59

Terry Essery

· RAILWAY HERITAGE ·
from
The NOSTALGIA Collection

ACKNOWLEDGEMENTS

Most literary efforts are not usually brought to a happy conclusion solely by the author - others are also involved, and so it is in this instance.

First I would like to thank my brother Bob whose idea it was to set down these chronicles and who was able to supply a wealth of detail and photographs from his vast library. Much appreciated too were unique photographs kindly provided by Messrs T. J. Edgington, P. Webb, J. A. G. H. Coltas, F. W. Shuttleworth and B. Jeuda.

Of course it would not have appeared at all had it not been for the marathon typing sessions of my wife Hazel, who not only learned how to decipher my hieroglyphics, but never even complained (well not much, anyway) when she permanently 'lost' her dining room.

A Silver Link book
from
The NOSTALGIA *Collection*

© Terry Essery 1980, 1994 and 2002

All rights reserved. No part of this publication may be reproduced, stored in a retrieval system or transmitted, in any form or by any means, electronic, mechanical, photocopying, recording or otherwise, without prior permission in writing from Silver Link Publishing Ltd.

First published in two volumes as *Firing Days at Saltley* and *More Firing Days at Saltley* by D. Bradford Barton Ltd in 1980
New single-volume edition, revised, enlarged and re-illustrated, first published by Silver Link Publishing Ltd in 1994
New two-volume edition first published 2002

All illustrations are by R. J. Essery or from the R. J. Essery collection unless otherwise credited.

British Library Cataloguing in Publication Data

A catalogue record for this book is available from the British Library

ISBN 1 85794 209 4

Silver Link Publishing Ltd
The Trundle
Ringstead Road
Great Addington
Kettering
Northants NN14 4BW

Tel/Fax: 01536 330588
email: sales@nostalgiacollection.com
Website: www.nostalgiacollection.com

Printed and bound in Great Britain

CONTENTS

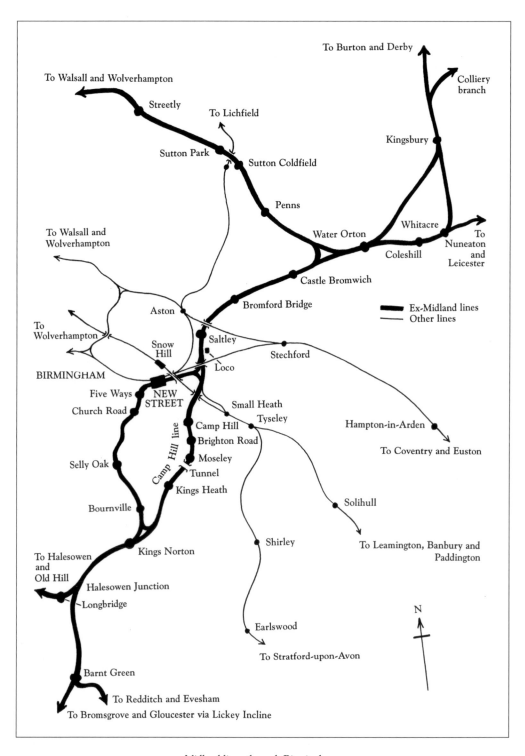

Midland lines through Birmingham

INTRODUCTION

At the close of Volume 1 I was rostered in the Control link at Saltley, and was feeling uncertain and unsettled about my future. The Control link formed the only pool from which firemen could be readily drawn to cover any unforeseen emergency, and I therefore found myself with several different drivers on as many different jobs in the course of a single week. While this had the advantage of broadening my experience at a faster pace than normal, it also meant that I never had time to get to know the ways of my driver or the job concerned. On many occasions I was literally groping in the dark without sufficient general knowledge and skill to execute my work as competently as I would have desired.

The manpower shortage naturally caused an excessive amount of overtime to be worked, and it was not unusual to relieve a westbound train at Water Orton or Castle Bromwich, and be relieved 12 hours later still without having reached Washwood Heath.

As the autumn nights lengthened, life developed into a humdrum seven-day week of bed and work with often precious little of the former, and many weeks passed when I rarely saw the light of day. All this activity tended to produce fatigue and a dulling of the intellect in both drivers and fireman alike, so that when standing on a bleak and exposed section of track for interminable hours conversation lapsed, and the ability to snatch a quick 40 winks took top priority. Not that this was always possible, for with the exception of Class '3F' and '4F' 0-6-0s, most engines were not built for relaxation and, in any case, being soaked and frozen on one side while at the same time being roasted on the other is not exactly conducive to sleep.

Looking back on that winter of 1951-52, it would be fair to say that it was the least happy and exciting period of my railway career. Based on the philosophy that the human brain endeavours to forget unpleasant experiences, it must have been so, for I remember less clearly the details of the individual workings of the latter half of my stay in the Control link than any other time. However, a marathon turn, again with Doug Pinkerton, who was never one to shy at overtime, stands out in my mind.

One December night we worked a 'Maltese' (at least four fitted vehicles next to the engine) to Derby North. This in itself was a pleasant change from local relief work, but we had been badly delayed during the journey and had already completed seven hours by the time we relieved a Class B freight bound for Washwood Heath at Derby North cabin. Our trip home was the usual stop-and-go ritual until we were turned in at Elford, roughly halfway between Burton and our destination, in the early hours of the morning. Here we remained for no less than six hours without moving a wheel, and standing at that exposed spot, wrong way to the weather on a freezing night, was an agony best forgotten. When eventually we did get the road we had been on duty over 15 hours, and the need for food and drink, both of which had long since run out, was getting more than somewhat pressing.

Even then a clear path was not yet available and another two hours or more had elapsed by the time we were finally relieved at Washwood Heath Junction. Feeling a little

the worse for wear, we walked to the shed and booked off exactly 19 hours after signing on, which was for me to stand as an all-time record.

With the coming of spring our spirits lifted, and I found myself looking forward once again to the prospect of being able to work the numerous passenger specials that I now felt more competent to handle. After all, I had another year's experience and physical development behind me, and it was logical to assume that this time I would get a rather thicker slice of the cake. Furthermore, it was now eight months since I had registered for National Service and, not having heard anything since, I was beginning to believe that they had forgotten all about me. The uncertainty of the past had consequently receded and I was fervently hoping to be booked with a driver who, like Doug Pinkerton, had a very extensive road card.

Alas, it was not to be, for when the May changeover lists were posted I found to my intense surprise that I had been promoted, not to another mate in the Control link or even to the next link, the Specials, but right up into the Trip link with driver J. Greatrex.

1
THE TRIP LINK

After the variations, the long hours, the uncertainties and general hurly-burly of the Control link, I unexpectedly found myself in the relatively well-ordered tranquillity of the Trip link in the company of an equally well-ordered and tranquil mate.

It was around this time I noted one of Nature's unexplained mysteries. Over the age of about 45, drivers tended to follow one of two courses with regard to their physical appearance. Either they seemed hell-bent on adopting the rotund hogshead model, or they took on the aspect of something resembling a bean pole. My new mate Jack Greatrex fell into this latter, generally longer-living, category. Jack, although only four years from retirement, was still blessed with finely chiselled features and undoubtedly must have been quite good-looking in his younger days. His temperament and demeanour was calm and quiet, but belonging as he did to the older school of ex-LNWR drivers, was set in his ways and quite a disciplinarian.

We first met in the lobby at 5.00 am on Monday morning prior to booking on for 28 Trip, a Bordesley job for which we prepared our own '8F' before setting out for the day's work. I soon discovered that everything had to be exactly right in every meticulous detail, and if only working a local tripper he would not take the engine off the shed if it showed the slightest defect. Had he been preparing a Carlisle, he could not have been more thorough. This, of course, meant that I too had to work to his high standard, which was, I must admit, a welcome change to the often slack attitudes found in the common working of my previous link.

For example, he insisted that the sanding gear was topped up and tested and that I spread a quantity of limestone over the grate before building up the fire. Furthermore, both injectors had to be proved satisfactory before moving on to the table, and although we would not be going within miles of the nearest water troughs, I had to operate the scoop while he inspected its action from beneath the tender. From the appearance of his somewhat faded but nevertheless well-pressed and immaculate overalls, I might have guessed that he was a stickler for cleanliness, so it was no surprise to find that all traces of coal and dirt had to be quickly banished from the footplate. Moreover, the tender had to be properly trimmed and the dust therein well and truly laid by a generous application of the slaking pipe, for he expected to finish up the week with overalls very little dirtier than when he started. However, since this fitted in very nicely with my own ideas on how a footplate should be kept, it proved no hardship, and in this respect we got on extremely well from the word go.

Bearing these aspects of his character in mind, it was therefore not unusual for us to book off the shed late, and on this first Monday we were something like 20 minutes awry when we finally departed. This delay was brought about by the need to obtain the services of a fitter and mate in order to attend to the sanding gear and a slight blow on the small ejector. When everything was in apple-pie order and we were trundling sedately, tender-first, along the up goods line heading for Washwood Heath Junction, I thought it was about time I got to know something about the job, and I questioned Jack accordingly.

'I've never worked a Bordesley tripper properly,' I said openly, since I wished to make this point quite clear. 'Just relieved one or two and brought the engine to the shed. What exactly do we do?'

'Oh, it's very straightforward,' replied Jack in his quiet, precise manner. 'We pick up a train at the junction or sometimes the West End, and work it into Bordesley. Then we shunt it as required, run over to the down sidings, collect another train from there and work it back over Hill 60, and then start all over again. Nothing much to it, really, but it involves a lot of waiting around, particularly in Bordesley, where we have to have a good clear path before crossing their main lines. The Great Western get very upset if we stop one of their expresses and, of course, we cut right across their up and down fast and slow lines when drawing out of the down sidings.'

I was able to picture the scene fairly clearly in my mind's eye, for I had studied this expanse of tracks at Bordesley hundreds of times when crossing over them on the Bank Pilots.

At Washwood Heath No 1 signal box we whistled three short, two short for the junction and continued to clank easily down past the hump of Hill 60 to the left. Stopping at the ground signal just beyond the junction box we waited some minutes for a path, and I took the opportunity to ask Jack about the other jobs in the link. It seemed that we worked as far as Kingsbury to the north, to Rubery up the Halesowen branch in the west, and to Aldridge over the Walsall line, while at the same time covering most places on Midland metals enclosed in this triangle.

Not having yet visited any of the venues mentioned I was about to question him further when the signal dropped and we hastily crossed over to the down sidings. Here, under the guidance of a shunter, we backed on our train and waited for the appearance of our guard. Jack, meanwhile, instructed me to position our headlamps for trip working, which was one lamp over the left buffer, and having done this I packed some coal under the firedoors and into the back corners. When

ignorant of a job's routine, it was always difficult to achieve the fine balance of just carrying the correct amount of fire; only experience could teach one that.

Shortly afterwards, Dennis, our guard, climbed somewhat laboriously on to the footplate in response to Jack's invitation to partake of a quick cup of tea. Holding the lid in one hand, he consulted a scrap of cardboard torn from a cigarette packet (guards, I found, universally seemed to prefer such pieces of cardboard to notebooks) and advised us that we had 48 wagons equal to 56 of mineral.

To clarify this remark, I should explain that for loading purposes a mineral wagon was calculated at 13 tons, but when a number of 16-ton wagons were in a train their extra weight had to be taken into consideration. In this instance we had 34 of the latter, which meant that another 104 tons was being carried. Dividing 104 by 13 gives the equivalent additional number of 13-ton wagons, which in this case was eight; therefore, although we only had 48 wagons behind the tender, they were equal in weight to 56 13-ton mineral wagons.

Having advised the yard staff that we were ready, Dennis duly returned to his brake-van, but a further 15 minutes elapsed before we were allowed to proceed. With a load of over 900 tons behind the tender we filtered out on to the down goods line and chugged sedately up the 1 in 326 gradient towards the West End. Being now somewhat familiar with the capabilities of an '8F', I decided to fire her lightly until we reached Duddeston Road. At this time I was just developing the technique of firing from the right-hand side of the footplate and, like most right-handed people, I found the action awkward and unnatural, but since all modern engines were built to be driven from the left-hand side I felt I must practice as much as possible until fully competent. Fortunately there is room on an '8F' to fire from either side, so initially I tended to ring the changes, using the driver's side to reach the front end only.

Passing the pilot sidings I had the pleasure of advising my old mate Bill that we required his assistance to Bordesley and that I thought his boiler front needed some attention, which

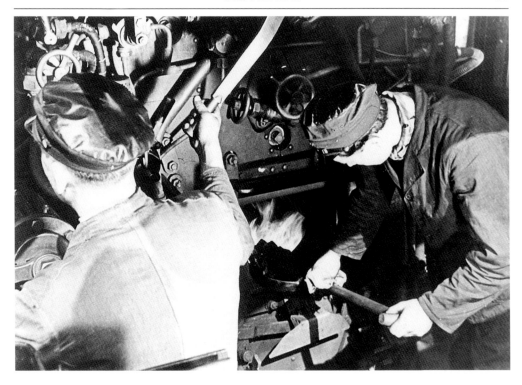

Above Although there was room to fire from either side in the roomy Stanier cabs, as depicted by this crew on an '8F', it was more convenient for the fireman to work from the right as shown. However, on long runs or during periods of prolonged heavy firing it was sometimes expedient to alternate sides in order to balance muscle fatigue.

Below This shows what a fireman should not do, coal spillage on the footboards forcing him to stand far to the left posterior-wise against the driver, while the anti-glare shield obstructs his swing.

needless to say brought forth a not unexpected rude gesture.

A long wait at Duddeston Road enabled Jack and me to relate some of our respective background history to one another, while at the same time it caused the usual difficulty of trying to strike the balance of keeping the fire reasonably lively without excessive blowing off. Fortunately, the thermal reserve of the full boiler of an '8F' was of great help, since one could virtually cover the run to Bordesley without resorting to use of the injectors, but it was on these jobs that I learned to leave a hole in the middle of the grate. By so doing the fire could be kept burning reasonably brightly with the back damper open a couple of notches, while the air entering via the hole prevented the firebox temperature from reaching too high a level.

When eventually we received the 'right away', all I had to do was dig the firing shovel blade into the live fire under the door and shoot it down into the hole, when normal firing could then be commenced immediately. This was the technique I used now, so that by the time Jack had finished calling attention to the fact that the signals were off by means of the whistle, I had already filled in the hole, had the firedoors closed and both rear damper and blower wide open.

Getting our heavy train moving from a dead standstill on the 1 in 105 gradient required full first regulator and maximum cut-off, but as Bill also opened up and our speed increased Jack was able to wind her up by degrees to around 55 per cent. Even so, this was making a pretty impressive volume of sound as we approached Brickyard Crossing, but despite the acceleration we had achieved at this point, our speed rapidly fell away as the gradient stiffened to 1 in 62. It was not Jack's nature to rely too heavily on the pilot and he quickly dropped her down to full gear once again for the stretch up to the Coventry Road overbridge. Just beyond we crossed over the facing points taking us on to the Great Western and, by the time we passed Bordesley Junction signal box, Jack had eased down to just a breath of steam.

'We have to be careful here,' he explained. 'From climbing at 1 in 85 it suddenly dips down to the stop signal at the entrance to the GW yard. If you come over too fast the train can push you past the signal and through the catch points.'

I soon realised what he meant, because Jack had to make two pretty hefty applications of the brake even though we were only travelling at a walking pace before we eventually shuddered to a halt at the signal. Some 10 yards beyond this lay the catch points he had referred to, and since the ground here bore no trace of weeds, I gathered that someone had been the victim of an embarrassing experience not too long ago.

We waited at the signal for some 20 minutes before the GW was ready for us. Bordesley is not a very salubrious part of Birmingham and although we had a fairly commanding view from the top of a 30-foot-high embankment there was little of interest to see, so we soon found ourselves talking shop. I quickly concluded that Jack was gently probing my knowledge of railway working, my understanding of engines and whether I was really interested in the job, without making it too obvious. Having once established that I was keen to learn more he adopted the role of tutor, and from then onwards for the duration of my stay with him we had at least one lesson per day on some aspect of railway life. This might take the form of a question-and-answer session about the function of locomotives or detailed explanations of the rules and regulations and why they were necessary.

Jack also supported the theory that firing was, or should be, a highly skilled art, and, like many other forms of physical endeavour, expertise more than made up for sheer brute strength. While he was no longer capable of practical demonstrations calling for great effort, his counsel was always much appreciated. However, I did consider his rather scornful regard of ex-Midland firemen a little unfair because I found good and bad firemen from all the pre-Grouping companies, but his attitude was quite typical of many ex-LNWR men who felt that even a navvy could fire the old Midland engines.

Our interesting conversation was abruptly terminated by a shrill blast on the GW head shunter's whistle calling attention to the fact that the signal was now off. We ran slowly into a lengthy siding, where for the next 20 minutes we were required to do some energetic shunting. Despite its bulk, an '8F' proved ideal for shunting a heavy train, for it had the power to accelerate smartly and, equally important, adequate weight and brake power to stop again. The only drawback was that it took a fair while and a lot of strenuous winding to move the reversing screw from full forward to full backward gear. Jack, never a hunky chap and now past his prime, was obviously happy when this unwelcomed exercise finally came to a conclusion.

Another period of waiting followed before a path was available for us to cross over to the down sidings, and I took this opportunity to observe the Western engines and their methods. Loyal as I was to the Midland Division, I had to admit that their locomotives in general were much better turned out than ours, while some of the 'Castles' and 'Kings' that roared by on the London expresses looked nothing short of magnificent in their gleaming Brunswick Green paintwork and polished copper and brass trimmings. Even the numerous Pannier tanks were impressively efficient as they went smartly about their shunting duties, while all around it was very apparent that the staff still considered themselves to be GWR men and a cut above the other divisions of British Railways.

Just before our signal dropped, I noticed one of our Saltley '8Fs', hauling a moderate coal train, come off the Bordesley Junction branch and without stopping head out on to the up slow line, where it accelerated with tremendous vigour in the direction of Small Heath. Puzzled by the sight of a Saltley engine working on the Western, I asked Jack what it was doing.

'Oh, that's the Long Marston,' he replied. 'One of the Group One jobs. They work a coal train up to Long Marston, which is the other side of Stratford-upon-Avon, then return with a load of empties. It must have been Percy Trotter. He's the only one in the link who works an engine like that.'

The name somehow rang a bell, then I remembered a very rough ride in a brake-van back from Water Orton one night when I had been working there on the shunter. When in the brake-van I had not appreciated his lack of finesse, but at least as a spectator I was forced to admire the determined way he handled that mineral.

Having run briskly across to the down sidings, we once more indulged in a period of shunting to make up our train, and when this was completed we settled down to wait for another path. I recalled what Bill had told me in the Bank Pilots about Bordesleys and it was undoubtedly true that, from the fireman's point of view, they were certainly not the most strenuous jobs at Saltley. As far as I could see the main object to aim for was to keep the fire as thin as possible and thereby use the minimum amount of fuel. This would then reduce the necessity to clean the fire and get coal forward during the 24 hours the engine was in service. A dozen shovelsful spread evenly round the box sufficed for the quick gallop back to Bordesley Junction, and thereafter it was merely a case of coasting down the bank to Hill 60. Here we followed the regular procedure of pushing the preceding train over the hump, and when this was done we shunted across the road to Washwood Heath Junction and started all over again.

On average about two round trips would be accomplished in an eight-hour shift but, as always, this could vary according to prevailing conditions. The main interest on these turns was the time available for discussion, and with a knowledgeable mate much could be learned.

Although the routine followed a general pattern, boredom was kept at bay by day-to-day variations, one of the welcome bonuses of railway work, and a new experience always seemed to turn up to add to one's store of knowledge. On the Thursday this took the form of sticking at St Andrews, an event that I had witnessed many times from the rear end when on the pilots but never from the train engine. After a prolonged dry spell, steady drizzle had made the rails very slippery indeed, and we unfortunately had an '8F' that was long overdue for a major shopping. She knocked and rattled in a most disconcerting manner even at low speed, and it was soon apparent that the wheels were badly in need of new tyres.

On arrival at Washwood Heath Junction we found that Dennis, our regular guard, had not turned up, and that his replacement was a pleasant young Pakistani whose lack of experience was only matched by his peerless enthusiasm. We later learned that he had not quite got the hang of what loading tables were all about, and he felt that it was his patriotic duty to couple just about everything in the siding to our tender hook. Under normal circumstances our all-up load would have been limited to manageable proportions by the number of vehicles we were allowed to take, but marshalled now to the rear end of our 50 mineral wagons were two special 'Weltags' carrying a couple of outsize steel ingots. These massive octagonal hunks of metal weighed over 80 tons each, but in his innocence our guard had regarded them as just two more mineral wagons. We therefore set out with a train equivalent to over 70 of mineral, a fact soon made apparent by the way we slipped and slithered up to the West End. Jack had to use a fair amount of regulator and full gear to move us up the 1 in 326 gradient and, because of the slipping, he was forced to use the sanding gear almost continuously.

'I'm sure our coloured friend has forgotten to take his brake off,' Jack muttered quietly in a puzzled way as he juggled with the regulator in an effort to keep us in motion. As far as we were concerned we only had 52 wagons in tow, but it felt as if we were still attached to the stop block.

Collecting our pilot en route we ultimately arrived at Duddeston Road, where during the usual wait I hunted around for a suitable bolt to insert between the upper edge of the baffle plate and the firehole mouth. Smoke baffles did not always fit too well and tended to drop down at the forward end, which in turn obstructed the free flight of coal from the shovel blade to the front of the grate. On the short steeply sloping grates of '3Fs' and '4Fs' this did not cause too much trouble, but on the longer, flatter grates of 'Black Fives', '8Fs', 'Crabs', etc, coal could be deflected downwards to form a ridge or hump halfway along the box. By reducing the gap between firebed and baffle, this ridge only compounded the problem until eventually the front end of the grate was starved of fuel. Therefore to correct this downward droop it was common practice to use a bolt or bolts of about half-inch diameter to act as a wedge, although care had to be taken of course so as not to foul the action of the firedoors, preventing their closure. Jack was the first driver to detail the importance of a sound and well fitting baffle, and in future I made it a matter of habit to never go off the shed with an unsatisfactory one. Many were so badly burned that they extended only a matter of inches inside the firebox, which because of incomplete combustion then produced a lot of smoke and inferior steaming.

Although somewhat out of context, it may be of interest to add that Bristol and Gloucester firemen often removed the baffles so as to get more coal into the firebox. They built fires up to a staggering amount, rising sometimes from the top of the firehole half way to the crown plate and burying the brick arch. So vast were these fires that I have relieved a through freight at Landor Street and worked it to Burton on Trent, doing no more than levelling the bed and filling the odd hole as it formed.

Having adjusted the baffle to my satisfaction, I built up the fire rather more than usual for a Bordesley, anticipating that we were going to have a struggle. Jack then climbed down and checked that the sanding gear was still functioning correctly by the time-honoured method of holding the back of his hand in front of the delivery pipe while I operated the valve.

At last our signal came off and Jack, having first given a prolonged 'crow' on the whistle, opened both sand valve and regulator. We eased slowly forward, gradually gathering speed, but any attempt at vigorous acceleration resulted in a slip, and Jack had to coax her along very gently indeed. The distants were off for St Andrews, but despite all his expertise with the regulator it was pretty obvious by the time we had passed Landor Street box that we were not going to build up sufficient momentum to stand even half a chance of getting up the bank.

'We're not going to make it,' observed Jack resignedly as we thumped slowly past Brickyard Crossing.

Having come to the same conclusion some little while ago, I had left the firedoors wide open so as to allow the steam pressure to fall back, for we had more than we could use and I wanted to avoid blowing off as much as possible. She would not keep her feet even on full first valve, and now that we were on the 1 in 62 section what speed we had rapidly fell away. It was frustrating not being able to transmit the power available to the drawbar, but with such poor adhesion we had no other choice, and after a final violent slip we came to a standstill some 50 yards short of St Andrews signal box.

'I'm sure we've got a dickens of a lot more on than 50,' said Jack, as I screwed the tender brake on as hard as possible. 'We should have come up better than that even though we were slipping,' he continued. I had not sufficient experience at that time to comment on the matter, but from my observations in the pilots we should have managed 30 wagons or so ourselves if the pilot was fully extended. After some 10 minutes we saw a column of black smoke move up behind the feather of white steam coming from our pilot's safety valves, and seconds later clearly heard the shrill, distinctive 'crow' whistle indicating that both were ready.

I quickly released the hand brake while Jack hooted our reply, then, after letting our engine roll back half a turn, he heaved open the regulator to the full first valve. There was a volcanic eruption from the chimney, the cab rattled and shook, and the wheels churned showers of sparks from the rails, but we did not move forward a single inch. Jack tried again as I leaned out of my window in an effort to see what the bankers were up to, but twin pillars of smoke and steam left no doubt that they were trying as hard as we were, and slipping just as badly. Jack made several attempts, but it was of no avail - the train might just as well have been welded to the track.

'I'm going to have a word with the bobby to see what's to be done,' said Jack, climbing down the steps after the final abortive effort.

Things must be bad if we can't get moving with two bankers, I thought. Having little to do but wait, I decided to see if I could improve our traction by the old method of applying grit to the rails. Leaving the steam brake on as a precaution, I descended shovel in hand to the ground and foraged around for some suitable material. I soon found what I was looking for in the form of a dark grey gravel lying at the side of the track. Although much coarser than sand, the chips were small enough for the purpose in mind and would crush under the wheels to form an abrasive layer. Scooping up a shovelful I quickly ran a trail along the surfaces of both rails for a distance of some 50 yards in front of our engine, and I had just completed this operation when Jack returned from the box.

'They're running a train up behind the bankers,' he said, 'which will then give us a nudge to get us started. Once on the move we should be OK with two pilots.'

I must admit that I had not seen this manoeuvre done before, but it seemed sound reasoning and would cause less delay than employing a third banking engine.

Once again the 'crow' whistle could be clearly heard from the rear and once again Jack heaved open the regulator. This time we moved forwards, did half a slip, then moved forwards again. After a couple of laboured revolutions Jack, taking heart from our new-found adhesion, pushed the regulator up to the horizontal and lo and behold we staggered on, gaining speed at every beat. My treatment of the rail surfaces proved very effective, for Jack was able to use both full gear and regulator until we were well and truly under way. Our exhaust crashed out in a deep-throated explosive roar that was absolutely deafening as I leaned out and regarded this unusual spectacle of an '8F' heading 50 wagons banked by two pilots, which were being pushed in turn by a '4F' hauling a train of some further 40 wagons assisted by yet another pilot.

Once off the gritted section we started to slip again, but our speed had built up sufficiently to enable Jack to come back to the first valve, which, with both pilots fully extended, enabled us to claw our way slowly up to Bordesley Junction. Jack took it very steadily indeed on entering the branch, but even so it required the combined efforts of the sanders and a bit of reverse gear to stop at the signal. It was only after we had shunted out the train that the true reason for our difficulties came to light, and needless to say our guard was given a lengthy and pointed lecture on the subject of loadings.

The Bordesleys, therefore, had their moments of excitement, but in the main they were leisurely, mundane affairs involving more talking than shovelling.

The following week I found myself working on the Kingsbury branch, a place I had never been to before but, like all new jobs, it proved quite interesting. The line served the North Warwickshire collieries of Wood End and Baddesley and, in addition to being steeply graded, it was not in the best of condition. Spice was added to this by the fact that one of the local drivers had recently run away down the bank with a loaded coal train. With commendable devotion to duty he had ordered his mate to bale out while, remaining

alone at the controls, he had managed to attract the signalman's attention with his frantic whistling. The runaway train was then duly turned into an empty siding where it would do least harm, but even so it ploughed into the stop block at a good rate of knots, reducing many of the wagons to matchwood.

With this rather daunting prospect in mind I keenly observed every section as we hauled our train of empties up to Baddesley with '4F' No 3912. The job itself was straightforward enough, involving a spot of shunting at Kingsbury sidings before departing with the empty wagons for the colliery. We worked tender-first up the bank to Baddesley, and this I found was a new experience, for I could not recall having worked a train in reverse up an incline before. Somehow the engine did not seem to steam quite as well, although no doubt this was mainly psychological, since the water level always showed a pessimistic reading and one could not afford to mortgage the boiler so much should the need arise.

No 3912, one of Saltley's old faithful Midland '4F' 0-6-0s, which took me on my first visit to the precipitous Kingsbury colliery branch, some 11 miles to the north of Saltley during 1952. The Trip link provided opportunities to learn some of the more remote backwaters around Birmingham rarely visited in other links. Behind No 3912 can be seen the skeleton of No 3 shed's roof, the result of wartime damage. Although No 1 shed's roof was replaced by a modern concrete structure, No 3 remained open to the elements.

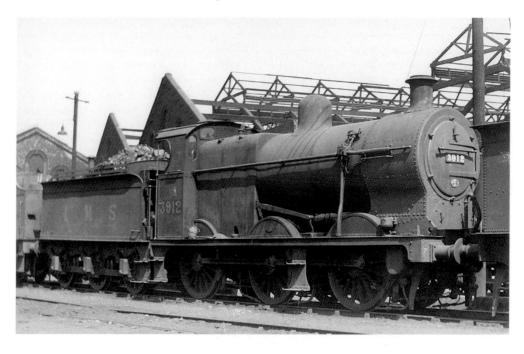

At Baddesley we indulged in some more shunting in order to make up our coal train, which was destined for Washwood Heath Junction. However, before descending the bank we had to have a certain proportion of the wagon brakes pinned down in much the same manner as was practised at the top of the Lickey Incline, and whether one kept the train successfully under control depended largely on the guard's skill in assessing this requirement accurately.

My speculations of a hair-raising run were quickly dashed, for Jack had to literally drag the train fully on to the incline before being able to shut off, then the hand brake alone was practically sufficient to keep us in check until we arrived at Kingsbury once again. Our journey to Washwood Heath was via the slow line that took in Whitacre and Coleshill, and I welcomed the opportunity to familiarise myself with this section, for there is no better way to learn a route than from the footplate of a coal train.

It was also just a sufficiently long trip to get to know the ways of a Class '4F' and experiment with firing techniques without the possibility of inviting too much trouble. I found in due course that they were basically similar to Class '3s' and responded in a more leisurely way to approximately the same treatment, but being superheated they always worked more efficiently when the elements had well and truly warmed up. This warming-up period of course took a certain amount of time, and if serious work was to be contemplated it paid to anticipate the event as much as possible and keep the fire bright, even at the expense of wasting steam through the safety valves.

Two weeks later I was introduced to another series of places I had never been to before. These were along the Walsall line from Castle Bromwich, and in summer it proved to be a delightfully pleasant run, since the route involved journeying through the very picturesque Sutton Park, where dense woods contrasted favourably with Birmingham's industrial areas.

At Castle Bromwich the track curves in a long sweep to the left on a low embankment where an excellent view could be had of the airfield on one side and the sludge treatment works on the other. At Park Lane signal box the line merged with the one leading down into Water Orton sidings, forming a triangle that was useful when an engine required to be turned. From Park Lane the line climbed at 1 in 157 over a bridge at Kingsbury Road, through Walmley and past Wylde Green golf course up to Sutton Coldfield, where a small goods yard lay on the down side surrounded by trees - a very pleasant spot in which to spend a leisurely half hour knocking out and picking up the odd wagon or two.

From the goods yard the climb continued up through the woods of Sutton Park, where holidaymakers could be seen enjoying themselves boating on the well-known Bracebridge Pool. Just beyond the park was Streetly station and, after passing Roundabout Wood, the line crossed the Chester road on a high embankment before proceeding up to Aldridge sidings, the summit of the bank.

Our trip terminated at this point, and after more shunting we returned to Water Orton with usually a light train of freight, bound for northern parts. As might be imagined, the work was not very exacting and made no undue demands from either side of the footplate, but in keeping with the majority of Trip link jobs it afforded the opportunity to get to know thoroughly all aspects of railway operations over that section.

After a further interlude of local work including another Bordesley, we were booked on the Rubery trip, our farthest journey west, and again this was interesting for me since it entailed breaking fresh ground once more. Following the general pattern of most trip jobs, loadings were not excessively heavy nor timings severe, for after climbing the bank to Kings Heath we acted as a pick-up until reaching Longbridge. Here was the site of the well-known Austin Motor Works, and the Halesowen branch made its way between the massive blocks of that extensive plant. The Austin works had its own sidings and, for that matter, its own motive power in the form of powerful 0-6-0 saddle tanks, painted in a distinctive bright green livery and invariably immaculately turned out. As may be imagined, a plant the size of Austin's daily

On a fine summer's day a pleasant hour or so could be spent leisurely shunting the yard and picking up an odd wagon from the goods shed in the tranquil surrounds of Sutton Park. In the Trip link most things were done at a leisurely pace whenever possible, which well suited the temperaments of the drivers, nearly all of whom were close to retirement. The generous platforms at Sutton were originally built to handle large numbers of visitors who came to the park by rail in bygone days. Beyond the goods shed on the left the tracks can be seen climbing beneath a distant road bridge, then up through the Park itself towards Streetly.

required a great deal of material and also facilities for removing the unending flow from the assembly lines; the sidings were, therefore, very busy indeed.

On arrival, we quickly shunted out our train and, while this was in progress, I was able to take note of the intense activity all around. Longbridge sidings were really in two parts, the section nearest to the junction being devoted exclusively to works traffic, while 200 yards further along the line towards Rubery were some more tracks laid to serve the locality in general, in addition to Austin's overspill. Here also were the twin station platforms over which tramped the feet of countless workers brought in from not only the city but also the dormitory towns lying to the west.

Having done our duty at Longbridge, we proceeded the half-mile or so up a 1 in 96 gradient to Rubery, where after a further shunting session we took our lunch before returning to Lawley Street, picking up at intermediate sidings as required. It was an

exceedingly pleasant little job, and terminating opposite the loco we were usually well placed for booking off at approximately the same time every day.

On Thursday a short-lived but nevertheless intense little heatwave had got well under way, and by the time we had completed our activities at Rubery and were settled to partake of our lunch, the early afternoon heat was oppressive. In fact, the trace of breeze that existed tended to draw heat from the boiler on to us so that conditions on the footplate were rendered almost unbearable.

Beyond the boundary fence, lush green meadows surrounded by shady trees looked more than a little inviting, so I decided to take my sandwiches and seek out a cooler spot. On the understanding that Jack would toot the whistle 5 minutes before we were due to depart, I took my leave. Finding an ancient and dilapidated stile I heaved my perspiring form over it and with a bottle of orange juice clutched in one hand and my sandwiches in the other, I headed through knee-high grass

Halesowen Junction was located 10 miles west of Saltley on the main line to Bristol. Here the Halesowen branch led off to the right, passing en route through the extensive Austin Motor Works at Longbridge. Austin had their own sidings and stud of locomotives, since in 1952 much of the materials consumed were still moved by rail. Workers' trains brought multitudes of workers from Birmingham and the Black Country direct to Longbridge station, which lay in the heart of the complex, and here Austin Motor Co No 5 is seen passing through the station with a rake of vans.

towards a fine specimen of a horse chestnut tree some 50 yards away. Relaxing on a bank of soft grass under its cool and ample shade I contently disposed of my lunch while reflecting on what a great life railway work could be.

On the far side of this green sea of meadow so brightly splashed with the yellows of buttercups and daisies was a herd of some 20 Friesians, their black and white bodies shimmering in the strong sunlight. As is the habit of bovine creatures, they were slowly moving en masse towards me, idly grazing as they came. Now, I've always been passionately fond of most of God's creation, from spiders to hippopotami, and possibly because of this I have frequently managed to hit up a pretty good relationship after only a brief acquaintance. Watching these gentle animals approach recalled an article I had read some two weeks before in a popular nature magazine by one Letitia Spode.

This dear lady had described in detail how she had held long conversations with horses and cows, and that she had first gained their confidence and friendship by gently blowing up their nostrils. Miss Spode pointed out that these creatures always greeted each other and became acquainted in such a manner, and if one was to make any progress at all an exchange of breath was absolutely essential before any conversation could commence. I must admit that at the time I thought she must have, if not exactly loose, a screw or two that were only just finger tight. However, I've

always been one to try anything new and felt that here was the ideal opportunity to put the Spode theory to a practical test.

The herd was now only 30 yards away and would probably have passed me by without a second thought, but I slowly sat upright and gave what I considered to be a very passable imitation of a virile young bull. As one, they stopped dead in their tracks and turned their heads towards me in that half sideways attitude peculiar to cattle. I mooed again, encouraged by the effect of my first effort. After cats, cows must surely rate a close second for their sheer curiosity, and these were no exception, for they all started ambling towards me with their necks outstretched, sniffing the air in order to catch my scent.

The largest animal, who was undoubtedly their leader, walked a few paces ahead of the rest. I rose slowly to my feet, giving at the same time another gentle moo. She stopped a yard away, thrusting her nose in the general direction of my face. Throwing caution to the wind, I leaned forwards and snorted into her dilated nostrils. She immediately responded and huffed right back at me. We repeated this performance some half a dozen times, and whether it was the smell of my recently eaten sandwiches or my own personal aroma that did the trick I do not know, but she suddenly gave a loud moo of what seemed to be approval and promptly nuzzled my chest, nearly knocking me over.

The ice was broken and, reaching down, I plucked a good handful of grass, offering it to her for appraisal. She gently took this from me and while munching contentedly I patted her neck and tickled her ears, quite delighted at the success of the experiment. It would seem that this Spode girl knew her onions after all. The rest of the herd had been standing back watching the ritual intently and now, having decided that it was quite safe to do so, wanted to enjoy a piece of the action.

While in all fairness their expressions could not be described as exactly smiling, their large brown eyes held a decidedly friendly gleam as they jostled around me for their handfuls of grass. After a hectic 5 minutes I was quite relieved to hear the pre-arranged whistle calling for my return. With the cows still in close company I grabbed my belongings and made my way back to the stile and, after bidding them a farewell moo, hopped over it to stroll leisurely across to the engine.

Jack was standing on the footplate between the uprights as I approached and when only a few yards away I noticed that he appeared to be looking beyond, rather than directly at me. His eyes widened and his jaw dropped.

'What the devil have you brought that lot for?' he gasped hoarsely.

'What lot?' I replied, glancing round, still unaware of the situation.

I staggered with surprise, for some 5 yards away was the herd leader plodding steadily after me, and strung out at precise intervals in a long line behind were her 19 sisters. They must have found a convenient gap in the hedge and decided to follow their new-found friend. Thinking that if I ignored them they might go away, I hastily climbed on to the footplate and set about putting some coal on, but no such luck, for when I looked over the side again a few minutes later I was greeted by the solemn gaze of 20 pairs of eyes, now arranged in a broad semi-circle around the engine.

Jock the shunter meanwhile hove into view round the end of a line of wagons, his cloth cap shooting into the air as he shied in amazement on taking in the scene. He seemed to be having difficulty in believing what he saw. His jaw was moving but no sound came from his lips and he was no doubt considering the wisdom of having had that last wee dram

at lunchtime. With a great struggle he pulled himself together.

'Where ha' all these beasties come fe?' he asked thickly in his broad Scots dialect.

'My mate brought them,' replied Jack simply, in his usual calm manner.

I thought that this statement was a little unfair and needed qualifying somewhat, and was about to elaborate when Jock interjected.

'What the devil for?'

'Dunno,' replied Jack, now obviously amused at the way things were going.

Jock scratched his head in an effort to produce another pertinent question.

'What does he intend to do wi' 'em?'

The conversation was getting ludicrous, so I thought it high time I butted in.

'I'll get rid of them,' I said resignedly, but that in itself posed a problem. How do you remove 20 love-sick cows from a railway siding when they seem very intent on staying there?

I climbed down and tried shooing them away, but that had not the slightest effect. I then tried mooing at them, but this only brought forth a chorus of moos by way of a reply and they moved in closer than ever. In desperation I turned to Jack.

'Are we all ready to go now?' I asked.

'Just as soon as you feel disposed to clear these animals from the track,' he said drily.

'Well maybe they will follow me in to the field and then when the last one has disappeared you give me a toot on the whistle and I will come belting back and join you on the move?'

I phrased this plan as a question since being a junior fireman I was used to having my suggestions countermanded. However, on this occasion the scheme received a nodding consent. Feeling rather like the Pied Piper of Hamelin, I found the narrow gap in the hawthorn hedge through which they had come and led my string of charges in a wide semi-circle across the end of the meadow and back towards the stile. Ten yards from this the whistle sounded above the clank of couplings being drawn taught, and without looking back I sprinted for and leapt over the stile.

Jack had got the 17 wagons making up our train moving at a pace rather more than I had visualised when outlining my plot, and after having galloped halfway back to Austin West Works I managed to fling myself on to the bottom engine steps. It took quite some while before I regained my breath, and having had his little bit of fun also, Jack let the matter rest until we arrived at Rubery the following day. We were immediately greeted by Jock, whose manner could only be described as distraught.

'Fe gaud's sake, Jack, keep ya mate on the injun today,' he expostulated. 'We had they beasties roamin' down to the motor works all afternoon and the farmer accusin' us o' trying ta rustle his stock.'

I thought it was all very comical really, but everyone else took a dim view of the affair and I was confined to the footplate for the duration of my stay. I need hardly say that it was quite some time before I tried talking to animals again.

Three weeks after this episode a buff-coloured envelope bearing an 'Official Paid' stamp was waiting for me on the hall table when I returned home from work. With mixed feelings I hastily tore open the flap and read the contents. It contained a brief letter requesting me to report to Aldershot, a travel warrant to facilitate this, and some instructions regarding what to take, which incidentally was very little.

I felt relief that the long wait and uncertainties were now over, but on the other hand the inevitable butterflies of not knowing quite what was in store for me over the next two years. My brother had related details of life in the army, and I must admit that some of the restrictions and severe discipline, not to mention other aspects such as lack of home comforts and leisure, held little appeal. However, I was resolved to make the best of matters and try and gain as much as I could from the experience.

In August 1954, after my service in the RASC, principally in Germany - the long-awaited day of my demobilisation arrived. After two years to the day I re-entered civilian life. I had learned many new things during this time - to drive, to shoot, to receive and give orders, but most important perhaps the ability to live in harmony with my fellow men. The army also taught me to appreciate all the things we normally take for granted in this materialistic age - one's home, good food and freedom of choice, a diminishing commodity nowadays, but precious nevertheless.

Despite familiar faces and unchanged surrounds, I felt rather like a stranger when I visited the loco for the first time to advise them that I was once more available. Until a place could be found for me in the bottom road group to which my seniority now entitled me, I was placed in the Control link.

Things had changed only in a few details, with the exception of the proposed staff amenity block, the footings of which were now laid out in the area between the tank house and the checker's hut. I also saw for the first time one of the new BR Standard Class '5s', which on the whole appealed to me aesthetically from most angles, and ergonomically I thought the footplate layout was a vast improvement on anything yet built. I was still, of course, at this stage trying to re-adjust to civilian life, but it was remarkable how quickly I slipped into the swing of things again.

At the end of two weeks, involving a variety of local jobs, I felt almost as though I had never had a two-year break, and even my muscles had ceased to ache and my hands were regaining their former toughness. On the Saturday of the second week the foreman called my attention to the roster board, where he pointed out with a friendly smile that I was now booked with driver Syd Lloyd in Link Three, Section C.

'Syd Lloyd?' I queried. 'What's he like?'

'Oh, he's a great chap,' replied the foreman enthusiastically. 'A real character. You'll get on fine with him, without a doubt.'

Well, I would soon find out, for we were to work the 8.45 pm Gloucester from the West End, booking on at 7.16 to prepare our own engine. I went home that night feeling for the first time that I could now be considered an experienced fireman, and looking forward very much indeed to next week's work.

2
THE LITTLE GLOUCESTER LINK

When I walked into the lobby just after 7.00 pm I asked Peter the clerk for my card in the usual way, and was told that my new mate had withdrawn it a few minutes earlier and was now waiting in the far corner for me. Looking across, I perceived a broad back hunched over one of the writing benches studying notices. I laid a light hand on the nearest elbow, and as the body rotated, I enquired casually into a passing ear, 'Syd Lloyd?' Facing each other fair and square, our eyes followed roughly the same path, starting at the crown of our caps, running south until reaching our stoutly soled boots, whereupon they quickly returned north but this time scanning east to west also. Although all this took no more than a split second, I definitely liked what I saw.

Twinkling grey eyes regarded me keenly over horn-rimmed spectacles, perched on the end of a well-formed if somewhat pointed nose, while distinguished-looking iron grey hair could be seen under his uniform cap which was set at a jaunty angle. That his build could best be described as rotund may well be imagined by the fact that, although he stood only 5 ft 7 in high, he weighed the best part of 16 stone. As our gaze met once more, the laughter creases around his eyes and mouth wreathed with a smile of genuine delight.

'Welcome back to the fold, Terry,' he said in a soft, husky voice, grasping my hand and pumping it with a warmth I had never experienced before with any other driver. I was very much impressed by his charming manner - sadly lacking in the majority of army personnel - and I therefore responded to this show of friendliness like a long-lost son. From that very first meeting a bond of true affection sprang up between us.

'I'm very glad to be with you, Syd,' I replied, managing to free my right hand at last. 'I'm afraid that I'm still a bit rusty on certain details after two years absence, so perhaps you would fill me in as we go along?'

'By all means, old son' he said with a smile. 'Just ask away.'

'Well for starters, what do we do on this job?'

'Oh there is nothing much to it really,' he replied airily as I signed my card. We prepare a Class "4F", go down to the West End, collect a train destined for Gloucester and work it as far as Bromsgrove where we get relieved. Then after sitting around for an hour or two we work any train the Control cares to give us back here. Usually it's a "Maltese" terminating at Water Orton, but this of course depends on how it is running, so we can bring anything else that is travelling north. Occasionally, if traffic is light or there is an excess of relief men, we return as passengers in the brake-van of a suitable train, but that rarely happens these days.'

'Doesn't sound too strenuous,' I admitted as we walked round to the engine board where we picked out our engine, No 4165, which was standing nearby in No 2 shed.

I discovered that the tool situation had not improved too much since 1952, and I was therefore obliged to forage for some items of equipment, as in the old days. However, with plenty of motive power coming on the shed at that time of the evening, it proved no great hardship and we rang off with some minutes to spare. Our guard joined us, and we departed for the West End at a leisurely pace on the up Camp Hill goods line.

It was on this job that I really came to know our guard, Les Suffield, quite well. In future years I was to tow him around the countryside for literally thousands of miles with a variety of drivers, and never once found him any different. He was a tall, thin, mild-mannered man, born and bred in the Hall Green district of Birmingham, and although only about 50 years of age, sported a head of almost white hair. His gentle disposition and serenity affected all he came in contact with, and listening to these two old friends chatting amiably reminded me - after army days - that such characters did still exist, so that by the time we reached the West End I was succumbing to their spell.

After backing on to the appropriate road, Les departed to check round the train, while I attached our headlamps in the Class A position, ie one on the smokebox and one over the left buffer. No 4165 seemed to be in pretty fair condition, but, not knowing her capabilities, the job, or Syd's methods of driving, I decided to play it safe and started building up a healthy fire in the rear of the grate with picked lumps. As I was manhandling a large piece over the mouthpiece ring, Syd passed the comment, 'Do you always wear gloves Terry?'

'Yes I do, as a matter of fact,' I replied, slightly on the defensive. 'I neither like getting burned nor any dirtier than I have to.'

'Don't blame you at all, I always did,' and then with a knowing wink added, 'The ladies are not very keen on dirty, calloused hands either.'

I returned his smile as the logic of the statement sank in, but before I could phrase a suitable reply he continued, 'That reminds me of the story about the Irish navvy and the shepherd girl. . .'

He then proceeded to relate this with a professionalism rarely seen off the stage. It was not so much the story itself but the way it was executed, with mime and expertly mimicked dialect thrown in, and to me it was extremely entertaining. This was the first inkling I had that Syd had quite a sense of humour, but just what a comedian he turned out to be I did not discover until later. The tears were still rolling down my cheeks when Les returned to advise us that we had 42 wagons astern and that he was all ready to go if we were. The ritual lidful of tea was proffered to him and graciously accepted, and when this had been disposed of, Les lowered himself to the ground.

'I see that Syd's started on you all ready,' he said with a benign smile, eyeing my still wet face.

'Yes,' I replied, 'and any more like that and we won't get up the bank very easily.'

'Oh, that's nothing, you wait a while,' he called over his shoulder as he departed in search of the yard foreman.

The significance of his remark was lost as I concentrated once more on building up the fire, and when this was done to my satisfaction I sat down to take a breather, for the night was still quite warm.

The trip to Bromsgrove was relatively

In all classes of locomotives, some engines always seemed much better than others. '4Fs' were no exception, and Crewe-built No 44165, seen here in LMS livery and numbering in its first year of service, 1926, was one of Saltley's favourites. I enjoyed this locomotive when I worked my first turn firing with Syd Lloyd on the 8.45 pm Washwood Heath-Gloucester. In BR days the locomotive retained its right-hand drive position.

Bromsgrove South signal box. Note the concrete relief cabin alongside, the scene of Syd's comedy shows and near the point where he nearly lost his life. On the down main line, approaching the water column but not intending to stop there, is BR Standard Class '5' No 73046, heading the 5.10 pm Cadbury's trade special from Bournville to Salisbury on 11 May 1956.

straightforward except that I found I had forgotten some of the details from Kings Heath onwards, and consequently was inclined to have either too much or too little steam at times. The descent of Lickey was a very well controlled one, rather too much so if anything, since we would have stopped half a dozen engine lengths short, had not Syd applied steam and dragged the train up to the column.

'I usually aim to stop slightly short if I can,' explained Syd as we filled the tank. 'You can always uncouple and run forward to get water while the brakes are being picked up, but you can't set back. Also it's our supper time that's being wasted then.'

I could see the sense of his argument, and mentally filed it away for the future.

We duly handed over to a set of Gloucester men and walked the few yards back to the relief cabin. Here I was not a little surprised and amused to find that Syd was greeted by, if not actual applause, certainly the nearest thing you can get to it without exactly clapping hands. Five sets of enginemen and two guards had previously been sprawled on the benches in differing attitudes of relaxation from snoring lightly to munching sandwiches. As one, they all sat up and began to take notice, and I suddenly became aware of an air of expectancy emanating from the gathering. This gradually heightened as Syd neared the end of his quite sizeable supper, a fact that he himself was not unconscious of, since he seemed to linger unnecessarily over the last few mouthfuls. I, meanwhile, relaxed in a corner enjoying a quiet cigarette while awaiting developments, feeling that something would soon happen.

Syd drained his second cup of tea, then, having replaced the lid on his can with exaggerated care, he looked up, beamed at his already attentive audience and said, 'Have you heard the one about the freshly ordained priest whose first appointment was to a remote country village in Wales?'

So this was it then, a free comedy show, and it must have been a regular affair because these other fellows had obviously known what was coming. Well I might have guessed, having already had a preview of Syd's story-telling ability at the West End, but even so I was flabbergasted at the marathon performance he gave that night. For two hours and ten minutes, story after story rolled from his tongue - each one had a religious background and each one was told with a skill worthy of a professional comedian.

Soon we were all writhing about in uncontrollable merriment. It was really a vicious circle - the more we laughed, the better Syd performed, which in turn made us more hysterical than ever. Always blessed with a vivid imagination, I frequently found my mind running ahead of the story, and consequently I was having convulsions long before the punch-line. Also, of course, the chain reaction effect was considerable in that confined hut, and we derived just as much amusement from seeing and hearing each other. One very fat old Gloucester driver in particular got me going. He had a most infectious deep guffaw and he heaved and shook like an enormous jelly, while the tears streamed in torrents down his face.

After about an hour he was gasping like a stranded fish and his booming belly-laugh was soon interspersed with a sizzling hiss as he fought for breath. Just when I thought he was about to expire for good, a Saltley crew arrived requiring relief and saved his day. Reluctantly he tottered off with his mate into the yard, still alternately rumbling and hissing with barely enough strength left to climb on to the footplate.

Men came and went without interrupting the proceedings, for there was no stopping Syd once he was in his stride. Finally, when my sides ached so much that laughing was becoming more of a pain than a pleasure, the Controller popped in and advised us of the train we were to relieve and that it had now passed Stoke Works Junction. I dragged myself after Syd as he bade farewell to his erstwhile audience, and as we staggered off into the darkness I could still hear the racket caused by his last parting quip.

Making one's way from the South signal box to the water column on the up line where relief normally took place involved a walk of nearly 400 yards. Not an unduly great distance for a stroll along a well-made path in daylight, but taxing enough when one's course was strewn with slippery sleepers, wooden ramps, cunningly concealed point rods and signal wires cleverly arranged to trip up the unwary. Darkness of course rendered matters doubly difficult since such lights that existed only tended to dazzle, and left the ground in deep shadow; watering eyes and limp limbs certainly did not help either.

Crossing the four tracks south of the station could also be a hazardous business even when visibility was good, and although I am jumping ahead in time, it would be appropriate to mention that Syd and I nearly came to grief here one winter's night some five months later. It was in late January and on this very same job. The Controller had informed us that we were not required to work home and were to travel back to Saltley in the brake of a Water Orton-bound semi-fitted. The news was not at all unwelcome since the prospect of travelling home in a cosy brake-van, with the chance of an hour's sleep, was a pleasant alternative to the footplate on this raw, cold night.

Two or three falls of snow over the past few days had accumulated to a depth of some 8 inches, which over the route we were taking had become impacted and very slippery with alternate thawings and freezings. Syd, holding a torch in one hand and a freshly mashed can of tea in the other, picked his way cautiously through a veil of meandering snowflakes, prior to crossing the tracks. The signals at Bromsgrove station were not visible, so we had to rely on our ears to tell us when it was safe to make our move. We had not, of course, to walk as far as the water column, but aim for a point some 35 wagons back. However, before we could reach this point our train clattered past on what Syd took to be the up fast.

'Come on mate,' he called over his shoulder. 'He'll only stop for bankers. We'll miss it if we're not careful.'

At this stage I was a yard or so behind Syd and about to step over the down slow rails when out of the gloom hurtled a Class '3F' hauling, or rather being pushed by, a mixed freight, travelling with the speed of an express and the silence of a ghost train. With our feet a twinkling blur we managed to leap out of the way, traverse the down fast and pause momentarily in the relative safety of the space between up and down fast lines.

Somewhat shaken by this narrow shave, Syd glanced round to make sure that I was alright and then, with head lowered, he stepped on to the up fast. Out of sheer habit I peered to the left and as I did so my heart stopped beating. A pair of dim snow-encrusted headlamps surmounting the equally snow-encrusted buffer beam of a 'Jubilee' were only a few yards away and bearing down on us at a terrifying speed, the engine's sound completely masked by the runaway goods. With Syd already halfway over, his decapitation was inevitable, and time seemed to stand still.

Grabbing the only thing available, his coat tails, I hauled backwards with all my might. As we crashed to the ground together, every ounce of breath was knocked out of my body, but I was vaguely conscious of wheels and wind and snow spray whistling past my ears far too close for comfort. With 16 stone of driver and two pints of hot tea lying on top of me I wondered if I might have achieved the same end with a little more finesse, but fear had lent me strength and I had literally yanked Syd right off his feet.

Both of us were somewhat stunned as we scrambled up, and it wasn't until we'd been settled for a while in the safety and comfort of the brake-van that the shock wore off and the full impact of what had happened hit us.

'Thank you, Terry,' Syd said soberly. 'I reckon you saved my hide just then. Do you know, I was under the impression our train was on the up fast. That's why I never bothered to look.'

'That's quite all right, Syd,' I replied, still feeling a trifle sore around the ribcage. 'I could hardly let you go to the great railroad in the sky without hearing the end of that last story, could I?'

The moral of this tale is that no matter how experienced one might be and how familiar one was with the job, walking across any

number of tracks was fraught with danger and demanded the utmost vigilance at all times.

This first night, however, was a balmy one in late summer with good visibility, and I was quite content to follow Syd, being as yet unfamiliar with the area. When we were about 50 yards from the water column, a 'Crab' 2-6-0 bearing 'Maltese' lights clanked past us and, although it was too dark to make out the number, Syd assured me it was ours. I had not fired a freight up Lickey, and the fact that it was to be a 'Crab' added spice to the prospect because it was a class of engine I was not very conversant with.

The Gloucester men had already put the bag in when we arrived and were gathering their things together as we climbed on to the footplate. She was blowing off despite the injector being on, which made conversation a little difficult, but the fireman did bellow in my ear, 'She be alright brother, and I've put 'e a good fire on.'

I glanced in the firebox and nearly fell over backwards in surprise, for the smoke deflector plate had been removed and a great mass of fire rose from the top of the mouthpiece almost to the crown. It was impossible to guess if the front half of the grate was properly covered, but by a quick calculation of the depth of fire at the rear, the mere process of shaking down should ensure this for some time to come.

With the departure of the other crew, I climbed on the back of the tender, retrieved the rake from the well, and dropped its triangular handle over the securing peg ready for immediate use. While standing in this exposed position, waiting for the tank to fill, I looked back along our train. A brilliant light was closing on to the brake-van; for a moment I was puzzled as to what it might be, then realised that it was 'Big Emma's' searchlight - the first time I had seen this 0-10-0 banker in action at night.

Back on the footplate once more, I cleaned up and looked around the cab while I had the opportunity to do so, and the benefit of wide open firedoors in which to do it. The general layout seemed to be a cross between an '8F' and a '4F', the only peculiarities being the curious circular seats, which protruded like flat-topped mushrooms from the footboards, and the fact that the tender was much narrower than the engine left one with a slightly insecure and exposed feeling, but gave excellent rearward vision.

Between the bouts of blowing off, Syd informed me that we had 46 vans in tow of which five were fitted, and he did not think that they would present much difficulty for No 2730. Within minutes the signals came off, and after giving the usual 'crow' whistle Syd opened the regulator and away we went.

From the starter to the end of the station platform the gradient is 1 in 186; even so, with 'Big Emma' weighing in at the rear, we bounded forward at a surprising pace until we were under the road bridge and on to the bank proper, where speed gradually fell away as more of the train got on it. We then settled down to a steady pounding beat on half the second valve and about 50 per cent cut-off.

I had initially closed the firedoors, an act usually referred to in the vernacular as 'boxing her up', but with the safety valves lifting I opened them some 3 inches and put on my injector, which at the present steaming rate just kept the water level steady at the top of the glass. I was also extremely pleased to see that, even with the doors parted and the injector on, steam pressure remained constant at 180 lbs per sq in.

With such an enormous fire in the box and things going so well, there seemed little point in doing anything other than enjoy the ride, so I poured myself a lid of tea and lit a cigarette. Trying to drink that tea made it obvious why these Horwich 2-6-0s were nicknamed 'Crabs'; with every thrust of the starboard piston the whole engine skewed literally to the right, while on the return stroke it gave a similar wiggle to the left, leaving one with the impression that if there had been no flanges on the wheels, she would have tried to climb the bank sideways. Apart from this the ride was smooth, while the crisp, deep-throated bark of the exhaust seemed to give an extraordinary incandescence to the fire.

Approaching the semi-automatic colour light signal halfway up the incline, I turned my back on these mundane matters and regarded the romantic glories of the night

Class '8F' No 48367 working hard with a long train of empties approaching Blackwell towards the top of the Lickey Incline in July 1956. Assisting in the rear is Class '9F' No 92079. Because coal wagons were reserved for the conveyance of coal only, trains of empties were a common sight travelling back to the northern coalfields. Certainly it was not unusual for Syd and I to return with one rather than our booked 'Maltese' semi-fitted.

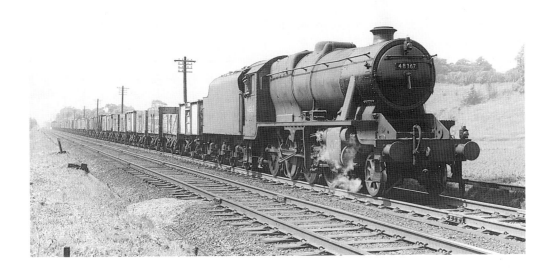

framed in my side window. A brilliant harvest moon, shining from a black velvet sky, bathed the gorgeous Worcestershire countryside in its soft mellow glow. General details could be seen for miles, but with no sharp edges or harsh shadows the view was given a beauty and serenity never to be observed in daylight.

With Blackwell in sight, I made a quick inspection of the fire and decided that there was now sufficient room for me to replace the smoke deflector plate. Once more I proved the protection afforded by wearing gloves, but even so, my overalls were smoking after only a few seconds' exposure to that searing heat. However, I felt happier with the plate in position, although there was still no need to add more coal at this stage.

Once off the 1 in 37 gradient our speed increased rapidly as 'Big Emma', with a huge column of sparks erupting from her chimney, gave a final full-throttle burst before dropping astern. Although still climbing at 1 in 291, Syd made reductions in both regulator opening and cut-off until we were rattling along at a fair old pace with hardly a sound from the chimney. I was most impressed by the ease which No 2730 handled her not inconsiderable load, and I began to develop a healthy regard for a 'Crab's' suitability to work fitted freights. A regard, I might add, that was to be considerably enhanced in the future when I came to spend many pleasant hours actually driving them.

The Linthurst advanced colour light advised us that we would be turning on to the slow line at Barnt Green, and once over the summit Syd shut off. Coasting down the 1 in 290, we rolled steadily through the deserted platform, and when the whole train was safely on the slow line, Syd eased open the regulator once more. With only a breath of steam on we hardly noticed the short climb at 1 in 297 up to Cofton where, upon entering the cutting, we were able to drift down through Halesowen Junction to Northfield where we were halted by signals.

Here the slow line officially becomes the goods line where the permissive block system operates, and we eventually found ourselves standing behind another freight train at Kings Norton. When standing on the slow line at Kings Norton and wishing to proceed down the Camp Hill line, one is trapped, so to speak, by traffic travelling to and from New Street station, so it was the best part of an hour before we departed from here. This, however, suited us admirably since neither of us wanted to dispose of our engine, which we would have been obliged to do had we arrived on the shed with more than an hour to complete before booking off.

All this time excess steam escaping from our safety valves had been a source of nuisance and eventually I was forced to close the damper in order to allow the fire to cool.

'Hasn't that 'tater roaster burned down yet?' queried Syd on seeing my action.

'No,' I replied. 'There is still a fair bit left - I don't know how they manage to get so much in.'

'Ah,' said Syd, mimicking a broad West Country dialect, 'when oiv filled the firebox up to the crown, I opens the smokebox door and starts at t'other end, packing it down the tubes - be a lot easier loik that.'

It was all very well having a laugh about carrying so much fire, but it could have its embarrassing moments, for one might have a quick run to Lawley Street or even Washwood Heath up sidings, and arrive soon afterwards on the shed with a box full, which of course made cleaning both tedious and difficult. Travelling to Water Orton, as we did on this particular night, gave one a bit of a chance, especially if delays occurred, but it was very tricky explaining the subtle difference to these good-natured Gloucester lads, who thought they were doing us a favour, between having a good fire on and too much.

After leaving Kings Norton we enjoyed a straightforward run down the bank, travelling main line to Castle Bromwich, then completing our journey on the goods line. Even so, I never had to put any more coal on, although it was necessary to level the fire and spread it around by means of the rake.

Quite heavy thundery rain broke out when we returned light engine to the shed, and I then discovered that 'Crabs' could be very wet when running tender-first. The disparity in width between engine and tender was a distinct disadvantage in this respect, and the only reasonably dry area was immediately in front of the firedoors. Eventually we booked off with an hour's overtime to the good, and as we walked to the cycle racks I learned that Syd lived in Walsall. For the 15 miles journey home he used an ancient Francis Barnett two-stroke that somehow surprised me since I had never imagined Syd as a motor cyclist. He was however, quite keen, so this was another common interest we had, and we stayed chatting for another half-hour on the merits of various makes, since he was contemplating a replacement machine.

As the week progressed I found myself looking forward to going to work more and more, with the revelries in the relief cabin the highlight of the evening. Syd's story-telling capacity was prodigious - each night he would pick a different subject or theme and pack in as many hilarious tales as there was time available, never repeating himself once. In fact, during the nine months I was booked with him I can only recall hearing a previous joke on a few odd occasions, and then they were varied in subtle ways to make them equally interesting.

For me, Syd was the perfect tonic for post-National Service blues, and within a week or two I was back to my former exuberant self, philosophically accepting set-backs and shortcomings and once again seeing humour in every aspect of life. I quickly found that we had quite a variety of jobs in the link, working regularly to such places as the Kingsbury branch and Burton to the north, Walsall - familiar ground to Syd, being an old Bescot man - and Bromsgrove, with occasional runs through to Gloucester, Worcester and - most interesting of all - Ashchurch via Redditch in the west. Under Syd's able guidance I soon buckled down to start thoroughly learning the routes to these mainly unfamiliar places, and during the rest of my stay in the link I devoted most of my energies to this end.

Nearly everywhere we went Syd was known for his shows, and indeed it was expected that he entertained the local clientele in his usual manner. We were therefore often detained for longer than was strictly necessary at certain venues in order that full benefit could be derived from his rare talents. He also gained

inspiration from local events for the writing of numerous amusing poems, which he scribbled down, usually on the backs of current train notices during odd moments of inactivity. I became his sort of unofficial critic since he would try them out on me before presenting the final work to a larger audience. For example, after two days on the Kingsbury trip job, while waiting at the Whitacre North starter, he suddenly looked up from his literary labours and announced that he had been meaning for some considerable time to write a poem about the exploits of the driver who got out of control there, and now had at last made a start. It was couched on the lines of 'There's a little yellow idol to the north of Katmandu' and was really very good indeed. I only regret that my memory does not enable me to reproduce the whole work, but it commenced:

'There's a funny little railway to the
    north of the River Thame,
The Kingsbury Branch to give the place a
    name.
Where they tell a thrilling story of a train
    that ran away,
On the night little Niggy sprang to fame.'

In its final form it was wildly applauded by all and sundry except driver Niggy, who did not seem to appreciate being reminded of the event.

Our next job of interest was a Landor Street to Derby mixed freight, which we generally worked with a Class '4F' 0-6-0 under Class B lights as far as Burton. I enjoyed this turn, not because it was particularly exciting as far as turns go, but it did afford me ample opportunity to study this important stretch of track at a nice leisurely pace.

From Water Orton we were diagrammed over the slow, then, after leaving virtually level track at Kingsbury Station Junction, we chugged steadily up the 1 in 460 rise to Kingsbury Branch Sidings. Gaining speed down the 1 in 460 past Cliff Sidings, we steadied on the 1 in 775 climb at Whatley Colliery Sidings and level run to Wilnecote where, as often as not, we were backed inside to allow the passage of faster traffic. Once a suitable path was available, the 1-mile fall of 1 in 837 to Kettlebrook enabled us to gain sufficient momentum to climb at 1 in 640 to Tamworth High Level and traverse the following undulations up to the 22½ milepost for Derby, without too much loss of speed.

Here the water troughs were situated, and once over these the fastest section of the route commenced. For over 2 miles the line descended at mainly 1 in 408 to Elford where, after a short rise of 1 in 366, it fell again, varying between 1 in 360 to 1 in 1509 right down to the level stretch approaching Branston Junction, where we were turned in on to the goods line. Almost outside the loco shed was the relief cabin and water column, and here a Burton crew took over to work the train forward.

After the usual hour or two wait, we would be advised by Control of the train we were to take back to Washwood Heath. Working home required a little more effort of course, since the gradients were mainly against us, but even with a '4F' it did not prove unduly difficult unless the fire was particularly dirty, in which case we would be turned inside at some convenient point if too much time was dropped.

It was in this link that I came to know, and to some extent appreciate, the qualities of the Class '4F' 0-6-0. They were essentially simple, robust engines, which, because they were not such ready steamers as the '3Fs', provided just that extra bit of challenge for a fireman, keeping his interest alive. They were quite a strong engine, too, and endowed with a surprising turn of speed when the need arose, although at anything over about 50 mph they became distinctly uncomfortable. However, on freight work they performed reliably and effectively, even if not too efficiently in terms of water and fuel consumption. Unlike the '3F', they required much more time to warm up and were at their best when on long non-stop runs. Consequently they did not respond anything like as well to the stop-go type of operation so prevalent at that time around Birmingham, and this may have been the basic cause of the reputation they gained for being somewhat steam shy.

A week later, when on a Walsall turn over the Sutton line, Syd introduced me to a novel and convenient method of cleaning the tubes. With a light load of only some 16 wagons we were hitting up a good pace between Sutton Park and Streetly and, although we should have been eating the job, our '4F' was not steaming particularly well. Admittedly the coal could have been better, but I was having a job to maintain 160 lbs per sq in and two-thirds of a glass of water. Syd concluded that the tubes might well be dirty and instructed me to mortgage the boiler and close the firedoors so as to bring the pressure up to 175 lbs per sq in. At the same time he increased speed and, when going at a fair gallop with half a glass of water and the needle on the red line, he wound the reversing screw back to about 10 per cent and heaved the regulator fully open. He then quickly dropped her to very nearly full gear, left it there for a few seconds, then returned it to the 10 per cent position. The exhaust immediately exploded in a great tearing roar, the like of which I had never heard before from a Class '4'. It was a most exhilarating racket that left the pulses racing and the eardrums numb. We looked astern and saw with much satisfaction a great pall of black soot hanging in the air above our now fast-moving train. Syd repeated the treatment twice more, but since on the last occasion the exhaust was nearly clean, concluded that most of the offending carbon had been removed.

Whether it was due to this forcible evacuation of soot from the tubes, or whether the enormous blast had lifted residual clinker and ash from the firebed, the fact remains that she steamed much more freely afterwards. Quoting the effectiveness on this occasion, I frequently persuaded Syd to repeat 'the treatment' on other jobs in the future. I did so partly because the fire actually required livening up, but in all honesty the main attraction was the fearful cacophony created by the exhaust, and I suspect that Syd, being still a boy at heart, quite enjoyed it too, since he never failed to oblige.

My next mate, Freddy Galloway, in the Bottom Passenger link, also subscribed to this method of cleaning the tubes, but with the added refinement of spraying a bucketful of sand in through the firehole when the blast was at its greatest. The scouring effect of sand travelling along the tubes at high velocity can well be imagined, and since we frequently had the same engine on a job all week, it paid to ensure that she steamed as well as possible.

From the moment I joined the Little Gloucester link I had been looking forward to working on the Redditch branch. This was the only lengthy section of single line over which Saltley crews regularly operated, and my brother had told me various tales of the problems that this entailed. Apart from the obvious one of picking up and dropping single-line tablets while on the move, Redditch Tunnel was quite the most formidable.

Although only 340 yards in length, it covered the best part of a short climb at 1 in 126 from Redditch South and, being single line, clearance around an engine was minimal. This meant that there was virtually no room for the exhaust to escape, and even under ideal conditions the atmosphere on the footplate was quickly rendered intolerable. To stick and then to 'blow off' was tantamount to disaster. Many men over the years had succumbed to heat and fumes, not to mention actual scalds and burns. I was, therefore, in a state of mild excitement when I arrived for work on that first Monday evening to work a freight to Evesham via the Redditch line.

We were allocated an '8F', although on occasions a '4F' 0-6-0 was substituted if the former were in short supply. However, on this particular evening we had No 8417, and providentially she turned out to be in quite good condition. Syd normally allowed me to go about my duties without interference, but during the preparation he did ask me to ensure that the sandboxes were well topped up, and we thoroughly tested the apparatus before leaving No 3 shed.

'It's important that they are working properly on this job,' he said seriously. 'It's quite a drag up through Redditch Tunnel, and I like to give it some stick!'

We rang out on time and duly arrived at the West End, where we found our old friend Les Suffield waiting for us.

'We've got a good load tonight, chaps,' he

called cheerily. 'Forty-six on altogether, 26 of mineral next to the engine.'

With the aid of a banker to Camp Hill, we ran fairly easily up to Barnt Green, No 8417 working well within her capacity and steaming like a kettle despite the mediocre mixture of fuel. The daylight had now faded as we trundled slowly from the down slow towards Barnt Green Single Line Junction box.

'I'll pick up the tablet to start with,' said Syd, 'just to show you how it's done. Then you can get some practise in as we proceed.'

The home signal was not lowered until we were almost at a standstill, then as it came off I noticed the bobby hurry out from the box and mount a small wooden stage that was dimly illuminated by a guttering oil lamp. With the engine checked by the hand brake, Syd pulled open the cab doors on my side, placed his right foot on the top step and holding on to the handrail with his left hand, leaned down with his other arm, crooked to receive the hoop containing the tablet. Hanging well out of my side window, I watched intently the whole procedure. At about 10 mph it seemed relatively simple and after a brief exchange of greetings, Syd hauled himself aboard, hung the hoop over the exhaust injector steam valve and remarked 'That's the easy part. It's a bit more tricky when you have to hand one over at the same time.'

In the light from the open firedoors I examined the tablet carefully, since I had never seen one before. The tablet, or token or key as it was sometimes called, was a substantial brass disc about the size of a small saucer, notched in a special way on the periphery. It bore the name of the section to which it related, and was contained in a strong leather purse attached to a hide-bound wire hoop some 2 feet in diameter. I later found that these tokens could also take the form of a truncheon-like bar of brass, equipped with a number of circumferential rings, in which case they were usually referred to as a staff.

Whatever their shape, however, they all served the same purpose, that of authorising the engine to be on a specific section of single line. Until the token had been inserted into the appropriate instrument at the end of that block, another token could not be extracted from either end. This, in theory at any rate, precluded the chances of two trains being on the same section of line at any one time.

Down the 1 in 74 gradient to Alvechurch station Syd kept the train well in check, leaving the hand brake hard on until the short level section some 3 miles from Barnt Green. From here the track undulated for another mile before the short rise up to Redditch North. The sodium street lights of Redditch, reflecting on the low cloud cover, provided sufficient illumination for me to just make out the rolling hills surrounding the town.

I joined Syd on his side of the footplate where, having removed the tablet from its hook, he was preparing to hand it to the signalman. As before, he lowered himself to the top step and holding the hoop as low as possible, dropped it neatly over the bobby's awaiting arm as we rolled slowly past. Between Redditch North and Redditch South there is a short stretch of double line through the station, so we did not require a token here. The signal was on at the South box, but instead of drawing up to it, Syd stopped halfway along the platform.

'If the signal is on,' he explained, 'it pays to stop well back. Then when we get the road we can have a bit of a run at the tunnel.'

During the descent from Barnt Green I had allowed the fire to burn down somewhat, and Syd now advised me to spread a thin layer of coal over the grate and put the blower hard on so as to burn the smoke off. It was desirable to create as little smoke as possible through the tunnel, and in future I developed the habit of building up the fire towards the end of our descent, and running the boiler level down, so that I could arrive at Redditch South with a hot fire, a full head of steam but with no more than two-thirds of a glass of water. Not only did this preclude any chance of priming or blowing off in the tunnel, but it also meant that maximum power was instantly available with the minimum of noxious gases.

When I had done this little task, Syd said, 'Pop along to the box and collect the tablet when the bobby's ready. I'll wait for you here, then when we get cracking you won't have the bother of collecting it on the move.'

The bobby was just extracting the token from the machine when I arrived, so I was able to dash straight back to the engine where Syd was testing the sanders once again.

'Okay,' I yelled, leaping aboard and winding off the hand brake.

'Now, if you feel you're going to suffocate,' said Syd with a smile, 'hold your handkerchief over your nose and mouth and get down as low as possible.'

I grinned back at him, thinking that he was laying it on a bit thick, adjusted the firedoors to leave a 3-inch gap, checked that all was well with the gauges, closed my side window, and sat down.

The station lights had been turned off long since and it was pretty gloomy, but on my journey to obtain the tablet I had noticed the dark patch of the tunnel entrance in the towering hillside just beyond the South box. Now, as No 8417 pounded towards it on full first valve and full gear, that black circle just did not seem large enough to accommodate her, and I ducked instinctively as we entered. Immediately I was conscious of pressure building up on my eardrums, and I swallowed desperately to equalise it. At the same time dense clouds of steam swirled into the cab and, despite the brilliant shaft of white light streaming through the firedoors Syd, bending forwards over the reversing screw, disappeared from view. The steam was thicker and hotter than I had ever known it and, coupled with the strong, acrid taste of sulphur, made my breathing both difficult and laboured.

The noise in the narrow confines of the tunnel was tremendous and caused actual physical pain, due to the pressure waves from the exhaust beat. After what seemed like an age, but in reality could only have been a few seconds, an enormous weight seemed to settle on my chest, and for the first time in my life I had to concentrate hard on the normally involuntary act of inhaling. The smoke fumes burned my throat and stung my eyes, while I was surprised to find condensed steam trickling from my nostrils. The temperature in the cab was rocketing upwards and my clothing already felt decidedly soggy, since apart from the wetting effect of steam on the outside, streams of perspiration were running from every pore.

I suddenly remembered what Syd had advised regarding the use of a handkerchief. Fumbling in my trouser pocket, I pulled it out already damp and quickly wiped over my face to soak it completely. Folding the cloth into a suitable pad, I then clamped it over my nose and mouth. It did nothing to lessen the effort of breathing, but the air entering my lungs certainly tasted much sweeter and did much to reduce the compulsion to cough.

Just under a minute from entering the tunnel, we thundered out of the other end, but it was a few seconds before I realised that our ordeal was over, so thick was the steam trapped inside the cab. In fact, the easing of pressure from my ears and the change in the exhaust note were the only indications. I quickly slammed open my side window and, hanging my head well out, drank in pure, cool night air. After a few moments, I had recovered sufficiently to cross over to Syd, who was still likewise engaged in purifying his lungs.

'Crikey, Syd,' I shouted, 'I certainly didn't think it was going to be as hot as that.'

'Well, I did warn you,' he replied, panting like a husky in a heatwave, his face still a bright vermilion. 'And that was a pretty good trip too. Wait until we get a rough one. The trouble is that there is so little clearance in the tunnel that it's like sitting on top of the chimney. The heat just hasn't time to dissipate before it reaches us.'

Syd had shut the regulator almost immediately after leaving the tunnel exit and we were now rattling down a 1 in 127 gradient doing 'half an hour in twenty minutes' as he would say.

'It's downhill to Broom Junction, about 9 miles,' he shouted, 'so you can put the hand brake on and let the fire run down for a while.'

I settled to enjoy the ride, although there was little to be seen of the countryside under the heavy layers of cloud, but I pottered from one side of the footplate to the other in an effort to make out some landmarks.

On about my seventh perambulation Syd, having checked our speed down to some 15 mph, suddenly arose, announcing that he would now show me how to give up and collect a new tablet at the same time. We were approaching Studley where the exchange had to be made and, as before, Syd lowered himself to the top step, but this time, since both hands would be momentarily occupied, he braced his body firmly between the uprights. Holding the tablet as low as possible in his left hand, he simultaneously dropped it over the signalman's waiting arm while scooping up the new tablet with his right. It was very neatly performed considering that there was barely enough light from the oil lamp over the stage to see the bobby, let alone the tablet hoop.

'You can try your hand in a couple of miles at Coughton,' smiled Syd as he placed the hoop over the exhaust injector steam valve.

As can well be imagined, I could hardly wait for those 2 miles to pass, but as usual when attempting something new I had mixed emotions. Two basic fears existed; the one of actual physical danger was of course foremost, since there arose the very real possibility of being dragged head first off the engine, then the lesser one of muffing the exchange, which would only result in injury to one's pride.

I need not have worried, however, for Syd made things as easy as possible by reducing speed to a mere walking pace, and my confidence grew steadily when I found that I could wedge myself securely between engine and tender despite their constant independent movements. Although it was just as dark as the previous stage, I was able to sight the hoop in good time, and scoop it into the crook of my arm without any difficulty. After proudly displaying the new tablet to Syd, I ventured to suggest that he could go a bit quicker next time.

'OK,' was the reply, 'but like everything else it requires practice and there's no point in trying to run before you can walk.'

He did, in fact, speed up on the subsequent changes as we trundled down through Alcester, Broom Junction and Salford Priors to Harvington. Just beyond that station the track undulated for a mile or so before climbing at 1 in 171, then at 1 in 68 up to the approach to Evesham North, where it descended once more at 1 in 104.

Single-line working terminated at the North signal box, where the GW line from Oxford ran parallel to the Midland tracks. Although interconnected, each Division had its own goods yard, station and loco in the Evesham complex and, as usual where they both came into close proximity, a certain amount of rivalry existed.

We deposited our train in the Midland yard, then ran forward to the nearby loco where, having turned our engine to face north on the outside table, we left it in the capable hands of the Evesham shed crew.

The second half of our job involved working a passenger train from Evesham station to Birmingham New Street. It originated at Tewkesbury and was crewed by Gloucester men as far as Evesham, where we took over. From here we stopped at every station, picking up commuters to Birmingham

and arriving at 8.45 am. This gave them just sufficient time for a brisk walk to their respective offices and shops, and woe betide us if we were late, since a veritable avalanche of complaints descended upon our heads.

Syd explained all this while we were restoring our tissues in the loco cabin, adding that the Gloucester men were not always as punctual as they might be due to delays at Ashchurch Junction. However, we were generally booked a Fowler 2-6-4 tank and, with only four or five coaches in tow, these could generally be relied on to perform well if the need arose to give them a bit of a thumping.

I had never previously worked a 2-6-4, nor for that matter a stopping passenger train, and this, together with the prospect of having a look at the Redditch line in daylight, kept me in a perpetual ferment of excitement. For once

Evesham Midland station presents a delightfully timeless scene evocative of Victorian stability and permanence. Set in the centre of a prolific fruit-growing area, Evesham boasted its own fruit store, which is the building on the left of the footbridge. Behind the camera the double track only extended a little further round the curve to Evesham North signal box, where it merged into a single line for the 22 miles to Barnt Green.

In contrast to the previous photograph, this view of Evesham looking south presents a picture of greater activity. 'Crab' No 42780, running with 'semi-fitted' lights, seems to be in the process of attaching more traffic to its train at the far end of the platform.

time dragged heavily, but eventually Syd announced that we had better be making our way to the station, and I desperately tried to control my impatience as we strolled leisurely across the intervening goods yard.

The dawn had broken clear and bright as we walked up the platform, and right on time No 2326 with four coaches behind her bunker screeched to an abrupt halt right opposite us.

'She be alright,' exclaimed the Gloucester driver, who seemed to know Syd quite well.

'Right, George,' replied Syd. 'See you tomorrow.'

And with that brief exchange we climbed through the narrow uprights. I had only been on the footplate of one of these 2-6-4Ts for a brief moment when in the shed link, so I glanced quickly around to familiarise myself with its alien surroundings. Tank engines, no matter how large, always appear to be confining on first acquaintance, and depending on whether it is summer or winter and how you view such matters, either claustrophobic or exceedingly cosy.

Being already quite a warm morning, the temperature in the cab felt a trifle on the hot side, but I was delighted to find an ample locker above extensive shelf space that formed part of the bunker. The footplate itself was restricted by two raised platforms on either side of the firing area, which elevated both driver and fireman when they were seated at their respective 'cut-outs', since no side windows existed on the pre-Stanier examples. It immediately struck me that this might make firing somewhat awkward for, having quickly inspected the firebox, I was surprised to find it as long as 8 feet. However, being steeply sloped after the fashion of a Class '4F' 0-6-0, provided that there was a good back on, coal tended to roll towards the front.

The firing shovel provided was of the short variety, since there was insufficient room to swing a long one, and this I found entailed having to shuffle between the shovelling plate and the firehole if the coal supply was becoming depleted. Also, to fire the front half of the grate required a fair bit of thrust from the rear hand, for one had to employ a pushing motion rather than a swing. The engine, though, seemed in good shape with the needle just below the red line at 200 lbs per sq in, water half an inch from the top of the glass and a healthy fire blazing in the grate.

With little else to do, I joined Syd to see our passengers safely aboard, and when the last had embarked our guard, having studied his watch for the umpteenth time, blew a shrill blast on his whistle. Syd immediately responded with a brief toot of acknowledgement, eased open the regulator, and No 2326 flowed smoothly into motion. I say 'flowed' deliberately, for the response was immediate, with none of the clanks or jerks that accompany many tender engines when getting under way for, of course, there was no drawbar or moving fall plate beneath our feet.

It was normal practice to watch the train out of the platform in case any doors were not properly fastened, since it was frowned upon by the company to lose passengers in such a manner. This morning it was just as well because after a couple of revolutions, a portly gentleman dressed in pin-stripes and bowler, clutching a briefcase and a tightly furled umbrella, suddenly appeared at the barrier and spurted across the platform with a surprising turn of speed. Syd snapped the regulator shut while the gentleman made a desperate leap through a door obligingly opened for him in the last carriage.

'That's Ponsonby-Smythe,' exclaimed Syd with mock affectation. 'The blighter does that trick nearly every morning - I'd almost forgotten him today.'

Our signal was off, but Syd kept the engine in check until I had scooped up the tablet at the North box, then he opened up to just about full first valve. A beautifully deep, crisp bark erupted from our chimney and we surged forward up the short 1 in 104 gradient in a most impressive way. I was amazed at the quality of the ride. Everything was so taut, with none of the jars, vibrations and clanks normally associated with footplate life.

As we surmounted an obvious hump in the track and descended the 1 in 68 gradient half a mile north of Evesham station, our speed rose rapidly, and Syd shortened the cut-off to about 20 per cent. Here the line runs through a continuous belt of smallholdings, and, despite the early hour, energetic market gardeners were out in the sunshine tending their crops. By the time we reached the 20 milepost from Barnt Green, we were hurtling along at an exhilarating pace with no more noise than a barely discernible exhaust beat and a subdued rumble from the wheels. Even at this speed I was able to leave the open can of tea on the drip tray without fear of spillage, while I quenched an ever-growing thirst from the lid.

'She rides well,' I bellowed in Syd's ear.

'Yes,' he replied. 'They're all the same, just like a 1st Class coach.'

I reflected briefly on the history of these fine engines. The design, originally drawn up at Derby in 1926-27 under the general direction of Fowler, benefited greatly from the Horwich influence of generously sized axleboxes, adequate piston valves and long-lap Walschaerts valve gear. Coupled with an efficient boiler derived from the Class '3P' 4-4-0s, a very lively engine resulted, which performed excellently right from the start. That the valve events and steam circuits were highly efficient was immediately obvious from the crisp exhaust beat, strong pulling capacity and effortless high-speed running. Although perhaps not as aesthetically pleasing as Stanier's taper-boilered 2-6-4Ts, I found myself biased slightly towards Fowler's design, mainly because of the quiet tautness of the ride, and their cosy warmth on a cold winter's day.

The coal was of good quality, but a number of large lumps had become wedged in the tunnel between the shovelling plate and the bunker, and I was obliged to open the enclosing doors to get at them. I then found that trying to swing a coal pick in those narrow spaces required a technique all of its own, and that if one was supplied with large coal it was better to leave the doors open so as to prevent a blockage occurring in the first place. This, however, did mean that extra care had to be taken to avoid barking one's knuckles on the open doors when actually shovelling.

I had just finished dropping the broken-up coal under the firehole mouthpiece when Syd shut off, and moments later we screeched to a halt at Harvington station. Once again, after collecting half a dozen passengers, we accelerated briskly away down the 1 in 291 incline before levelling out for the 2-mile run to Salford Priors. The engine was steaming like the proverbial old kettle and I was enjoying myself immensely on this bright autumn morning.

At Salford Priors there existed an old graveyard for retired steam-rollers and traction engines. Unique and beautiful pieces of machinery so much sought after today by avid enthusiasts, but looking, even on that glorious morning, rather pathetic and forlorn in their uniform coating of rust.

We blasted off once again in fine style up the 1 in 370 towards Broom Junction, after which it would be uphill all the way to Redditch Tunnel, some 10 miles distant. I found that I was tending to fire the engine after the initial hard acceleration and, by leaving about an inch of space at the top of the glass, I was able to prevent blowing off by judicious use of the injector when entering and standing at the stations. This allowed me to give tablet swopping and the passengers my undivided attention when appropriate.

Broom station was unusual in that it sported an island platform in the centre of a loop of twin tracks. Apart from being the junction with the Stratford line, it was one of the few places where trains from opposite directions could pass. We were, in fact, booked to do that with a westbound freight. This normally arrived first and waited for us, in which case I would exchange the tablets at the south end of the platform. If, as sometimes happened, the freight was late, I would give up my tablet there, and we would linger in the platform until the signalman brought us the one for the next section. On this particular morning all was well and, having collected the fresh tablet and a fair crowd of passengers, we set off dead on time through the very pleasant stretch of countryside leading to Alcester.

Alcester station was sited on a 1 in 125 incline and Syd gave a most impressive display of fireworks as we hammered away, with incredible vigour and surefootedness, to the accompaniment of a really cracking staccato blast produced from a full first valve and 50 per cent cut-off. Despite the last miles to

Above The island platform at Broom Junction where Syd Lloyd made his flying stop and the signalman came to grief during a tug-o'-war over a tablet. With stooks of corn ripening at one side and verdant parkland at the other, it was a delightful setting and, in summer at least, pleasant to work in Broom Junction North box, which can be seen to the left of the platform in the middle distance.

Below A closer view of the same platform. Even in the 1950s oil-lamps were still in use so that on a dark winter's night 'spot the tablet' could prove quite an exciting game.

Coughton station being at 1 in 107 we fairly romped up with no more than 20 per cent cut-off, the boiler producing so much steam that I was obliged to leave the firedoors wide open; as may be imagined, that did little to cool the already hot interior of the cab.

The departure from Coughton was slightly easier at 1 in 368, but this stiffened to 1 in 120 approaching Studley; even so No 2326 kept to time with consummate ease and, although I was having to do a fair amount of coal-cracking in addition to my other footplate duties, I was, all in all, having quite an easy time, and my opinion of these 2-6-4s rose to new heights.

We literally raced up the 2½ miles to Redditch Tunnel, gaining time hand over fist with no trace of undue effort. As we coasted down through that black hole at speed, I was able fully to appreciate just how little clearance there really was now that it was daylight. The following February, after a week of severe frost, I recall watching with great fascination our boiler and chimney ploughing through masses of enormous stalactite-like icicles that festooned the brick lining. It

certainly paid to keep one's head well inside going through that tunnel, whatever the occasion.

It was Syd's practice to gain sufficient time from Studley so that the tank could be replenished from the column at the end of the up platform at Redditch without delaying our departure. This, of course, was not always possible if we were already running late, but the 2-6-4s had so much power in reserve that, provided we had the road, it was easily accomplished. I found that a tank engine had to be positioned very precisely when filling up from a water column, and if the hose was on the long side it was quite possible for it to foul a steel plate situated just below the filler cap, in which event a kink and an unwanted bath would result. However, Syd had it accurately marked and we experienced no difficulties on this particular morning.

Redditch was the largest town on our route, and from on top of the boiler I watched with considerable interest quite a large crowd of travellers scramble aboard. Having taken our fill, I pushed the column arm clear and, as instructed by Syd, fastened the tank lid with

Ivatt Class '4MT' No 43036 at Studley & Astwood Bank in April 1957 working the 5.10 pm New Street to Ashchurch. These 'Doodlebugs' were exceedingly lively and ideally suited to stopping passenger work.

its retaining clamp. This was most important with a tank engine, since under heavy braking, water will surge forward and erupt out of the filler like an outsize fountain, causing considerable wastage.

Right on time we eased out of the station, Syd keeping her on a light rein until I had collected the tablet from the North box. He then opened out on to the following gradient of 1 in 200, to take a run at the 4-mile climb up to Barnt Green, which terminated in a lengthy stretch at 1 in 74.

Syd pushed her on to the second valve for the first time, and at about 25 per cent cut-off we attacked the bank in a most impressive style, the exhaust ringing out sharp and clear across the surrounding hills. We were checked by signals at Barnt Green Single Line box, so handing over the tablet was no problem, although Syd had to give her some stick to lift the train up the final couple of hundred yards of 1 in 74 to Barnt Green station.

From here we had a mainly downhill run for 4½ miles to Kings Norton station, and this section provided the only stretch where we could work up anything like express speed. I tried to take a rough timing from the quarter-mileposts at Halesowen Junction and was surprised to find that it appeared to be as high as 70 mph, for the ride was rock steady and the noise minimal.

I was unfamiliar with the main line from Kings Norton to New Street, so I spent as much time as possible observing this from both sides of the cab. With only 5 miles of mostly downhill work to go, I could afford to run the fire down, which of course left me more time than normal to take notes. Accelerating briskly out of Kings Norton station, we entered a sharp left-hand curve carrying a 35 mph speed limit, which, after straightening out, took us down past Bournville loco and on to Bournville station. Stopping at this picturesque wooden structure built on a high embankment gave me a fine bird's eye view of the well-known chocolate factory.

A series of sweeping left and right-hand curves, albeit on level ground, covered the next mile to Selly Oak station. We were not booked to stop there and, although the gradients were mainly level or in our favour, the nature of the track precluded any further high-speed running. At Church Road Junction, just over a mile from New Street, where a branch line runs down into the old Central Goods Depot we plunged into a deep brick-lined cutting, interspersed with five short tunnels. The gradient here was 1 in 80 and it was necessary to count the tunnels carefully in order to ascertain our exact position in the all-pervading gloom. It was useful to know that a water column was available at the end of one of the disused platforms at Five Ways since, if checked by signals, sufficient water could be taken on to get one to Saltley loco if things were getting desperate in that department.

From the last smoke-filled cavern we suddenly burst out into New Street station, clattered over the points outside No 5 signal box, and eased to a halt at the signals halfway along No 8 platform, 1 minute before time.

Almost immediately a small swarthy shunter made an agile leap into the 4-foot and started to uncouple us from our train. Meanwhile, having been previously briefed by Syd, I hopped on the platform, dropped the headlamp from the top of the smokebox to the centre of the buffer beam, and fitted the other one under our bunker. Ensuring that we were now free from our train, I rejoined Syd who was leaning over the uprights appraising the hordes of pretty young office girls rushing unheeding to the exit barriers.

However, not all the passengers were unappreciative of our efforts, for a couple of distinguished-looking middle-aged gentlemen came up to Syd and congratulated him on our prompt arrival.

'That's nice,' I remarked, as it was the first time I had heard such comments from the public.

'Oh, they are a pair of regular enthusiasts,' he replied. 'Stop-watches out on every section. Mind you, they are just as quick to tell me all about it if we are late.'

Our signal came off and we trundled slowly down to No 2 box, the sound of our motion being considerably amplified under the great grimy glass roof that spanned the Midland side of the station. We waited for the departure of the Bristol-Sheffield express standing in the adjacent No 7 platform headed by *Rooke*, resplendent in gleaming green paintwork, looking the very epitome of a real passenger engine. A deep-throated hoot on her whistle was followed by a powerful hiss of steam as she flowed into motion. Those great drivers gave a brief slip before they found a secure foothold and then she was gone, thundering down into New Street Tunnel, accelerating her 11 coaches as if on a roller-coaster.

Soon it was our turn, and we too snorted briskly into the hanging smoke clouds under Birmingham's well-known shopping area. It was quite apparent that all movements in and around this station area were conducted with an alacrity not to be found in any of the surrounding goods yards, where a more leisurely attitude seemed the order of the day.

Heading south from New Street was rather awe-inspiring on first acquaintance since, after hurtling out of the tunnel, one found oneself galloping down a 1 in 58 gradient that almost instantly reversed to uphill at 1 in 57 past Proof House signal box, giving the impression that somehow one had been suddenly shunted on to a switch-back. This of course accounted for the incredibly swift departure of the Sheffield express. Dipping into a stone-lined cutting, we descended once more, this time at 1 in 100 under the London line, and moments later we were passing Landor Street box, to be quickly shunted on the shed.

Leaving No 2326 on one of the arrival roads with a full boiler, plenty of pressure and a low fire, I ended my first day of what I considered to be the most pleasant job in the link. Working with Syd, no matter what turn, was invariably an experience to look forward to, but somehow the Redditch line always seemed to produce that little extra in excitement that made all the difference. Maybe it was because of the passenger duty, the single-line operation or the dreaded Redditch Tunnel, but something always seemed to turn up.

I well recall the week's work some three months after my first trip. Continuous torrential rain for several days on end had caused the River Avon and its tributaries to burst their banks and produce heavy flooding in the area. It was so bad in some places that the water came right up to the tracks, and left us wondering if the line could possibly stay open if these monsoon-like conditions persisted. What upset Syd, though, was that he was unable to collect blue-legs, those mushroom like saprophytes with a kidney flavour, much coveted by the local country folk. He had, over the years, pin-pointed a number of prolific beds and it was his practice to stop the train whenever suitable and quickly harvest a pound or two. Regrettably the floods destroyed those beds and they, like many other wild mushrooms, seem to have departed permanently from our fields.

On the Thursday it was our misfortune to be given a Class '8' that was considerably below par, coupled with a load that was at top limit. The sand in our boxes would appear to have succumbed to the exceptional weather and, being wet and lumpy, it was not flowing as well as it might. This caused us a fair amount of trouble climbing the bank to Camp Hill, so we were anticipating another struggle up through Redditch Tunnel.

I was by now quite experienced in the procedures, and we had stopped well back from Redditch South with a good but well-burned-through fire, a full head of steam and three-quarters of a glass of water. I collected the tablet from the signal box, getting soaked in the process despite being huddled inside my heavy company-issue rubberised raincoat.

'OK, Syd,' I yelled as I scrambled aboard.

Syd, also dripping wet, since he had been out giving the sanding gear a poke and a tap, heaved open the regulator. We staggered forward, slowly accelerating the heavy train, our wheels finding sufficient grip to take full gear and full first valve, as we pounded up to that black hole. No sooner had we entered than we started to slip, the sanders no doubt having given up the unequal struggle. I had already taken the precaution of applying to my mouth a damp handkerchief formed into a pad and held in place by a wiper knotted at the back of my neck. Even so, the searing blast of hot steam and gasses that now came into the cab literally took my breath away.

Immediately, Syd - looking more like a train robber than a train driver, since he too was wearing an improvised gas mask - disappeared from view. From now on I felt very isolated and more than a little helpless, although of course I had to ensure that we had maximum pressure without actually blowing off. I soon felt the tremendous vibration cease and sensed by the regular pressure waves that once more our exhaust was beating out a steady if somewhat slower rhythm. Then we started slipping and this was again only controlled by constant juggling with the regulator. Every time we regained our feet our speed had fallen, until we seemed to be making hardly any headway. Indeed, we might well have been travelling backwards, for I had now lost all sense of time and movement, and could see nothing whatsoever more than 2 feet from my eyes. I was already squatting on the floorboards with my back against the cabside, and even here the heat was intolerable and the fumes choking, while rivers of hot water seemed to be flowing from every pore.

Must check the pressure, I thought, as I staggered to my feet, grasping the injector wheel for support while peering myopically at the gauge. Good lord, the needle was on the red line! I tottered over to drop the tender water feed, and as I did so we slipped yet again. Another searing blast of scalding steam shot in through the uprights, catching me full in the face, and I reeled back, groping once more for the injector steam valve. Hanging on to it with my left hand, I beat desperately against the handle with the palm of my right hand, strength ebbing from my arm at every blow. If only I could have breathed it would have helped, but I was choking as I hung there in the hottest layer in the cab, burning up inside as well as out. Finally the valve spun open and I dropped to the footboards with senses swimming, holding my face as near to the floor as possible in order to gain some relief from the suffocating heat. Despite the general clamour and vibration, I could hear the injector singing and decided that at least one crisis was now over.

I was now conscious of a roaring in my ears, a thumping like a steam hammer right in the centre of my cranium and a body that felt like lead. It slowly dawned on me that I was being steadily asphyxiated, and the uppermost thought in my mind was how to get out of this inferno. If a healthy young fellow like myself was slowly going under, how the devil was poor old Syd, at more than twice my age, coping? Had he in fact succumbed already, and even now was I the only one still conscious on what was about to become a runaway train?

I crawled across the footplate and found he was, in fact, in the act of closing the regulator, and the resulting jerk would have sent me back to the footboards had I not managed to cling on to the conveniently sited anti-glare shield. Syd in one frantic movement disappeared out of view left, slammed open the side window and remained draped over the arm rest heaving like a stranded walrus. The dense clouds of steam seemed to be rushing out of the cab, and instinctively I rushed with them, collapsing over the side doors. We were out!

Tearing the handkerchief from my mouth I gulped in great lungsful of fresh air and, turning my face upwards, delighted in the luxury of feeling icy cold rain which was still coming down in torrents. Syd likewise, between fits of coughing, was enjoying the providential cold shower, but with one hand on the brake valve, was already controlling our descent. I wound on the tender brake, shut off the injector, then treated myself to some more fresh air. After a few minutes I felt sufficiently recovered to see how Syd was faring and crossed to his side. He was gulping down tea between the odd convulsion, but his breathing now seemed less laboured.

'Crikey, that was a bit rough,' I remarked hoarsely.

'Yes, you can say that again mate,' Syd croaked in a whisper. 'Just about as bad as I've ever experienced. To tell the truth, I'd have backed out if I thought we could have made it, but by the time I realised that I had had enough, I did not have sufficient strength left to wind the bloody screw into reverse, so I had to keep going.'

It was typical of Syd to make a joke about such a close call, for a close call it certainly was. He must have suffered more than I, since he had been obliged to remain at least semi-upright in order to operate the regulator. However, by the time we had reached Evesham and eaten our supper we were both pretty well back to normal and no permanent harm seemed to have been done, although it was an experience we had no desire to repeat too often.

With the same job the following February, after a week of icy weather, we were delayed on the Friday night outward trip by a tragedy again involving Redditch Tunnel. Six ponies had broken out of their field adjoining the tunnel and had entered it to enjoy the relative shelter and warmth therein. Regrettably an up freight train arrived soon afterwards and in those narrow confines there was no escape for the poor animals. The crew, who were completely unaware of their presence until their mangled remains began to be churned up on to the footplate, suffered severe shock, and the whole line was held up until the matter was investigated and cleaned up.

Being dark we fortunately saw nothing of the carnage, but we arrived so late at Evesham that we barely had time to get to the station before our passenger was due. As frequently is the case when things start going wrong, they continue to do so and our train was 18 minutes late on arrival, due, so we learned, to icing in the coaching stock brake system before setting out. This problem arose from time to time in extremely cold weather and was caused by condensed water freezing around valves and in brake pipes, preventing the brakes from releasing when a vacuum was created by the train engine. Indeed it was then a fairly common sight to see wads of oil-soaked cotton waste burning under such afflicted trains in an effort to thaw them out.

We quickly relieved the Gloucester crew and immediately appreciated the cosy warmth provided by the Fowler 2-6-4T. By the time I had done a check of fire and gauges including, on this occasion, the carriage warming system, which I always endeavoured to keep on the maximum of 50 lbs per sq in, we were ready to depart.

Syd was in a determined mood and had pushed the regulator right across as soon as the last coach was out of the platform. We had 2354 on this occasion and she was in beautiful condition, responding like a thoroughbred, her exhaust shattering the freezing air as we raced headlong for Harvington. This high-speed burst, together with a well-judged, full-brake-application stop, sliced 2 minutes off our deficit, and an equally energetic spurt did the same for us by the time we hammered away from Salford Priors. This thrashing meant, of course, that I was working harder than normal, but at least it kept me warm. Also I had now become expert in the art of exchanging tablets; in fact, it was a matter of some pride and I was constantly hinting to Syd that he might go a little faster so as to test the limits of my expertise.

In the low-lying area between Salford Priors and Broom where the river is in close proximity to the track, patches of freezing fog had reduced visibility considerably. Whether it was because of this, Syd's evident exuberance, or a combination of both, I do not know, but we made a very rapid approach to Broom station. Through years of practice Syd knew the points where a full application of the brake at a given speed would ensure stopping in the platform without recourse to easing off. This practice of single and late application of course saved valuable seconds when in a hurry. However, trains are not as consistent as cars in this respect and variables inevitably arise. No two sets of stock have exactly the same braking power, nor are the conditions always the same on any two consecutive days. As it happened, we had a good set, a fact discovered by Syd on our two previous stops, but unfortunately at Broom freezing fog had deposited a layer of ice on the rails, with the consequence that some of our wheels locked. What was intended to be a rapid stop two-thirds of the way along the platform resulted in a very frantic one, with the engine right at the extreme end of it.

It will be recalled that the signalman here stood on the approach end of the platform to exchange tablets, and this particular bobby was always rather nervous of the operation. He had been working the South box only a matter of some three months and from the start it was obvious that he did not enjoy the tablet-swopping part of his duties, for he would stand as far away from the track as possible, dithering first on one foot and then on the other as if undecided whether to go through with the business. As a result I found myself performing split-second acrobatics to accomplish the desired result. He was a podgy, Billy Bunterish young man, and on this morning as we flew into the platform I discerned a look of abject horror on his pallid features as I wedged myself tightly between the uprights in preparation for the fastest exchange I was ever called upon to make.

His previous dithering was not dithering at all compared to his antics now. Holding the old tablet low with my left hand, I aimed for the other gyrating hoop with my right and instantly felt a tremendous tug, which had I not been able to grab the handrail securely, would have pulled me from the footplate. Annoyed, I glanced back and was surprised in the extreme to see him gambolling head over heels up the platform in a most astonishing manner, half hidden by dust and grit. Seeing him suffer thus mollified my resentment somewhat, and having hung the tablet over the injector steam valve, briskly set about adding more coal to the fire.

Popping my head out to see how things were going a few seconds later produced a second surprise, for I was perplexed to see the bobby only a few yards away limping towards us. His fat features, even more pallid than usual, were contorted with pain, while he vigorously rubbed a limp right arm that seemed about 3 inches longer than when I last saw it.

'Why didn't you let go?' he wailed, wiping tears from his eyes with a coat sleeve. 'You nearly pulled my arm off, and anyway you've got the wrong tablet.'

'What do you mean, the wrong tablet?' I demanded, a strong feeling of irritation beginning to well within my breast.

Syd was by now taking an amused interest in the discussion, and collecting the tablet from its resting place, examined it studiously.

'Its certainly the Salford Priors to Broom one,' he exclaimed. 'How did that happen?'

I was absolutely flabbergasted and could not for the moment account for this conjuring trick. However, there was no time to debate the cause there and then for our guard was already trying hard to blow the pea out of his whistle. So, quickly collecting the correct tablet, we thundered out of the station leaving a disconsolate bobby trying to brush platform chippings out of his curly locks with his one useable arm.

Analysing this debacle I came to the conclusion that the signalman, whom Syd described as 'a bit of a fairy', had managed to strike the tablet I released with the one he was offering me. This had the effect of knocking it up so that my right arm collected it instead of the correct one, and since he also by now had his own right arm through the hoop but pointing in the opposite direction, a rather unequal tug of war occurred. Some 200 tons of train moving at 20 mph is a useful ally, and consequently the poor signalman had rather the worse end of the deal, but on reflection we were both lucky, for a serious accident might have resulted.

We attacked the relatively easy gradients up to Alcester with sufficient verve to cut another 2 minutes off our schedule, and during that time I was able to build up a really thick fire for the long climb to Redditch. Syd did not disappoint me and, using full regulator and never less than 40 per cent cut-off, we hammered up the 1 in 107 to Coughton at a scintillating speed, the exhaust ripping out from the chimney like an artillery barrage.

Getting away from Coughton produced another splendid display of pyrotechnics, and we were gaining time handsomely all the way to Studley. Although I was kept pretty busy with the shovel, we had as much steam as we could use; indeed, I was hard put at times to prevent her from blowing off. Halfway between Studley and Redditch Syd came over to examine the tank water gauge.

'We'll have to pick some up,' he bellowed. 'Thought we might save some time by not getting any, but it's far too low to risk it.'

So saying, he crossed to his own side and lengthened the cut-off another half turn. This was the price one had to pay for thrashing the engine. After all, one cannot obtain energy out of thin air, so consequently both fuel and water consumption increased enormously. Since we had to take on water, we might just as well work harder still, and gain a few more valuable seconds.

We approached the tunnel in an ear-splitting fury of sound, then all was suddenly quiet as we coasted at high speed into its black maw. Peering intently ahead through the spectacle glass, I was amazed to see clusters of large icicles hanging down from the roof at the far end. Instinctively I ducked my head as 2534's smokebox and chimney tore them off, causing a flurry of tinkling ice splinters to come bouncing back along the boiler. As we emerged, still going at a fair old pace, I was just able to lasso the lamp over the signalman's stage with the tablet since the bobby was still running down his steps as we flashed by.

Syd executed a brilliantly judged, if somewhat abrupt, halt on exactly the right mark for the column, and I had scampered along the platform and was opening the tank lid hardly before the screech of our brakes had died away. Syd likewise had moved with great alacrity and the water was flowing almost before I had the bag in place. From my elevated position I was able to take a breather and once again observe the crowds of passengers hustling aboard. Now, Worcestershire is well known for its beautiful girls, and none finer were to be found anywhere than at Redditch. It was generally considered that one of the perks on this particular turn was being able to appraise the merits of these lissome young souls.

I had just noted that the tank was three-quarters full when my attention was drawn to a vision of absolute loveliness gliding across the platform towards the first coach. I had seen some real beauties here before, but this one was incomparably the cat's whiskers. Syd too had seen her and turned round to feast his eyes on the spectacle. I goggled at the delightful creature as she drew near and received not a haughty stare but a most marvellous, radiant smile that seemed to pour sunshine and warmth into that gloomy February morning. The pulse quickened in response and the station seemed to swim before my eyes.

One hears of strange effects when men are thus smitten, but on this occasion the whole bally station was moving off stage left. The penny dropped. it was not the station that was moving, it was me, or rather the engine. The dashed thing was so eager to get going that it was taking off all on its own!

Many drivers of passenger and for that matter fitted trains evolved the technique of holding the engine brakes on while at the same time recreating a destroyed vacuum with the small ejector by wedging the retaining hook on the combination brake valve against the steam brake actuating arm. This allowed steam to enter the engine's brake cylinder while the brake handle was in the off position, and was a useful expedient when standing in a station for a short period to ensure that the train did not move when the necessary vacuum had been created. On BR engines separate steam brakes were fitted, but ex-LMS ones had no such useful facility available.

Syd had done just this, but in his haste he may not have positioned the hook quite correctly, and as the vacuum built up, pressure against the hook caused it to move away, releasing the steam brake. Being on a falling gradient, the train started to glide slowly forwards under the influence of gravity.

'Hey up, Syd, we're moving!' I yelled, alarm giving power to my voice as I shuffled along the moving tank top, undecided whether to try and throw the bag out or try and keep it in.

With a frantic leap Syd hurled himself on to the footplate and made a full brake application. He was, however, a split second too late. I had tried to pull the bag free, but the thick leather hose was rigid from the pressure of water running through it, and as the tank opening slid away the inevitable happened. The end of the hose kinked - forming a sort of U-bend - which caused the full flow of water to be directed vertically upwards like a huge gusher. I was bending directly over the opening, still wrestling away, when the violent eruption caught me amidships.

The powerful jet of icy water shot underneath my overall jacket, ballooning it out with such force that it nearly lifted me off my feet. For a second I stood there, a blown-up carnival effigy with water spraying out of both sleeves and around my neck like some unique animated fountain, then I staggered clear, soaked to the skin. The icy shock had taken my breath away, but there was no need to shout, for Syd came racing back and had already pounced on the shut-off valve.

Unfortunately for him the bag at last jumped free and the twitching hose, still disgorging umpteen gallons of water per second, swung back to position itself right over his bent form. It was now Syd's turn to receive a ducking, and my unspoken sympathy went out to him as he disappeared under that foaming, icy deluge.

A lesser man might have made a run for it, but Syd, with his now unshielded head hunched down between his shoulders (his cap was floating majestically down the platform on the crest of a small tidal wave), stuck to his post, and although he spun the control wheel faster that I've seen a control wheel spun before, he was quite as wet as me by the time the torrent ceased.

With teeth already chattering, I screwed down the lid and squelched back to the footplate to be joined seconds later by an equally squelching Syd whose face was even now turning a shade of light blue. We said nothing, partly because there was nothing much to say, partly because our dithering jaws rendered this difficult, and partly because the guard was already blowing his whistle and we had to get under way. My soaked clothing clung so tightly to my body that it was difficult to move, but I managed to collect the tablet from Redditch North box, although I found the act of firing impossible. As we pounded up the 1 in 91 gradient I removed my jacket, shirt and vest and draped these over the boiler front. I then put in a most energetic burst of firing in an effort to combat what felt like ice crystals forming in my blood stream.

Halfway up the bank I was down to only socks, boots, underpants and my uniform cap and leather gloves, while Syd had similarly divested himself of his saturated garments. It was then that we suddenly noticed ourselves, Syd in his long johns and me in my Y-fronts. Our eyes met and we simultaneously saw the comedy of the situation. Possibly it was reaction to the shock of being drenched, but we both doubled up in uncontrollable laughter.

Redditch station in 1963. With heavy Evesham-bound freight trains, drivers tended to stop well back in the station on the easier 1 in 283 gradient and send their fireman forward on foot to collect the tablet. This enabled them to have a charge as the following 1 in 126 section up to the dreaded tunnel.

'God' cackled Syd apoplectically, 'you look flamin' ridiculous.'

I could only gurgle and point vaguely at his long johns and cap - speech just would not come. Firing was murder without the protection of clothing ,and I lost most of my body hair in the searing heat. On the other hand, I had not until then realised how draughty a 2-6-4's cab could be, nor how cold the metal sides became in frosty weather. Modesty and a fear of getting my most precious parts frozen prevented me from opening the side door and lowering myself to hand over the tablet in the conventional way at Barnt Green Single Line. I did, however, score a bull's eye on the bobby's arm by tossing the tablet at him hoopla fashion. We both crouched low as we entered the station, for in those days 'streaking' had not become fashionable and we did not wish to alarm the female clientele.

It is amazing how the railway 'bush telegraph' works, though, and it was obvious by the time that we steamed into Northfield that a message had been passed down the line to the effect that the crew of the Ashchurch slow was doing a Lady Godiva on the footplate and up to no good. The bobby's face was pressed hard against the windows of the box as we passed beneath, and his goggling eyes goggled even more as he glimpsed our naked forms. Fortunately there can hardly be a more efficient dryer of wet clothes than the boiler front of a Fowler 2-6-4T, and although somewhat stiff, our garments were perfectly fit for wearing after leaving Kings Norton.

The luxury of getting dressed again was indescribable, and although there may be much to commend nudism in the right place and at the right time, I can definitely state that the footplate of a locomotive on a cold February morning does not fall into either category. The capers we got up to on that last dash into New Street were both hilarious and exciting, but we finally shuddered to a halt on platform 8 only 2 minutes adrift, which was a pretty good effort considering our preoccupation with other matters.

With the coming of spring the last couple of months with Syd seemed to speed by.

However, as much as I disliked the idea of leaving him in May, it soon became apparent that instead of moving into another section of Group Three, I would be going into the Passenger Group, such was the pace of promotion then. This prospect was a powerful palliative and considerably softened the blow of our parting, since by now I had acquired a strong taste for this type of work.

When the fateful day at last arrived a quick glance at the new rosters confirmed that I had in fact gone into Link 2, Section C and was booked with a chap called Fred Galloway. Syd and I bade each other a fond farewell, but life is an endless flowing stream with new adventures around every bend, and to be perfectly honest I was really looking forward to that next bend in the Passenger Link.

On my way home I reflected on the events of the past nine months. Syd was not such a great railway enthusiast as some other drivers, but he was certainly one of the outstanding characters at Saltley. He had not pushed enginemanship and railway dogma down my throat, rather he had let me find my own way, demonstrating and explaining only when I wanted to learn. He no doubt realised that I needed to settle down slowly after the disruptive influence of military service, and being an expert in the psychology of human nature, considered this was the wisest method. It was most fortuitous that I had been booked with him after demobilisation, for his balanced and stable philosophy of life and wise council did wonders for me during this difficult period.

I had never driven an engine, except for shed movements, during the whole of the nine months, but then I never felt the need to. I had, however, developed both my firing technique and route knowledge considerably and was now as supremely fit as any 21-year-old should be. Furthermore, I was enjoying life immensely, work was sheer pleasure and I awoke every morning eager to live that day to the full. I will always be eternally grateful for the privilege of working with Syd Lloyd, and will forever benefit from the influence he had upon me during those formative years.

3
THE PASSENGER LINKS

In the past I had frequently felt overdressed when in the company of some of my colleagues, but when I was introduced to Freddie Galloway on that first afternoon with him, I was conscious of just the reverse. Although I had made an extra effort with my appearance that day, I could not match the dapper figure that now confronted me.

Fred stood only about 5 ft 2 in tall and, although in his early 50s, carried not an ounce of surplus flesh. In fact he looked positively fragile and could not have weighed more than 7 stone dripping wet. From his shining uniform cap down to his equally highly polished expensive shoes, he was the picture of sartorial elegance, and even his spotless overalls were neatly pressed. His face was sharp and alert, wearing that cheeky, slightly belligerent expression so common in many small men. However, from the purple capillaries tracing his complexion it was obvious that he was fond of alcoholic refreshment.

We were booked to work the 5.15 pm to Redditch, so after the usual formalities we got down to the business in hand and sought out our engine, 'Doodlebug' No 3013, which was standing already prepared in Woody's Sidings. It was in a bit of a mess, so while I set to work with brush and slaking pipe, Fred went off to make the tea.

I had not fired a 'Doodlebug' on any form of road job before, and this prospect, together with the fact that it was to be on a passenger turn, left me feeling as happy as a lark. With the rest of the cab now looking spick and span, I was just putting the final polish on Fred's windows when he returned. Instead of being delighted at the gleaming footplate his face clouded over.

'Damn, I meant to tell you not to wet the floorboards on my side.'

He went on to explain that he suffered from recurrent bouts of phlebitis in his left leg and he was quite convinced that standing about on a wet floor did nothing to help this painful condition. Notwithstanding this slight setback, I turned the conversation to our coming work and asked for details.

It appeared that we travelled down to Saltley Carriage Sidings, collected a train of four or five coaches, ran empty to New Street, then worked the 5.15 pm stopping train to Redditch. There we ran round our stock, shunting it into the carriage sidings adjacent to the old loco shed and waiting until about 9.15 pm when another shunt enabled us to back down into the station in readiness to work the 9.35 back to Birmingham. After that we returned our stock to Saltley, then ran on to the loco, leaving the engine to be stabled by the disposal crews. It was a straightforward job, and one of Fred's favourites, since during the long wait at Redditch he could retire to a convenient hostelry and indulge himself in the local brews.

'What do you think of these engines?' I enquired as we rolled towards the carriage sidings.

'Not a lot,' he retorted. 'They are cold and draughty things in winter. Mind you,' he continued, seeing that I was eager for further qualification, 'they run well enough, but they only steam when you haven't got the injector on.'

I was a trifle disappointed by these remarks since, as previously explained, I held these

Left Ivatt Class '4MT' No 43013 with its original double chimney. In this form the class earned a reputation for being steam-shy, but later fitted with modified single chimneys they were capable of some very useful work.

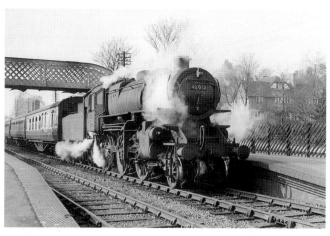

Below left In this view No 43013's double chimney has been replaced by the decidedly more handsome single version, which also improved steaming. However, in this view No 43013 has more than her share of leaks, with a bad blow from what appears to be the steam supply pipe joint to an injector and another at the front of the boiler, which may be a delivery pipe defect on that same injector. While cold weather emphasises a steam locomotive's exhaust and makes for more spectacular photographs, it also shows up such blows, which could cause annoyance by restricting vision.

I found these locomotives lively performers, although because of their remarkable efficiency the injectors had to be used very circumspectly.

Ivatt 2-6-0s in high regard. This regard, however, was fostered purely from their ease of disposal, and I realised that now I had to view them from an entirely different angle.

As initially introduced with double chimneys they had gained, for good reasons, a reputation of being steam shy and, as with many other things, first impressions die hard. A considerable improvement had been effected by fitting single chimneys, but even so the difference was not so great as to reverse immediately general opinion. I recalled reading that the brilliant engineer, S. O. Ell, had during the course of experiments at the Swindon Test Plant improved the continuous steaming rates of these 'Doodlebugs' quite dramatically. Minor modifications had brought about this miracle, since only a reduction in the chimney taper and that of its

choke from 1 ft 2¼ in to 1 ft 0¾ in was necessary. No 3013 had a single chimney, but since she had obviously not been shopped for some considerable time, it was a pretty reasonable bet that she had not yet received Mr Ell's treatment. Apart from this, though, everything else seemed to be in splendid condition, and I decided to reserve my verdict until the end of the trip.

Having coupled up to our train and with empty stock lights on the buffer beam, I started to prepare the fire. At 23 square feet, the grate area was not over-large, and I thought it prudent to ask Fred's advice.

'What's the best method of firing these?' I enquired.

'Keep a good back on, but very thin at the front,' was his immediate reply. 'Much the same as a "4F", in fact.'

The answer seemed logical since the grate sloped down to the front in a similar manner, so I started manhandling some large lumps in the back corners. Being essentially mixed-traffic engines, they were not always coaled with the best grades, and today our fuel was a mixture of large lumps and slack. However, I was fairly confident that we would not get into too much trouble, working a stopping train to Redditch. As usual with passenger work, very little time was wasted and no sooner were we ready than the signal came off and away we went.

Immediately No 3013 showed that she could handle her five-coach load with nonchalant ease by the brisk manner we accelerated up to Duddeston Road. There the distants also came off and we were able to take

a run at the 1 in 90 section up to Grand Junction. Entering New Street station from the London end is even more exciting than from the western approach, since not only is there the thrill of the switchback beyond Proof House, but the Rugby and Bescot lines run in parallel to the Midland tracks and a short race often results.

We soon arrived on platform 10 where a crowd of passengers were already waiting for us.

'Make sure she doesn't blow off,' advised Fred as I leaped off to rearrange the headlamps.

Fortunately there was little fear of that just yet, for I had deliberately allowed the steam pressure to fall back to 180 lbs per sq in. Returning to the footplate I began building up

Birmingham New Street station, Midland side, in September 1952. Both platforms 9 and 10 were departure platforms for westbound trains. Standing on the centre road, just simmering at the safety valves, is No 41025, one of the original Midland 'Compounds', stabled at Gloucester (22B). It was especially important not to blow off in New Street. The arched glass roof greatly amplified sounds and trapped smoke, and if loco crews transgressed in those aspects of engine management, they quickly drew wrath upon their heads. *F. W. Shuttleworth*

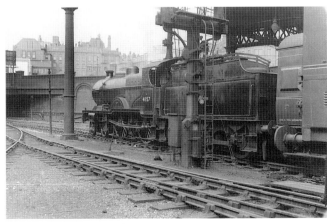

Standard 'Compound' No 41157 heads a westbound stopping passenger train at New Street's No 10 platform. This was one of a batch of 25 engines built by the North British Locomotive Co in 1925. Thirty-four years on, it was still able to handle these secondary duties competently.

The westbound exit from New Street. 'Compound' No 41123 piloting 'Jubilee' No 45626 on the 8.15 am Newcastle-Cardiff wait to depart on the stiff climb up through the tunnels to Five Ways.

the fire, keeping both blower and doors wide open so as not to create too much smoke, a heinous crime in New Street. Again I was amazed how quickly the injectors topped up the boiler, and reminded myself that they would only have to be used in short bursts.

At 5.15 pm everything in my department was as it should be. The needle was on the red line, the water was just in sight at the top of the glass and the fire, well built up, was burning brightly. Unfortunately something was blocking our path because, although our guard had given us the 'right away' whistle, the signal remained stubbornly in the on position. I was now on the horns of a dilemma, whether to let her to blow off, or inject more water into the boiler, which was already as full as it ought to be. Deciding that she could probably take a little more, I chose the latter option and knocked the steam pressure back 5 lbs per sq in. In the future I found this annoying problem arose fairly frequently, and I adjusted my departure preparations so that we often set off slightly low on water, rather than be a noisy nuisance while in the station.

With the valves just lifting, the signal came off at 5.18 and Fred, who had been impatiently hopping from one foot to the other, yanked back the regulator. A couple of sharp barks erupted from our chimney as the wheels gave a half-slip, then, finding her feet, she blasted off into the series of tunnels leading up to Five Ways. The benefit of our little 5 ft 3 in driving wheels was most noticeable as we stormed up through those smoke-filled catacombs, the exhaust ringing out sharp and clear and at a much faster rate than normal. Some of the impression was no doubt psychological, but even so there was no doubt at all that these Ivatt '4s' got off the mark, and climbed banks surprisingly well.

We stopped at every station along the route, so there was no problem with steaming; in fact I was unable to decide at the time just what No 3013's limitations might be. Certainly the lively acceleration proved ideal for a stopping passenger train, and even better than that of the 2-6-4 tank engines, although the ride was nothing like as stable and the noise level definitely higher.

On the final stretch from Barnt Green to Redditch, Fred introduced me to a young couple who had recently moved into an old but picturesque lineside cottage. I do not know just how the relationship came about, but he made it a practice to arrange for a large lump of coal to fall from the tender as we were passing by. In the past I had engineered such accidents for the benefit of signalmen and platelayers, but never before for anyone not working on the railway. From the cottage it was only a matter of minutes before we gave up our tablet at Redditch North and rattled into the station, where we disgorged our remaining passengers.

While they were streaming by I hopped down in the 4-foot and uncoupled our engine, when a simple shunting operation enabled us to run round our train. We then dragged the stock forward on to the up line and finally backed into the siding alongside the loco where we would have to wait until 9.15 pm.

Having well filled the boiler and dropped some lumps of coal under the door we both washed, and as I prepared to eat my supper Fred announced that he was going to slip off for a pint. Not harbouring any such inclinations I preferred to remain with the engine, although I did find it rather lonely, particularly when the dark winter nights arrived, and in future I always made a point of carrying an interesting book with me.

Later on, as Fred's confidence in my capabilities improved, he would save himself a walk by taking his leave at the station, allowing me to stable the train, and for that matter bring it back again, single-handed. Needless to say I enjoyed this spot of driving, coupled with the responsibility involved, and considered it more than adequate compensation for being left alone.

Fred always returned in excellent spirits after his little binge, and was usually very talkative. Although initially I had doubts as to whether his ability to drive was impaired in any degree, I found that I had no cause to worry. Despite his lack of inches, Fred could hold his drink as well as anyone.

On this first occasion he was back in good time, and advised me when to start building up the fire again. He also recommended opening the tender doors and thoroughly wetting the coal, since travelling tender-first with a 'Doodlebug' at speed caused a blizzard of coal dust to swirl around the cab.

This wetting of coal could be overdone on occasions, particularly if there was a high slack content that absorbed large quantities of water before it was well and truly laid. In this event one would tend to find oneself firing a heavy black slurry, which was hardly conducive to promoting a bright, hot firebed. However, it was in freezing weather that one really had to take care, as I discovered on this very same turn the following winter during a severe cold snap. After backing into the siding I had liberally hosed the mixture of dust and slack in our tender in the usual way, and then settled to read a book that I had just bought. We were halfway up the bank from Redditch on the return journey when I found that coal was no longer falling down on to the shovelling plate. Thinking that some large lumps must have become jammed I opened the tender doors to investigate and thereupon found a vertical wall of slack, frozen as hard as concrete. I was forced to literally hack out every shovelful for the remainder of the trip, and while this effectively combatted the intense cold, it kept me very busy, to say the least.

In the merry month of May there was no such problem, although the night was chilly enough for me to agree with Fred's verdict that these Ivatt '4s' were cold and draughty when running tender-first. In all other respects, however, they were well designed for this purpose and vision was as good as on any tank locomotive. The return run was uneventful and No 3013 mastered the job effortlessly; not many people patronised this train, so the stations were largely deserted, but even then departure times were strictly adhered to.

Later in the week with the same engine I came to curse the fact that they were fitted with twin regulator handles. It was often debated as to the logic of retaining this unique arrangement on 'Doodlebugs' because, although the regulator could be operated from either side of the cab, the brake and reversing screw were located on the driver's side. A theory was offered that Ivatt, realising that these engines did not steam too well, sympathised with the firemen and gave them the facility of being able to surreptitiously close the regulator when in times of difficulty. Whatever the reason, this extra handle could be positively lethal at times.

There was a permanent way restriction of 15 mph at the 3 milepost from Barnt Green and, after traversing this, Fred opened up for a quick burst on the following level stretch. Anticipating his final shut off accurately, I bent down and started to close the rear damper, which, on a 'Doodlebug', took some little while since it was effected by means of a wheel operating on a screw. I had half completed this when the world suddenly exploded in a myriad of stars, and I found myself dazed and not a little puzzled, sitting on the floor. As the pain and confusion in my head eased slightly I slowly realised what had happened.

During our sprint away from the slack, Fred had opened the regulator on to the second valve for a short while and it had become 'gagged'. To free it he had yanked it fully open just as I was bending forward, and that hefty bar of steel had caught me right on top of my head. Fortunately, being pretty nearly solid bone, no real harm was done, although I sported a lump the size of a golf ball for a day or two. Needless to say, afterwards I always experienced a slight pang in the cranium when operating dampers on 'Doodlebugs'.

Two weeks later we were booked on the 5.5 pm Birmingham to Leicester and, not having been there before, I was looking forward to it even more than the Redditch job. A 'Compound' was allocated for this duty, so at last I was able to try my hand with one of these famous Midland engines. The 4-4-0 wheel arrangement deceives the eye, so that at a distance they do not appear particularly large, but when in close proximity their true size becomes obvious. I was surprised at the length of the firebox when I first glanced through the doors on boarding No 1109 in No 2 shed. The engine had been prepared, but we had to take her outside and, since moving a 'Compound' was always an exacting operation, I concentrated on raising maximum pressure as

soon as possible. She was in a filthy state and Fred left me to clean up while he went and made some tea.

I had already secured the turntable when he returned, and warned the crew preparing an engine on the pit opposite that we were about to make a move. Fred eased gently on to the table without any problem, but I noticed that he seemed a long time backing out after I had called him from the shed entrance. I climbed on to the engine steps for the short ride down to the next set of points.

'The bloody reversing screw is as stiff as hell,' yelled Fred, looking rather red about the gills.

Casting my mind back to the good old shed link days, I recalled that 'Compounds' were inclined to be a bit heavy in this respect, which is possibly why they required 24 turns on their low-geared screw from full forward to full reverse.

I dropped off and, setting the points for the departure road, called Fred forward. I had already walked up to the water column and No 1109 still had not moved; I rightly concluded that Fred was having another struggle. Eventually he arrived, sweat glistening on his forehead and cursing profusely.

'Never had one as stiff as that,' he grumbled as we filled the tank. At the time I did not attach much importance to his comments since my thoughts were more on how I would fare with my own duties.

With some minutes to spare, we booked off the shed and ran over the points on the up Camp Hill line prior to crossing on to the down main. It was here that Fred first asked me to try the gear. Normally, reversing screws can be wound quite easily with one hand, but with this one I had to use both hands and a fair bit of effort to obtain the desired result.

'Wouldn't like to do a day's shunting with her,' I replied to his inquiring look, for Fred had a habit of cocking his head on one side like a bird when asking a question.

Muttering under his breath, he climbed back on his platform and opened the regulator. It was then that I noticed that, due to his lack of inches, this was also a bit of a struggle for him. Fortunately, 'Compound' regulators were equipped with twin handles in the form of a V, so that they could be pushed and pulled at the same time.

The action of the 'Compound' regulator was unique in that opening it to the halfway position allowed high-pressure steam to be admitted to the two outside cylinders only, and in this condition she operated as a simple engine. When speed had built up to a sufficient degree, opening the regulator further allowed 'compounding' to take place by admitting high-pressure steam to the inside cylinder, which in turn exhausted in to the two outside cylinders. The regulator could be then eased back in the normal way until on final closure the sequence of events would be repeated.

Ascending the bank up to Grand Junction I first noticed how swiftly No 1109 covered the ground. The exhaust beats were deceptively slow, but her large driving wheels had an enormous stride, and it was only when one studied the trackside that the pace became apparent.

After arriving in New Street we had to wait some 10 minutes before backing on to our

train of six coaches, and then a further 5 minutes before receiving the whistle to start. During that time I was able to build up the fire and get everything else shipshape, although I left plenty of room in the boiler because our first stop was Saltley station only 2 miles away and all downhill at that.

We were both watching when the guard gave us the tip and, answering with a toot on our flute-like whistle, Fred clasped both handles of the regulator and heaved it open. There was a loud hiss at the front end but nothing else happened. A string of curses came from Fred's lips as he opened the taps and laboriously wound the screw back to full reverse. With the taps closed again, he quickly opened and shut the regulator, which this time caused us to nudge back on our stock.

Another long hard wind into full forward gear was followed by a generous opening of the regulator. Immediately a shattering explosion of sound erupted from our chimney as the wheels spun violently, and then we were off, pounding down into the tunnel with a much louder and sharper exhaust than I would have thought possible from a 'Compound'. In

Freddie Galloway found Standard 'Compound' No 41109 very reluctant to move in either direction; it was obvious that the valve events were a trifle odd, since the exhaust roared in a most un-'Compound'-like manner. She pulled exceptionally well up banks and ran like the wind, but had a voracious appetite for coal. She was built at Derby in 1925 when 'Compounds' were very much in favour.

virtually no time at all we were coasting past Saltley loco and braking for the station. Here, amongst a dozen or so passengers, were three sets of enginemen I did not recognise, and concluded that they must be Leicester crews on their way home. Since the platform was on my side, I was obliged to keep a look out for the guard, and this time when he waved us away No 1109 blasted off with no hesitation whatsoever, much to Fred's relief.

By the time we had passed Washwood Heath Junction, he had the regulator right over so that she was then on 'compound'. Much to my surprise, the blast did not subside to the customary hiss, but continued as a peculiar, loud, syncopated beat which seemed to indicate that the valve events were somewhat unusual to say the least. Just what was wrong we never found out, but we fairly hurtled through Castle Bromwich station, and I was then able to assess the ride at speed.

There were no knocks in the motion, but there was a certain amount of lateral movement in the axleboxes that seemed to accentuate a natural rolling tendency. However, on the whole the ride was good by any standards and we were certainly covering the ground very quickly indeed.

Once more we accelerated out of Water Orton station without any problems, at least not on Fred's side, although I was having the unusual one of her steaming too well. I ought to qualify this statement because an engine cannot really steam *too* well; No 1109 was steaming better than I had allowed for, mainly I think due to the unusually fierce blast burning fuel at twice the normal rate.

Up the bank from Whitacre Junction was real stirring stuff working on simple engine, but by Shustoke we were compounding again with little diminution of exhaust volume. By the time we breasted the summit I was sweating profusely from my efforts, but I was able to take it slightly easier on our dash down to Nuneaton. Here we struck trouble again and Fred had to mangle away at the reversing screw before she could be persuaded to go forwards.

From now on the line was unfamiliar to me and this always makes firing just that little more difficult, since one has to rely on the driver's advice, and he is not always cognisant with all the facts. Fred recommended that I kept a good fire on because Hinckley, our next stop, was approached up a 2-mile bank mainly at 1 in 160, and after that we were 'right away' to Leicester.

We were dead on time arriving at Hinckley, but when we came to depart No 1109 would not budge an inch. Resignedly Fred wound it into reverse, and still she would not move. At this stage he was just about all in, so I pounced on the screw and, when in full forward gear, heaved open the regulator. There was a slight shudder, but nothing more. The guard was whistling frantically all this time thinking that we had both dropped off to sleep, and the Station Master was walking up to investigate the matter. Fred tried to indicate our difficulties by sign language without much success while I wound the confounded screw back through all its 24 turns. I could now appreciate Fred's distress for, although I was probably twice as strong as he, I was now beginning to puff and pant. Desperately heaving up the regulator I breathed a sigh of relief as the wheels revolved, unfortunately giving the passengers a hefty jolt as they did so.

Then came the long wind forward until we could again move in the correct direction, but I finally accomplished this, happy to do so because I was sort of driving, and Fred was quite happy to let me expend my energy. With another jerk we set off some 4 minutes late, and I stepped down from the driver's stand to allow Fred to regain his rightful position. That 4 minutes had to be regained and here was the ideal place to do it, for, after an initial fall of 1 in 320, the next 2 miles dropped at 1 in 162. With the regulator wide open we fairly bounded down that bank, our exhaust beating back at us in a great tearing un-'Compound'-like roar.

We hurtled through Elmsthorpe station at the bottom of the incline at a speed that left no doubt why 'Compounds' were labelled 'greyhounds' in their heyday. In fact, to use one of Syd Lloyd's expressions, 'telegraph poles were going past like palings'. The short rise of 1 in 351 up to Stoney Stanton Sidings was barely noticed and we continued our headlong flight over the falling gradients past Croft Sidings, Narborough and on to Blaby where, despite another slight climb, Fred was obliged to ease up for Glen Parva Junction. Here the Rugby and Bedford lines merged from the right, and frequently we were checked on this complex. However, today we had the road and, after observing the 25 mph speed restriction, we were able to sprint into Leicester right on time.

After refurbishing our engine on the nearby loco, we were required to work the 9.00 pm back to Birmingham. This was again a stopping train, but it involved rather greater effort since we had more uphill work. However, No 1109 was well up to the task and she steamed as well as ever, providing I kept baling in a plentiful ration of coal. Her reluctance to start unfortunately still persisted, and Fred was very glad when we finally left her for the disposal men on Saltley shed. His term for 'Compounds' - 'one-arm bandits' - seemed most appropriate in her particular case.

I very much liked the Leicester runs and we fortunately had a number of them in the link. The 11.15 am was interesting in that we were booked a Class '4P' 2-6-4T, and I was at last able to make a direct comparison between the Stanier and Fowler varieties. We always ran bunker-first to Leicester, and to be quite truthful there was little to choose between the two types. They both pulled well and ran like deer, riding beautifully at high speed. Because of their side windows the Staniers were perhaps a little less draughty, but on the other hand their cabs and fittings tended to rattle rather more, so we never really cared which type was allocated.

Possibly one of the easiest jobs was working the 12.50 am parcels to Leicester. We were relieved in the station there and, after walking across to the loco, we collected a 2-6-4T and backed on to four or five coaches standing in the bay. We were booked to heat the stock before working it forward as the 5.50 am early morning workmen's train to Birmingham. Needless to say no effort was spared to couple up as soon as possible, and while we ate our supper I gave the steam heating apparatus full pressure. Then, after filling the boiler to capacity and putting a good charge on under the door, we retired to the first coach to slumber peacefully in comfort for some three hours or so. When vitality is at its lowest ebb it is surprising how alert three hours' sleep can make one, but then it was just as well, because sometimes we miscalculated and awoke to find passengers already boarding the train and the engine low on fire and water.

There were also a couple of regular Derby turns in the link and an occasional run to Gloucester, which kept our hand in on these sections. It was on a return working from Derby on a very wet and grey autumn Saturday afternoon that I first got my hands on a BR Standard Class '5'. I had been eagerly awaiting such an opportunity since entering the link, and now at last we were able to sample a brand new engine straight out of the works.

We only had this job on Saturdays and,

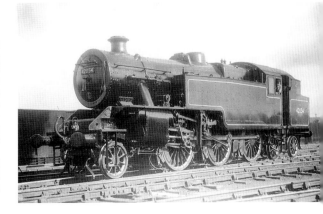

The Leicester stopping passenger trains provided an excellent opportunity for crews to make comparisons between various locomotives. The 40 miles of undulations supplied the right mix of gradients and fast stretches while plenty of intermediate halts gave ample scope to test acceleration with various loads. The three designs of 2-6-4 tank engines were one such exercise - all were superb, and there was little to choose between the Fowler, Stanier and Fairburn versions. I only regret that I never had the opportunity to try a BR Standard.

Pictured here at Crewe is Fairburn No 42054, one of two allocated to Saltley. Built at Derby in 1951, it had a shorter coupled wheelbase and was some 2½ tons lighter than the Stanier design.

being a through express stopping but once at Burton, it was worked all week by the top link men. Conservative by nature, Fred was not too pleased with the prospect of having to drive this unknown type for the first time on what was just about our most exacting job, in foul weather conditions. Initially he protested about taking her, but the Derby men were both enthusiastic and persuasive and, while the tank was filling, quickly showed us the unfamiliar controls. The driver lightly dismissed Fred's objections.

'Just like a "Black Five" only better,' was the parting verdict, and the fireman was just as positive about her steaming capabilities.

On receiving the 'right away', Fred tugged open the regulator and off we set. As might be expected with a brand new engine, everything felt delightfully taut, with no knocks or rattles, giving an immediate sense of confidence and well-being. The exhaust was sharp and clear, but pitched somewhat higher than that of a 'Black Five'; as we thundered out of the station with ten coaches behind the tender she seemed very determined to show us what she could do.

Unfortunately we soon caught up with a fitted that was making slower progress than Control had anticipated, but at least the delay gave us an opportunity to have a closer look at our charge. The back of the boiler, compared with other LM engines, was particularly neat and free from the plumber's nightmare of pipes that cluttered even Stanier's latest designs. The general layout seemed ergonomically ideal, with all the driver's controls positioned around him, while likewise the fireman's controls - including both injectors - were within easy reach of his seat. These seats were excellent, being of the fixed variety, comfortably padded, and an immense improvement on anything I had yet seen.

The cab, attached directly to the boiler, was not subjected to the stresses and different movements as on previous types, and was particularly free from noise, although it did give rise to a unique drumming sound as the wheels passed over rail joints. Furthermore, since the footplate extended right back to the tender in a continuous area, the fireman had a more stable platform on which to work. My only reservation was the design of the shovelling plate, which was formed into a hump along the leading edge. While this tended to prevent small coal from rolling on to the footplate, it did require a different angle of attack when shovelling, but I found in due course that this was only a question of adaptation.

Another desirable feature was the provision of twin whistle handles mounted so that they could be operated from either side of the cab, and I have already described the glorious chime whistles originally fitted to these standard Class '5s'. Even Fred, on this first trip, used it far more often than was strictly necessary. The GWR-type gauge glasses and protectors were also very neat and easy to read, but what really held my interest was the provision of two other instruments, namely a steam chest pressure gauge and a speedometer. Here for the first time I was able to note the actual pressure achieved from the various regulator settings, and an instant read-out of the effect it was having in terms of mph.

Fred did complain of the strangeness of the brake handle and the reversing screw, the former being horizontal instead of vertical, and the latter lying longitudinally instead of the usual transverse position. However, he did concede that the seat was comfortable, although because of his short stature he had to bob around a good deal more than the designers had no doubt intended.

Strange or not, after leaving Burton we had a clear road and, although the steam chest pressure gauge showed no more than 160 lbs per sq in on full first valve, the speedometer needle was hovering in the upper 60s all the way up the bank to Tamworth, where I tried out the water scoop. It was lower geared than that of a 'Black Five', and while it operated quite freely, I was a little slow in extracting the blade, so that a couple of hundred gallons of water sloshed back over the leading coaches. Had it been a hot, dry day, complaints would soon have been forthcoming - as it was, the deluge passed unnoticed in the torrential rain.

Beyond Tamworth our pace gradually increased and, although Fred notched her back to 15 per cent cut-off, the needle crept into the lower 70s, at which speed she was commendably smooth and quiet. Further checks approaching Birmingham caused us to arrive in New Street some 3 minutes in arrears, but by that time I was thoroughly converted and an out-and-out enthusiast for BR Standard locomotives. Fred, like many other drivers, regarded them with a somewhat cooler eye. He and his kind required more than one trip to pass any balanced judgment, and in fact a year or two passed before the majority of drivers accepted them as competent, reliable engines.

Being human, Fred at times had his moments of fun, and one particularly amusing incident happened whilst working the West Pilot turn on Christmas Eve that year. The West Pilot was regarded in the link as a sort of rest job, since it never involved much work. A '2P' 4-4-0 was allocated to perform this duty, which consisted of spending most of the night standing by in New Street station in case any westbound train required assistance. Only once in the whole 12 months were we called upon to pilot a train through to Gloucester, and this was because part of the engine's brick arch had fallen down. Therefore only a few short bouts of shunting broke our nightly relaxation, which on a '2P' could be very comfortable indeed for the fireman.

The tool box on the fireman's side was just about the largest on any engine and formed a very adequate bed. Not unnaturally, the drivers tended to allow firemen to drive on this job, under the pretext that it was good training for learning the intricate moves in New Street station. Be that as it may, I suspect the true reason was that they could make full use of the very inviting tool box during the lengthy quiet periods.

Christmas Eve was cold and frosty and New Street station, normally busy, had been a veritable hive of activity all evening. At 11.00 pm it was still crowded with cold and hungry passengers from end to end, awaiting the innumerable specials that, regrettably, were not always running to time. In those days the restaurants and snack bars, such as they were, closed down around 10.30 pm, which was neither enterprising nor considerate.

We were standing in the bay on No 10 platform when the manageress of the restaurant approached us with a sack of onions that were decidedly on the turn and causing her establishment some considerable embarrassment. Here I must point out that it was a fairly common practice for such garbage to be disposed of in the firebox of the nearest loco, since one would be lucky to find a more efficient incinerator anywhere. I was therefore not surprised by the request, and after bidding her a Merry Christmas, heaved the odorous sack on to the footplate and prepared to dump the contents into the fire.

Fred, whose sense of devilment was no doubt heightened by the extra tot or two of hard stuff he had taken with his nightly pint, stopped me.

'Don't put 'em on the fire,' he said with an air of mystery. 'Throw them on top of the brick arch instead.'

'What for?' said I, puzzled by this unusual instruction.

'You'll see,' he replied with a twinkle in his eye now evident. 'They'll roast slowly on there, and then you just watch their mouths water.'

He waved a hand indicating the mass of humanity stamping their feet and flapping their arms on No 9 platform. Perhaps this was a little unkind, but my curiosity was now aroused and I readily admit to having felt a few pangs of envy since we were to 'see Christmas in' working on the footplate while everyone else was seemingly enjoying this festive occasion.

Removing the deflector plate, I quickly 'fired' the onions on to the top of the brick arch, spreading them over the whole area as evenly as possible, where they started to sizzle away in a most satisfying manner. Within 2 minutes of completing this task, we were asked by the shunter to take a van down to the north end of the station and stand on the centre road, prior to backing it on to a westbound mail train due shortly.

As anyone knows, even a single pound of onions produces a considerable aroma when frying in a pan, so one can well imagine the effect of half a hundredweight cooking merrily away. As we puffed gently through the whole length of the station, this most appetising

Class '2P' locomotives were booked to Station Pilot duties at New Street. If all went well no greater effort than a few minutes light shunting was called for during a shift. The fireman's seat was long enough to lay full length on, which is possibly why drivers frequently decided that it was a good opportunity for firemen to learn 'station movements' while practising their driving. Occasionally, however, a passenger train required assistance, then the old '2P' had to hitch up her skirts and travel at a quite indecent pace at the head of an express to Gloucester or even Bristol.

It was on the West Pilot that Freddie Galloway tantalised cold and hungry passengers with the smell of roasting onions one Christmas Eve. *F. W. Shuttleworth*

smell was trapped under the great glass roof and percolated into every corner, while 400 or so heads turned this way and that, trying to detect in vain the source of their torment. . .

The year with Fred passed very quickly and, although I did no real driving, I received a thorough grounding in passenger work, which incidentally required a whole new range of techniques. It was a really enjoyable year, but during the second half a longing for faster, harder, more exciting jobs grew, and neither the link nor Fred was able to fulfil this.

He was a very competent and careful driver who had the happy knack of being able to run punctually from point to point without constantly consulting his watch. He would, wherever possible, try and regain the odd few minutes lost, no matter by what cause, but he would not flog any engine or run at exceptional speeds for the sheer fun of it, and in my youthful enthusiasm I yearned for a driver who would do both these things and also explore the limits of the engines and my capabilities.

At the annual link change my prayers were well and truly answered when destiny brought Tommy Charles and me together.

He was the very epitome of what I then considered a driver to be, and while I needed

him so he, as it turned out, also needed me. It may sound a trifle arrogant, but by enthusiastic encouragement and an untiring willingness and ability to fire at exceptionally high rates, I enabled him to drive with an unrestrained abandon that produced performances that would have made the designers themselves shake their heads with disbelief. Every day we both delighted in proving that a steam locomotive, enthusiastically even if uneconomically handled, was capable of just about double what was normally expected of it.

Tom and I were both on the same wavelength in as much as we considered that the crew's attitude was the main limiting factor to a steam locomotive's performance. Most drivers were kind, mature men at heart who had arrived at their positions only after many long, hard years with the shovel. It was therefore not unreasonable that they should be sensitive to their mate's labours, and cause them no unnecessary work since, after all, the company only required them to run to schedule. To the majority of firemen, footplate life was only a job, a job that was demanding enough even when working to the minimum requirements, so that an excess of physical effort was to be avoided if at all possible. Furthermore, not all crews were aware, or capable, of exploiting the tremendous reserve of energy that could be stored in the boiler and firebed. Thorough route knowledge and keen anticipation could tap this reservoir and exploit it to produce short-term efforts way above the considered norm, which is why some startling performances appear on record.

Everyone in the passenger links seemed to know of Tommy Charles, and when the new rosters were posted they were quick to tell me just what I was in for. With this prior knowledge of Tom's methods in mind, I lost no time in airing my own theories and attitudes, telling him that as far as I was concerned he could not drive an engine too hard or too fast, and that I was fully prepared to bale coal in as fast as he could knock it out as long as I could still stand up. Having this 'carte blanche' invitation did wonders for Tom's outlook since I later learned that several firemen had refused to work with him on the grounds that he worked them too hard, and he had not unnaturally been a trifle hurt by this criticism. It took a few days before he realised that I meant exactly what I had said, and during this period I made a point of deliberately standing by his side spurring him on to even greater efforts when occasions arose. After that we fully understood each other and it was then that the sparks really began to fly.

Tom had joined the LNWR in 1919 after having served in the Royal Navy as a torpedo-man during The First World War. It is now well known that LNWR men drove their engines harder than just about any other railwaymen, and Tom, well schooled in this method, liked to hear the exhaust beat, no matter what the type, load or conditions. Moreover, the fact that he was slightly deaf only meant that an engine had to be opened up just that bit more to achieve the effect!

In his mid-50s, Tom resembled an amiable rhinoceros - tough, thick set and utterly dependable. Nothing seemed to upset or disturb him, even when near disaster loomed ahead, and during my stay with him I heard no complaints about anyone or anything, although he had to endure a painful open ulcer on his left shin, a legacy from the war. Tom took life as it came, obstacles and difficulties were part of that life and it was no use whining about them - they were there to be surmounted and surmount then he did, for he was by nature one of those strong, silent men of action.

After only the first week I discovered that he was susceptible to a little encouragement, provided that it was subtly presented. We were working the 1.55 pm slow to Leicester, which was in itself a bit of a misnomer since timings were quite keen and the train ultimately ran through to Great Yarmouth. Usually a 'Black Five' was allocated along with eight corridor coaches, although this could be made up to ten at the height of the holiday season. I was already enjoying myself very much on this turn because the loadings, the frequent stopping and starting and the gradients combined to necessitate giving the engine a fair bit of stick, and Tom was prosecuting this in a manner I had not previously experienced.

On the Thursday I was delighted to find that we had a BR Standard Class '5' and looked forward to see just how she would perform. Tom, as usual, showed no particular emotion and hammered on in his normal enterprising way, until we reached Hinckley. This, as previously mentioned, was the start of the fastest stretch, but unfortunately we were booked to stop at Elmsthorpe only 3 miles further on. I felt that this stop was a cruel quirk of fate for, had we been able to run straight through to Leicester, Tom would doubtless have worked up some exceptionally high speeds by the bottom of the bank.

As it was, we set off vigorously enough using full first valve and, after half a mile or so, 25 per cent cut-off. With help from the gradient our speed rose steadily and, as it did so, I stepped over to Tom's side of the cab to see what the speedometer was reading. Without any alteration to the controls the needle gradually crept past 70, and steadied on 74 mph.

'Do you think she would reach 80?' I enquired. Tom looked up at the speedo as if noticing it for the first time.

'Should do,' he replied in the manner of a schoolboy seeing a new game.

He brought the regulator back to the fully open position, and immediately the steam chest pressure gauge indicated 220 lbs per sq in instead of its former 170. I noticed a slight sharpening of the already rapid exhaust beat, and the speedometer needle started to creep upwards again - 75, 76, 77 mph. Elmsthorpe was now getting perilously near, but having been set a target, Tom seemed determined to achieve it at all costs. I suppose that had we sufficient time, 25 per cent cut-off would have taken us well over 80 mph, but we were now rapidly running out of road, therefore Tom dropped down to 35 per cent forcing the engine along above her normal effort.

It was amazing what a difference that extra 10 per cent made; the exhaust increased to a ferocious staccato roar, while at this speed the individual beats were barely discernible.

The effect on the speedometer was equally dramatic, for the needle started to move quickly towards the 80 mark. It had just touched 82 mph when Tom slammed shut the regulator and made a full brake application. As usual with trains, there was initially little apparent effect and, looking ahead to see just where we were, I was horrified to see Elmsthorpe station looming towards us at a tremendous speed. Then, as the brakes overcame the momentum, our pace slackened noticeably, but even so it was quite apparent that we were not going to make a controlled stop in the orthodox manner, and I stood behind Tom fascinated by the spectacle.

The leading edge of the platform hurtled past and then all too quickly the trailing end swept by at a pace greater than I would care to have alighted at. Four coach lengths beyond this we jerked to an abrupt halt with the vacuum gauge still registering zero.

'Didn't think that we were that near,' murmured Tom, as cool as if this happened every day of the week. 'Still there are four coaches in the platform - only holds five anyway,' and with that we watched the few alighting passengers sorting themselves out with plenty of time to spare because, as usual, he was running well ahead of schedule. On arrival at Leicester I had time to reflect that if Tom was willing to put up this sort of performance on a stopping train, I could look

forward to an exciting year ahead on some of the other turns.

It was on this 1.55 Leicester that I discovered his eyesight was nearing the minimum acceptable standard. All enginemen, of course, had to pass periodic eyesight tests, and although this presented no problem at his last one, he admitted that a number of signals under certain conditions were proving difficult to sight.

Most of the passenger and top link drivers were in their 50s and 60s, and for their age a better-sighted group of men would be hard to find, but there is no doubt that their vision was not as keen as it had been 20 years earlier. Fortunately experience and constant practice largely compensated for this, but passenger drivers discovered any problems of this nature first because of the higher speeds that their jobs demanded, and Tom travelled at a higher speed than most.

With this problem frankly exposed, I soon learned the whereabouts of those difficult signals, and also the ones that were sighted first from my side of the cab, so that like many other experienced firemen I was able to act as a sort of advanced warning system for the driver.

Gradually I became used to Tom's exceptional everyday driving methods and these were then the norm by which I judged other performances. Like every other driver, Tom occasionally, by dint of circumstance, or merely through joie de vivre, produced an extraordinary effort out of the blue, and these episodes are indelibly printed on my memory.

For example, after only a few weeks together we were booked to work the 4.00 pm Bristol Parcels from Birmingham New Street to Gloucester. After perusing the engine board we found that our engine, No 4744, was already prepared and waiting in the shed yard. This was a Caprotti 'Black Five', and although I had never worked a Caprotti before, I was well aware that they were not held in high regard by the majority of drivers. This stemmed from a reputation of not being able to pull very well on banks and of being indifferent steamers into the bargain. On the other hand, all drivers readily admitted that on the level or downhill they ran like greyhounds and could be linked up to almost mid-gear.

Naturally I was very keen to see what Tom would do with one and broached the subject as we walked over to her.

'What do you think of them, Tom? I've heard that they are not too clever on uphill work.'

'Never had any problems,' was the studied reply. 'Think the trouble lays in the fact that they've got a louder bark than the Walschaerts "5s", and most drivers wind them up too much.'

I then remembered what Doug Pinkerton had told me once. He had been working an express one night with a Caprotti and found to his amazement that on the easy gradients down to Gloucester he had been running for many miles at 7.5 per cent cut-off in back gear! It was therefore logical to assume that there was a good deal of truth in Tommy's theory.

Climbing aboard No 4744 I was more than somewhat surprised and a little annoyed to find that she had been coaled from end to end with ovoids, and the footplate was 6 inches deep in these little synthetic 'eggs'. We had a little time to spare, so after a quick check around Tom went off to make the tea, while I set about the task of cleaning up. First I sought out an old firebar from the disposal pit, which I wedged between the bottom of the tender doors and the shovelling plate. This was the usual method of reducing the flow of small coal or ovoids, which tended to flood on to the footplate with the movement of the engine. Also shovelling off the floor was much harder work than off the shovelling plate, apart from the annoyance of walking on the things and the dust they produced when crushed underfoot. I then cleared all traces from the footplate, packing the ovoids under the firedoor and around the sides of the firebox, swilling the remaining dust away with the slaking pipe. This was just completed to my satisfaction when Tom returned saying that he had rung out and as soon as the signal came off we could go.

From the first shudder as we moved out of the yard, to when we came to a halt in New Street, a steady stream of ovoids rolled on to the footplate, so that once more we were wading knee deep in the things. There was still some 20 minutes or so before we were due to depart, so I decided to deposit this lot in the firebox as well. By the time I had finished, a very thick bed of ovoids was lying on the firebars except for a hole some 3 feet from the mouthpiece. This was of course necessary to prevent the generation of too much steam and help reduce the production of smoke, which even then was belching from the chimney in greater volumes than was strictly desirable.

No 4744 had been out in service for some considerable time, and as was common with many engines fitted with rocking grates and hopper ashpans, she had been subjected to a certain amount of misuse. At some period in her life a fire had been dropped into the ashpan before first opening the doors, and the resultant excess of heat had distorted these doors, preventing their proper closure and admitting a considerable quantity of air. I therefore could not control the draught to the firebed as well as I would have liked; however, on the other hand the fire was burning through evenly over the whole grate area.

The needle was on the red line by the time we backed on to our train, but since I had deliberately arrived with only half a glass of water I was able to prevent blowing off by use of the injector. Our guard, whom I deduced knew Tom quite well, came up to us while we were being coupled on and, with tongue in cheek and an apologetic smile, announced that we had a gross load of 364 tons.

'I'm afraid there isn't a pilot available, Tom - 320 tons is your limit unassisted, so it's up to you. Will you take 'em?'

Without any hesitation Tom nodded his consent. I'm quite sure that he would have done so if asked to take double this load, for it was his philosophy to give his engine the lot and see what happened.

The guard disappeared, but it was already 4.10 pm before our signal dropped, and knowing that an express was shortly due to follow us, Tom was in no mood to hang about. Everything was in good order from my point of view. In full gear, which was 85 per cent cut-off on a Caprotti, Tom opened the regulator; No 4744 took a pace forward, checked, and

Caprotti 'Black Five' No 44757 leaving New Street on the Sheffield-Gloucester on 8 June 1953. It would seem to be coaled with the very smoky 'eggs' so prevalent at this period, but the smoke seen here is a mere trifle compared to the 'blackout' that Tommy Charles and I produced at the same place with No 44744 when working the 4.00 pm New Street to Bristol parcels.

then almost immediately the regulator was heaved right across. An almighty explosion of sound shattered the air, reverberating under that great arched roof like an artillery barrage as the wheels spun in a gigantic slip, and the area round New Street station was transformed from brilliant sunshine to a darkish midnight within a matter of seconds. The enormous draught produced by that slip had well and truly stirred up the fire, and although the blower was hard on and we were once more moving with a wide open regulator, a great towering column of jet black, oily smoke was erupting from our chimney.

I had left the firedoors wide open in an effort to burn the smoke, but so much was now being produced by that thick bed of ovoids that it was beyond the capacity of the firebox to consume it with the draught available at our present speed. As we pounded into the first tunnel a blow-back between each beat occurred in the form of a great red cone of flame that flattened itself menacingly against the tender doors; I shrank back in my corner, fascinated at this spectacle. I had never experienced anything quite like it before and, apart from thoughts of becoming singed, I was fearful that my shovel, which was in the line of fire, might lose its handle.

Through the thick smoke and steam now streaming into the cab I could see Tom's bulk, as unconcerned as ever, leaning forwards over

the screw with one hand poised on the horizontal regulator handle, taking little or no notice whatsoever of these footplate pyrotechnics. After all, this was the fireman's business and he was quite confident that I would cope with it.

Up through the tunnels to Five Ways the cacophony was deafening, for under full gear and regulator we were accelerating our train up the 1 in 80 in a manner that totally belied the load we hauled; I was left wondering how Caprottis could possibly have acquired their reputation for not pulling well on banks if they were all like this one. When we finally broke out into daylight I was delighted to note that the needle was still glued to the red line, although the water level had fallen to half a glass, so it was necessary to put on the injector and start ladling in ovoids with great gusto. Under the incredibly fierce draught generated by a wide open regulator and 50 per cent cut-off, they burned at a demoralising speed; fortunately it was only necessary to scoop them up and let fly in the general direction of the mouthpiece since the blast then took over and distributed the ovoids in much the same way as a mechanical stoker would.

Over the level stretch beyond Church Road Junction our pace increased rapidly, and as we roared through Selly Oak station the exhaust had risen to an absolutely earsplitting staccato bark that had my pulses racing, for not even

Tom had previously hammered an engine like this. In seemingly no time at all we were through Bournville and shutting off for the 35 mph restriction round Kings Norton station junction, and I used this opportunity to turn on the live steam injector in an effort to top up the boiler because the exhaust injector had only managed to maintain the half glass level from Five Ways. The firebed was also now only a third as thick as when we had started and I frantically fired all round the box as fast as I could shovel before Tom opened up again.

This he did as soon as we were on the straight and, after shutting off the live steam injector, I paused on his side of the cab, taking a quick breather while blinking through rivers of sweat across at the carriage sidings. To my delight I saw Freddie Galloway gesticulating wildly from the footplate of a Class '5'. He was trying to convey in mime that Tom ought to give her some more. That was hardly possible, for with the boiler at 225 lbs per sq in, the regulator horizontal, and the cut-off at no less than 60 per cent, the cylinders were handling just about as much as they could take. The exhaust, as it thundered off the brick-lined embankment rising above us on the up side was nothing short of shattering.

Some days later I saw Fred in the engineman's lobby when booking off, and he remarked jocularly that I looked about 2 stone lighter than when I was booked with him.

'No kidding,' he went on, 'we could hear you all the way up to Barnt Green!'

This may have been something of an exaggeration, but with the wind in the right direction they no doubt heard us for some considerable way because we stormed through Cofton cutting at 45 per cent, and even on the down grade of 1 in 297 approaching Barnt Green Tom did not condescend to shorten the cut-off beyond 30 per cent. Here, with our speed well into the 70s, the impression of sheer power was indescribable. Never before had I witnessed such a sustained effort with a steam locomotive.

Despite these tremendous demands made on the boiler, the steam pressure gauge was still showing 220 when Tom finally shut off for the descent of Lickey. However, the water was again down to half a glass since the exhaust injector had not kept pace with usage, and I quickly brought the live steam injector into action as we started down that notable incline. As previously mentioned, the fireman can usually depend on a few minutes' respite

Caprotti 'Black Five' No 44744, one of a batch built at Crewe in 1948 with plain axlebox bearings. These locomotives initially gained a reputation for being weak on banks, although all agreed that they were very fast and very free-running. Tommy Charles soon disposed of these notions when working the 4.00 pm New Street-Bristol parcels with this same locomotive. Despite having 364 tons behind the tender (44 tons over-load) he made a nonsense of the loading tables, giving a scintillating performance on the rising gradients up to Blackwell, and indeed gaining time hand over fist all the way along the route.

while coasting to just beyond Bromsgrove South, but not so on this occasion, for the firebars were now only covered by a very thin incandescent layer. I was therefore obliged to pack in more fuel with undiminished vigour, knowing full well that this would be my last opportunity to build up an appreciable bed before reaching Gloucester.

Being now truly warmed up and having had all the cobwebs blown out of her, No 4744 showed us that she was as fleet of foot as any 'Black Five' in the region. Past Stoke Works, Tom, with wide open regulator, gradually pulled her up to 15 per cent cut-off, and over the following easy gradients our speed rapidly built up, certainly the fastest I had yet travelled on a steam engine, and I only wish that she had been fitted with a speedometer so that I could have recorded the peak reached at the bottom of the 1 in 385 drop to Eckington. I also wished that I had had a coke shovel available, since I could hardly bale in ovoids quick enough with the standard implement to keep pace with the excessive rate of combustion. Despite our tremendous speed, she rode very well indeed and, although the footplate was one frantic seething mass of motion, there were no excessive bangs or rattles, while the furious tearing roar of the exhaust could be clearly heard above everything else.

Approaching Cheltenham it became obvious that not only had we wiped out our 10-minute late start, but had begun to catch up the preceding train, for we ran into a series of signal checks. In a way I was glad of the opportunity to build up the fire again for the final spurt to Gloucester, although I had no complaints with the way No 4744 steamed. Admittedly it had required a great deal of physical effort, for I had been firing almost continuously all the way, but the needle had barely left the red line and although I was a bath of perspiration, I was still feeling in fine fettle.

With a clear road once more, we thundered away from the station, accelerating with a most impressive display of power using full regulator and 30 per cent cut-off and consuming ovoids at such a rate that I was now obliged to open the tender doors. With

Gloucester almost in sight we literally hurtled past a Western express running parallel to us. This caused black looks from its crew, but gave us a great deal of boyish satisfaction. Despite a further check just north of Gloucester station, we glided to a halt at the end of the platform 4 minutes to the good and, having put the bag into a now virtually empty tank, handed over to the relieving Bristol men.

They were pleased by our early arrival, but not at all happy about the depleted fuel supply nor the fact that it was composed entirely of ovoids. However, you can't have everything in life, so we left them to it and wandered off to a small pub Tom knew of just outside the station. Standing at the bar I suddenly realised how thirsty I was, and within minutes sank three pints of ice cold cider shandy. Adequately satisfied, we returned to the messroom for a well-earned bite, happy in the knowledge that as a team we had performed well above the required standard - Tom confident that I was both willing and able to supply just about as much steam as he could use, and I now confident that I could meet his demands, no matter how excessive they might prove to be.

From then onwards Tom's driving became even more dynamic, but I had no regrets, for despite the extra physical effort this involved I constantly exhorted him to break new records. Strangely enough we were never once short of steam. On the contrary, we even made engines that were supposedly steam-shy perform as never before, as this next incident will illustrate.

The 5.00 pm Derby slow was crewed on weekdays by men from that Mecca of the old Midland Railway. An Ivatt Class '2P' was allocated, and they worked this down on the 1.30 pm slow from Derby. After terminating at New Street station the engine was brought on to Saltley loco and refurbished by our shed men while the train crew restored their tissues in the canteen. However, on Saturdays the 5.00 pm became the 5.15 pm, and its return working was entrusted to ourselves in Link 2, the Derby men travelling home on the train as passengers.

While in the shed link I had at times been involved in refettling the Ivatt Class '2Ps' and

Ivatt Class '2MT' 2-6-0 No 46446 just out of the paint shops at Crewe. When extended to the limit, these engines could perform surprisingly well. In fact, the harder they were worked the better they steamed, as Tommy Charles proved on his boisterous 'demonstration run' with the 5.15 pm Derby slow. Being the first modern LMS locomotives designed to handle light duties, these '2MTs' were generally well received by crews, who particularly appreciated their ease of servicing.

thought them grand little engines, since, being fitted with self-cleaning smokeboxes and rocker grates, they were very easy to work on. I was therefore looking forward to actually firing one, particularly since it was to be for the first occasion.

On climbing aboard No 6446 I was a trifle disconcerted to find that she was coaled with what appeared to be a tender full of slack, the surface of which was broken by the odd large lump of dull, poor-grade coal. Following previous exploits with Tom, my confidence was running at an unprecedented high, but this was rather dispelled when, after just having cleaned down, two sets of Derby men clambered on to the footplate.

'God!' exclaimed the leading driver, 'have you got to take this camel back?' Before either of us could ask the obvious 'Why?', he continued.

'We worked her down this afternoon and lost 9 minutes - 9 minutes on a slow!' At this juncture, he spread out his hands and, looking up, appealed to the cab ventilator for sympathy. 'I booked her for not steaming, didn't think they would have the cheek to turn her out again, and Christ, we had a lot better coal on than that rubbish you've got there. You'll be in trouble with that lot. I say, you'll be in right trouble with that lot, won't they, mate?'

I glanced across at his fireman who was nodding his head in vigorous confirmation. He was a tough looking fellow, several years older than myself and obviously no novice. If he had had problems with a familiar engine and reasonable coal, then how would I make

out? I quickly transferred my gaze to Tom and received all the assurance the trace of a shrug can give one. Tom's face betrayed no alarm, but then it never did, so I decided to play safe and build the fire up some more.

But here was a problem, for there were already six of us on the not over-spacious footplate, and now three guards, seeking a ride up to New Street, came scurrying on board and mingled with the crowd. I found myself jammed hard against the open side window, barely able to lift an arm, let alone find sufficient room to swing a shovel. I was therefore obliged to adopt a passive role during our protracted journey to New Street, and by the time we arrived there, no more than 160 lbs per sq in was showing on the clock, while the boiler level was down to half a glass.

The delays incurred outside the station left me little time to put matters right, although when our passengers finally left the footplate I was able to quickly drag out a few of the exposed lumps of coal and drop them under the door. One advantage of a grate area of only 17 sq ft was that even a few lumps covered a fair percentage of the bars. Leaving the blower hard on, I hared round to the front of the engine, for the shunters had already coupled up, and positioned one headlamp on the smokebox. I hated having to dash around like this when the engine was not in a condition to my liking, but we were due away at 5.15 pm, and even now it was 5.18.

I was able to get in another half dozen shovelsful before we received the tip to depart, 4 minutes awry, but steam pressure was still 10 lbs per sq in light at 190, and the water level was showing only half a glass. With six well-filled coaches behind the tender, and a late start into the bargain, Tom didn't pussyfoot about and immediately yanked the regulator well across the quadrant. If any reader has never heard the wonderfully crisp, sharp exhaust of an Ivatt Class '2P', I can strongly recommend a visit to the Severn Valley Railway at Bridgnorth, Shropshire, where they operate a beautifully preserved example in the form of 46443. Even on the modest requirements of this line they sound more impressive than just about any other type and, when opened up, have a bark closely akin to that of a Bofors gun.

We executed a typical Tommy Charles New Street getaway, the little 5-foot driving wheels spinning viciously on a perfectly dry rail, touching the equivalent of 70 mph without moving an inch, while the exhaust rose to a shattering crescendo. Then with barely a pause to obtain adhesion we were off, thundering down through the tunnel, into the switchback at Proof House and on to Grand Junction, all the time accelerating furiously under full gear and regulator. I had witnessed some pretty vigorous getaways since being with Tom, but from a cold start this certainly took the biscuit, and the rapidity with which our wheels revolved only accentuated the fact. How so much steam could pass through cylinders measuring only 16½ in x 24 in to make such a racket was truly remarkable, but pass through it did and the sound as we dived into the cutting leading down to Landor Street Junction was splendidly exhilarating.

Our first stop was Saltley, and as Tom shut off I quickly knocked on my injector and glanced at the pressure gauge, expecting the worst. However, I was pleasantly surprised to see that it was on the 190 mark, although having mortgaged the boiler somewhat, the water very nearly disappeared from sight under heavy braking for our brief halt.

There was just sufficient time to flash a few shovelsful of coal round the box before we were on our way once more. Tom was absolutely ruthless in his working of the engine, for with the regulator wide open we were past the West End before he deigned to touch the reversing screw, and even going through Bromford like a bat out of hell, the cut-off was no less than 40 per cent.

With only half a glass of water in this very small boiler, the reserves were slender indeed, and while using steam at this rate I decided that it would be tantamount to folly not to leave the injector on continuously, no matter what effect it had on the steam pressure. Furthermore, this fearsome blast was consuming fuel much too fast to use the firing-after-shut-off method I had employed on previous stopping passengers. I therefore opened the firedoors, flipped up the small bottom flap and sprayed slack and fines over this as fast as I could shovel. Judging by the trail of rich, black smoke we left billowing in the air far behind us, a certain amount must have passed through the tubes unburned, but most of it was obviously doing some good, for the pressure fell no lower than 175 prior to shutting off for Castle Bromwich.

Here I found and broke up some large lumps of coal that had become exposed, and with these I was able for the first time to build up a respectable back on the fire. The short sections between Water Orton, Coleshill, Whitacre and Kingsbury provided just the necessary amount of respite to allow both the water level and steam pressure to gradually attain their optimum readings. The blast generated by Tom's merciless hammering kept the fire at a really fierce white heat, so that by the time we left Kingsbury station she was ready for just about anything. This was just as well because with the perception of years of ingrained experience, Tom sensed that all was now as it should be and properly set about showing the world what an Ivatt Class '2' 'Mogul' could really do.

We departed from Tamworth dead on time for the longest non-stop stretch of our journey. Had one not known Tommy Charles, it might have been imagined that, having pulled back the lost 4 minutes, we could have taken things a little easier over the generally falling gradients to Burton-on-Trent. However, with water to be picked up over the troughs, our departure from Tamworth was as aggressive as anything Tom had achieved to date, and we thrashed away in a devastating blaze of smoke and sparks and sound. With the tank topped up, we started the descent down to Elford, first at 1 in 484 and then beyond Wiggington at 1 in 408, while all the time I was working like a madman, spraying in fuel over the bottom flap mechanical-stoker-fashion.

As our speed rapidly built up, Tom, sitting as phlegmatically as ever, gradually linked her up, keeping the game little engine at the absolute limit of her front-end capability, until at Wiggington he finally settled for rather more than 30 per cent. We had the benefit of a stiffish tail wind in addition to the favourable gradient, and from the lively, cavorting footplate it became obvious that No 6446 was now travelling a good deal quicker than her designers had envisaged. Approaching Elford the crisp, clear exhaust beats began to merge until they became one long, incredible, continuous harmonic roar. Never before had I heard an engine worked in such a manner, and indeed only once more in my life was I to experience the indescribable exhilaration that this ultimate effort produced.

Our headlong dash from Tamworth had lowered the boiler level to the halfway mark despite one injector being in continual use, but just before Tom closed the regulator for the inevitable signal checks at Branston Junction, I could not resist showing off by dispensing with that injector for a few moments. This allowed the needle to come right up to the red line, so the instant Tom shut down our safety valves lifted, indicating to the world in general, and the Derby men in particular, that we still had plenty of steam.

Not unexpectedly, we had gained so much time that we were held for several minutes in Burton station, but I welcomed this delay since it enabled me to fill the boiler, build up the fire and drag some coal forward, for I was now obliged to work with the tender doors open.

When our guard finally blew his whistle, Tom did not let up one little bit; on the contrary, he hammered up to Repton & Willington just as vigorously as on any previous section and knocked another couple of minutes off our schedule in the process. From here, which was our last stop before terminating at Derby, Tom really went mad. The adverse gradients, varying from 1 in 387 to 1 in 1861, did not allow the extraordinary high speeds we attained at Elford to be repeated, but in terms of horsepower generated in the cylinders there could not have been much in it.

Being on top of the job and now able to run the fire down, I was well placed to observe cut-off settings, and with a wide open regulator and 200 lbs per sq in on the clock, never once did Tom link up beyond 40 per cent. I realised later that he was demonstrating just what could be done with the engine, and he could not have done so more effectively than over this last stretch for, with the benefit of a clear run, we screeched to a halt in Derby station exactly 3 minutes in front of time. Admittedly the schedule was not particularly exacting, but with a load of six coaches and an engine that was reputedly a poor steamer, it was no mean feat.

For more than a century Derby had a profound influence on railway practice both on the Midland Railway and the LMS. This period view is of platform 1 in its original condition; it was completely modernised in the 1950s, and was invariably crowded with passengers when the Carlisle and Glasgow fitted freights from Water Orton sped boisterously through on their long journey north. Being 40 miles from Birmingham it was a convenient point to change crews, particularly on freight duties, when a round trip from Birmingham could represent more than eight hours' work in those days of severe congestion. However, it provided just sufficient distance for Tommy Charles to demonstrate how to work the 5.15 Derby slow on his epic run with the Ivatt '2MT' No 46446.

The climax to this tale occurred while we were still standing in the platform waiting to be detached. During the final run in I had been able to swill down the footplate and have a wash myself, so that on arrival everything was spick and span with a full head of steam and the water an inch from the top of the glass. Voices raised in argument caused me to look over the side, and I then found myself confronted by the two sets of Derby men we had taken up to New Street as passengers and who had, of course, travelled home on our train.

'There you are,' said one of the drivers, 'I told you it was the same engine.'

The other driver who had worked her down to Birmingham just goggled and, thrusting his head between the uprights, stared round the cab in stark disbelief.

'Well they must have done something to her at Saltley,' he mumbled as he turned away, and off they all went, still arguing.

'What do you think they did to her at the shed?' I asked of Tom.

'Don't suppose they did anything,' he replied, with a sort of smirk. 'The trouble is, these chaps probably charge the firebox, and then when she doesn't steam too well, work her lighter and lighter until it's all choked up, instead of putting a bit of blast on the fire. I've always found that these "2s" like a good thrashing. Never did harm any engine.'

There comes a moment in every being's life when he or she hits an all-time high, achieving the ultimate peak performance that is never again exceeded. This applies to just about every form of human endeavour from playing golf to composing grand opera. So too, is it true of machines, particularly machines as full of human characteristics as steam locomotives, and when all the good variables come to work together for a while, then that is the time when records are broken. Should, by some strange chance, the appropriate human and mechanical peaks be achieved at one and the same time, then wonders can occur. Such a wonder was brought about on the last occasion Tom and I worked the Bristol to Sheffield Night Mail together from Gloucester to Birmingham. That night belonged to Tommy Charles and *Galatea*, one

of the 'Jubilee' 4-6-0s. This was their supreme effort, and I am forever grateful for the privilege of having witnessed it and indeed for having played some part in making it possible. My own peak in terms of sustained physical effort was yet to come, but without doubt this run with Tom was the most enthralling, fantastic performance I was ever to enjoy during my railway career, and it stands head and shoulders above all others, to be remembered and relived for the rest of my days.

The Mail was normally worked weekdays by Bristol men as far as Birmingham, where they were relieved by a Sheffield crew. However, on Sunday mornings it was routed the hard way, via Worcester, and this one turn fell into our own Link 2, Section B. Tom and I had taken a late-night passenger train down to Gloucester and, having completed a relaxed supper in the station messroom, were all ready for our coming exertions. We were due to relieve the Bristol crew at 2.50 am, but it was something like 3.05 when No 5699 *Galatea* trundled in with no fewer than 14 coaches behind her tender.

Even in the dim platform lights I could not fail to notice the gleaming green paintwork of a recent shopping, and my heart gave a little skip of joy, for nothing raised my spirits more quickly than having a 'new' engine.

'She's a beauty. Steams like a kettle even with the dampers shut,' were the only words spoken by the Bristol fireman as we scrambled aboard.

Having dumped my kit into the locker, I hastily climbed on to the back of the tender and thrust the water column bag into the tank. As the water flowed in I was able to take stock, and was delighted to find a tender full of best-quality hard coal, real black diamonds that had a ring when struck with a pick and could be split with absolute precision by a single blow. Moreover, it was already well broken and neatly trimmed, and since this required no further attention I descended to the footplate.

Unbesmirched paintwork, shining brass handles, polished copper pipes and white unscarred footboards heightened the impression of newness as I glanced at the

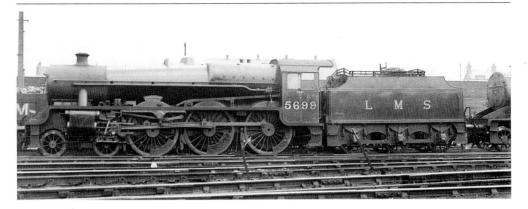

Above *Galatea* is seen here at Newton Heath 19 years before her magnificent effort with the Night Mail on the Lickey Incline. When first introduced in 1934 with a GWR-style low-degree superheater, 'Jubilees' gave poor performances. Urgent attention was given to rectifying this, and when *Galatea* was built at Crewe in 1936, changes to superheating, draughting, boiler and firebox had been incorporated, which then proved very successful.

Right This view of the curve between Holmes and Rotherham was taken in 1951 from the footplate of No 45699 *Galatea* when hauling the 9.04 am Derby-York. Although the background is different and, in this instance, in daylight, the view reminds me of departing from Gloucester with this locomotive on the Bristol-Sheffield Night Mail when Tommy Charles really made the sparks fly. As with Gloucester, the relevant signals are first sighted from the fireman's side. *Pat Webb*

gauges, which showed the water level an inch from the top and steam at 220 lbs per sq in. A short inspection of the long firebox revealed a perfect fire, well burned through and in the classical shape; everything was too faultless to be true.

Here then, was a freshly shopped '5X' in superb condition, with a perfect fire burning in her box, backed by a tender full of Grade 1 coal, hauling a heavy load over a demanding route containing one of the steepest banks in the country. The control of this juggernaut was in the competent hands of just about the most determined and fearless driver on British Railways, aided and abetted by a fireman whose enthusiasm for speed and power was only exceeded by his ability and willingness to

work. With the added incentive of a late start and a desire to get home to bed as soon as possible, we had all the ingredients for an extraordinary run. Just how extraordinary it was to be I could not of course imagine at that stage, for although I was by now well used to Tom's methods, we had not worked a '5X' together and I was very much looking forward to see what he would do with her.

After filling the tank I had sufficient time to fire ten quick shovelsful round the box before we received the 'right away' - 15 minutes late. Tom eased her out of the platform while I busied myself with sighting the signals that were first visible on my side.

'OK, Tom!' I yelled. 'We've got the back 'un.'

The blast sharpened and that beautiful double-three beat that the '5X' played with such virtuosity sounded like music in my ears as I bent to flash another quick ten round the box. The run to Cheltenham was not spectacular due to the numerous permanent way restrictions in operation on that section. However, it did serve to prove what a magnificent piece of machinery *Galatea* was. It also enabled me to get used to the longer firebox of the '5X', build up the fire and experiment with injector settings.

Having to draw up at Cheltenham because of our inordinately long train caused a further delay, but finally the whistle blew and we were off at last. A brief half slip and *Galatea* quickly accelerated the 420-odd tons out of the platform and down the favourable 1 in 196, her piercing blast crashing out into the still night air. Tom, as always, was determined to pull a bit back, but it was not to be - just yet. Down the 1 in 306 bank to Cleeve, *Galatea* started to get into her stride. Everything had that superbly taut feeling of new machinery, her 6 ft 9 in driving wheels turning so smoothly that one might have been in a 1st Class dining car. With no knocks, no rattles and no violent lurching, speed was deceptive and only the rapidity of our exhaust beat, giving six pulses to one revolution of the wheels, indicated our true pace. If only all locomotives were like this!

I was really enjoying the ride when I noticed that the distant for Cleeve was on and shouted across to Tom. A quiet oath indicated that he too had seen the signal at caution, and correctly guessed the cause. Since we were running 20 minutes late, a fitted freight had been turned out in front of us and we had caught it up. Needless to say, we were obliged to follow at a sedate pace until Abbotts Wood Junction, where we turned left to Worcester while the fitted carried straight on to Stoke Works Junction.

At last, with a clear road, Tom opened up to some purpose, attacking the rise to Norton Junction with great vigour, and then fairly rattling down the 2-mile descent of 1 in 363 to Wylds Lane. Slick work by the GPO at Worcester saved a few minutes, but knowing Tom this was where the real effort would

commence, to try and haul back the massive deficit that had now accrued. I therefore strove to prepare for the coming onslaught, filling both firebox and boiler to their practical limit.

Without so much as a shudder No 5699 surged forward, and before our last coach had cleared the platform we were on full first valve and still in full gear. Out of Worcester Tunnel she stormed, the very epitome of power, blasting up the short incline before dipping down to Blackpole Sidings where, as our pace quickened, the double-three beat took on an even crisper note. Over the easy gradients to Droitwich Tom linked up to about 30 per cent and, although the distants were off, he kept her on a tight rein until past the Kidderminster line junction, and then he really let rip.

Over went the regulator, right across, at the same time dropping the screw to 40 per cent. Out through that sleepy little spa we thundered, making enough noise to wake the dead, accelerating hard before the 2-mile climb of 1 in 158 up to Stoke Works Junction. The fury of the exhaust had now risen to incredible proportions, and, taking a quick breather from what was by necessity almost continuous firing, I suddenly became aware of what appeared to be a miniature volcano erupting on top of the smokebox.

Despite the thickness of fire I had managed to maintain, a continual stream of blazing coal and cinders was being hurled high into the air by this enormous blast, and sparks could be clearly seen bouncing off even the last of our 14 coaches. '5Xs' had a reputation for throwing fire out, but here the whole countryside was illuminated by this firework display. *Galatea* certainly had the bit between her teeth now, and it was a wonderful sight to behold. So great was the evaporation rate due to this unmerciful hammering that the exhaust injector could not maintain the water level and I was obliged to supplement it with bursts from the live steam injector, but even so the needle never left the red line.

Since the tender doors had been open for some time now, I was having to drag coal forward, apart from breaking up numerous large lumps, so that I was never still for a second, but this was a small price to pay to witness such a fantastic spectacle. However, I was very thankful indeed of the brief respite afforded by our halt for bankers at Bromsgrove. This was my last chance to make sure everything was in perfect order before our assault on the 1 in 37.

With both injectors singing away, topping up the boiler and just keeping the safety valves closed, I was able to make my final preparations to the fire. A dozen accurately placed shovels brought the bed back to a perfect shape, preventing any tendency for holes to be dragged in that great incandescent mass.

The two Class '3FT' pilots had by now rolled into position and I leaned well out of the side window to listen for their distinctive 'crow' whistle while at the same time trying to regain some breath. The shrill call came clear and bell-like in the still night air. Before the echoes had died away, Galatea bellowed her reply and Tom heaved open the regulator.

Turning both injectors off, I took a quick look astern to see that all was well and noted a tall column of sparks indicating that at least one of the pilots was trying hard.

Acceleration over the first few yards through the station before we reached the base of the bank was impressive, but as we started the steep climb, No 5699 settled to a steady ponderous beat. Almost immediately I was obliged to put the exhaust injector on again and take up the shovel, for the regulator was now wide open, and although pressure showed a full 225, I had every intention of keeping it there.

Halfway up the bank Galatea was incredibly smooth at 50 per cent cut-off, showing as before no signs of shortness of breath. Then suddenly, without any warning, she checked in her stride, as if some giant hand was dragging her back. Somewhat baffled, I glanced enquiringly across at Tom who, as calm as ever, merely muttered a few oaths of vaguely nautical origin. Loosely translated, these meant that he did not think that the bankers were contributing much to the overall effort as of now. He was quite correct in this assumption; they were not contributing one iota, although of course we were quite

unaware of the details at that time. It took a couple of weeks before the full story of what had occurred filtered along the grapevine.

Apparently the fireman of the leading banker, while commendably enthusiastic, was still very inexperienced and had filled the boiler to such a degree as to cause excessive priming. This, apart from forcing his driver to close the regulator, also led to a simultaneous failure of the ejectors and consequential, if only temporary, application of the brakes. Despite rapid action by the driver, our 14-coach train actually left the bankers (this was the snatch we felt) and it is to his lasting credit that he was able under such difficult circumstances to once again take up position at the rear of the train without so much as a shudder being transmitted to the occupants. Unfortunately the priming was so severe that we had almost reached Blackwell before he was again able to do any useful work.

A lesser driver than Tom would not have taken up the unfair challenge and would have shut down while waiting for the pilots to recover. A lesser locomotive than Galatea would probably have given him no other option, but by now Tom knew his engine and without further ado he wound the gear down to the full forward position of 75 per cent cut-off! Fortunately, all this happened in less time than it takes to tell, and our speed had only diminished slightly. With a wide open regulator and 225 lbs per sq in on the clock, the 'Jubilee' responded like the magnificent thoroughbred she was. The exhaust crashed out in an unbelievable volume of sound, reverberating across the hills like a gigantic, unending thunderclap. Galatea had the lot!

Imperceptibly at first, but increasing all the time, the exhaust beats gradually quickened. The impossible was happening; Galatea was actually accelerating this huge load of 420 tons up Lickey with practically no aid from the banking engines! The sight and sound of this wonderful locomotive in full song inspired me to redouble my own efforts, and I was already working like mad, but the reward was on the pressure gauge and the boiler was as full as it should be. With Blackwell in sight, she seemed to gallop forward in a triumphant blast of energy, while twin columns of sparks at the rear showed that the pilots were trying desperately to make up for their midbank lapse. We caught a fleeting glimpse of unlit platforms and a through freight waiting to descend and then we were away and heading for Barnt Green with the bankers already left far behind.

On the falling gradient of 1 in 290, Tom wound back the reversing screw, for our speed had by now increased to the point where, once again, single exhaust beats were barely discernible and an ever-increasing column of fire was rocketing from our chimney. Fascinated, I went over to Tom and glanced at the gear indicator, which was showing, as near as I could determine in the reflected glare of the fire, 45 per cent. Seeing me do this, he looked up enquiringly.

'She OK at that?' he shouted above the uproar, genuinely seeking my opinion, since after all I was responsible for generating the steam being consumed at such a colossal rate.

I bellowed my consent, adding in what I thought was a jocular manner, 'In fact, Tom, I should drop her down another half turn.'

Knowing him as I did, I should not have been surprised when he promptly complied with my suggestion, but I was surprised nevertheless, for not even Tom had thrashed an engine like this before.

Beyond Barnt Green and still on a favourable gradient, acceleration was truly fantastic. The continuous jet of fire now erupting from our chimney was bouncing and rattling along the full length of the train, lighting our progress with a glare that gave it the appearance of some phantom from the underworld.

I had built up an immense fire while climbing the bank and had continued firing heavily until Barnt Green. Provided that they enjoyed an uninterrupted run from Blackwell, the majority of express drivers shut off at the road bridge just beyond Halesowen Junction signal box. From here, since the track is still falling at 1 in 301, they coast down through Northfield and along to the severe curve at Kings Norton Station Junction some 2 miles distant, where speed has to be reduced to 35 mph. I calculated that even consuming fuel at this terrific rate, *Galatea* had more than

enough in the box to last until Tom's own shut-off point, which was likely to be somewhat beyond that of the majority.

As we thundered down through the cutting towards Halesowen Junction I made no attempt to fire the engine. The mere act of opening the doors would have now admitted too much cold air, and although the water level was down to little more than half a glass, the pressure gauge was showing a full 225 lbs per sq in. We were living off our fat, so to speak, calling up the vast reserves of energy stored in the firebed and boiler, because *Galatea*'s prodigious effort was far beyond normal continuous steaming rates. This was the wonder of steam locomotives; skilfully handled, they could perform at twice their accepted output for short-lived but crucial periods, and thereby work a miracle.

Tom did not even have his hand on the regulator as the road bridge flashed overhead, and he still made no movement to close it when the distant for Northfield loomed up. I had never seen anyone hold on past this point, so I decided to dispense with the exhaust injector for a few moments since I wanted to maintain full pressure right up until the end, for surely he must shut off soon.

Galatea's exhaust had by now risen to a terrible, shattering ferocity, a continual thunderous roar. Never in my life had I experienced such a vast cacophony of sound. She seemed to be tearing out her very heart and soul for us, and the emotion of this caused a lump to rise in my throat, particularly when I saw that the needle was still immovably fixed to that red line. How could she possibly stand up to this murderous treatment and continue to steam? It was incredible to think that '5XPs' were temperamental in that respect when first introduced, and quite amazing what a few years development could produce.

I caught a fleeting glimpse of the bobby's goggle-eyed face pressed hard against the windows of Northfield signal box and as I looked back along our train, as far as the eye could see a veritable blizzard of fire and flame swirled and danced around the coaches; I recall wondering if the firebars themselves would be the next to go. Never before or since had I travelled through Northfield at such a speed; in fact, this moment represented the ultimate I was to experience in terms of sheer speed and power while on the footplate.

Then, with a final tremendous volcanic blast, we roared under the road bridge beyond the station where the distants for Kings Norton could be sighted. Three seconds later, Tom slammed shut the regulator while at the same instant making a full brake application. This time the sparks and flames came from the wheels!

Quickly knocking on both injectors, I was now able to have a peep at the fire, or rather what was left of it. I had expected to find it somewhat run down, but I was frankly amazed to discover only a thin layer of white hot cinders with some firebars even showing through in places. Still, at least it was clean! It was a case of back to the shovel, and from Kings Norton I had the rare experience of firing in earnest as far as Five Ways.

As previously explained, a fireman can normally devote the last few minutes to dragging forward coal, cleaning down the footplate and making sure that everything is in apple-pie order for the relief crew on arrival at New Street. On this occasion it was a very hard fight indeed to keep enough fire in the box to get us to Five Ways, for we still had nearly 5 miles to travel and Tom meant to exploit every inch of it. As the brake blocks released from the wheels on the last coach rounding Kings Norton curve, so Tom heaved up the regulator to the horizontal again and *Galatea* once more shattered the calm with her explosive roar, swaying majestically through those numerous bends from Bournville to Selly Oak, and then on to Five Ways. Here at last she was allowed to coast down through the tunnels into New Street.

I could not help wondering as we finally rolled to a halt at the end of platform 7 just what Tom might have achieved with a 'Scot' or a Stanier 4-6-2! However, the relief fireman's adverse comments regarding the amount of coal we had consumed quickly brought me back to reality. The poor chap would have to spend most of his time in the tender, so perhaps it was just as well that the 'Lizzies' were not allocated to our area.

'Jubilee' No 45676 *Codrington* having an easy time with the 4.40 pm New Street-Gloucester stopping train, seen here passing Bournville on the down line in October 1963. When travelling in the other direction, only 4 miles of mainly falling gradients separated New Street from Bournville, and when working passenger trains firemen were usually able to tidy the footplate ready for the relief crew. Eight years before, Tommy Charles still had the regulator wide open when *Galatea* thundered through here with 14 bogies, so it was a case of heavy firing all the way. *T. J. Edgington*

I joined Tom as he made his way to the exit intent on catching our shed bus, which always contrived to meet the Mail. The faintest of smiles playing around his mouth was the only indication that he was well pleased at regaining so much time from Worcester, for we had arrived only 2 minutes adrift. On the other hand I was still all of a tremble with the excitement and exertions of the past hour or so. Out in the station yard our guard caught us up, and from his manner seemed to be somewhat agitated. We knew him well as a conscientious railwayman who enjoyed a great sense of achievement when his train made up lost time.

'Hey, chaps!' he cried, 'I've had the very dickens of a job with a young soldier who caused an almighty panic running up and down the train shouting that it was on fire and wanting to pull the cord. Took me all the way from Barnt Green to convince him that it was only sparks from the engine. Mind you,' he added in an aside to me, 'I rather thought that you were chucking out more than usual even for Tom.'

Two sets of our colleagues had also travelled home as passengers in the train, and one of the drivers who was in Link 2, Section 1 overheard this last remark.

'Chucking out more than usual!' he exclaimed. 'I've never heard such an infernal racket in all my life. We couldn't sleep a wink this side of Worcester. Thought it must be Tom, though - no one else drives like that. Whatever did you do for him to give you a rollicking like that - have a row at Gloucester?'

I dismissed the question with a light laugh, for he was obviously impressed but did not want to admit it. To have made a hard-bitten top passenger driver sit up and take notice when he dearly wanted to sleep was proof enough that Tom had produced an exceptional performance. What a pity a dynamometer car had not been attached, or even a skilled observer to take timings, because I am pretty sure that some interesting figures would have been recorded. As it is, I have only got my memories, which fortunately are still as vivid as on the day it happened.

Some while before Tom and I parted company it became obvious from the roster sheets that promotion was going ahead at such a rate that I would miss the Top Passenger Link and go straight into Group 1. This was in many ways a disappointment, for I had been looking forward to working the Birmingham-Bristol and Birmingham-Sheffield expresses, particularly since most of these were allocated '5XPs'. On the other hand, to become a top link fireman had for many years past been my main ambition, and to be perfectly honest, after the scintillating performances Tom achieved almost daily, I felt that even the Top Passenger Link would prove something of an anti-climax. After all, I knew of no other driver who would consistently hammer engines in the Tommy Charles manner, and I preferred to leave my memories of passenger work unsullied by lesser feats.

Furthermore, in November 1955 I had been married, and could well use the fatter pay packets that went hand in glove with the greater percentage of night work and overtime to be found on freight duties. In addition, I had purchased a powerful new sports motor cycle, which provided all the speed and excitement one could wish for. I was never happier than when riding this as far and as fast as possible, and did so at every opportunity. With this alternative expression of power and speed so freely available, I began to realise that there was more to being an engine driver than merely thrashing a locomotive to its limit just to see what it could do. Moreover joining the elite in Group 1 only served to strengthen this realisation and bring home the fact that in the not too distant future I would be required to pass out as a driver myself.

Bearing this sobering thought in mind, I decided that I should now cease to treat work as an exciting game and buckle down to the task of acquiring the vast amount of knowledge and technique necessary to be successful in that very exacting role. I could not possibly have been more fortunate in this respect, for when in May I fervently scanned the rosters, every bit as nervous and excited as when I was a Passed Cleaner, I discovered that destiny had placed me in Section D, the Long Marston link, with none other than Percy ('Piggy') Trotter.

4
THE LONG MARSTON LINK

When it became generally known that I was to be matched with Percy Trotter, just about every driver and at least half the firemen of Saltley offered their commiserations at my misfortune.

The picture painted was not a rosy one - indeed, it was downright daunting if even half the descriptions of his character were to be believed. He was supposedly a self-opinionated, garrulous tyrant who spent most of his time arguing with everyone about everything, and amused himself in between sessions by telling his fireman in plain language just how incompetent his every action proved him to be.

To be forewarned is to be forearmed, and having taken much of this well-intentioned advice with a pinch of salt, I resolved to be the essence of happy geniality, which I had found in the past proved effective in deflecting even the most vicious verbal lashes, and to follow his wishes whenever possible, for after all Percy was to be my chief for a full 12 months. Obviously I would now have to be most punctilious in my work, and the week prior to our first meeting I spent many hours with Rule Book and *Questions for Enginemen* in my hand, brushing up on matters I had neglected during the last hectic year.

My confidence was running pretty high when I booked on for our first turn together. Providentially it was the lowliest job in the link, being no more exacting than a Kingsbury tripper, slipped in to provide a rest week from the hurly-burly of the other 11. Despite the fact that I had arrived a quarter of an hour before time, Percy had booked on some 15 minutes previously and was already hard at work preparing our engine, Class '4F' No 4209 stabled in No 2 shed. I soon discovered that it was his practice to arrive anything up to an hour before he was booked. That he did so was partly out of necessity, since the Corporation bus service did not always obligingly key in with our train times, but mainly because the official preparation time allowed was insufficient for his purposes. His oiling was the most comprehensive of any driver I have ever known, and his inspection so meticulous that only a portable X-ray unit might have revealed more.

It was therefore in the hot, smoky interior of No 2 shed, under the shadow of No 4209, that I first confronted 'Piggy' Trotter. There was no need for me to ask his name, for apart from obviously being engaged in oiling the engine, his descriptive nickname fitted perfectly. He was a biggish man, some 5 ft 11 in tall and about two-thirds of that measurement around the waist. Come to think of it, most of his 16-odd stone seemed to be distributed around those swollen equatorial regions, since his body ballooned progressively outwards, then tapered down to inordinately slim ankles, accentuated by the wearing of bicycle clips. These lower limbs were terminated by small feet that appeared too tiny to support the vast bulk above. As a matter of fact, his ankles were rather on the weak side and caused Percy to hobble about in a most ungainly manner at times.

His fleshy face was an unhealthy purplish hue, indicating high blood pressure and a liking for a pint, and this colour spread down over double chins sporting a two-day grey stubble to the top of his chest, which was revealed by an old-fashioned, open necked collarless shirt worn summer and winter irrespective of prevailing weather conditions. I later found that Percy rarely felt the cold and his one and only concession to a freezing day was the donning of an old silk scarf knotted loosely around his ample throat.

A thin-lipped slit of a mouth, permanently pulled down at the corners, gave him an unfortunate sneering expression, even when he was not actually sneering, and small light blue eyes set rather deep and close together did nothing to improve matters. Short, sparse grey hair combed into a divided fringe, Oliver Hardy fashion, completed one of nature's less aesthetic pieces of handiwork. I could see at a glance how he might have come by his nickname, for there was no denying the strong resemblance to an overfed porker, but from what I had been told, the obdurate stubbornness of his character had also considerably influenced the choice of phrase.

As I rounded the front of our engine, Percy had just topped up the feeder he was holding in his right hand and he acknowledged my cheery greeting with an abrupt nod. Depositing the feeder on the framing, he wiped his sweating forehead with the back of his hand, adding another grease smudge to the half-dozen already there, then with over-elaborate movements he pulled out a large pocket watch that he held at arm's length, perusing it by squinting down his nose. I had never seen a chap lean so far back from the hips as Percy. It was an ingrained habit of his, derived no doubt from the necessity of adjusting his centre of gravity to counterbalance the weight of his paunch; since this also tilted his head back, it only served to emphasise the built-in sneer. This study of the time was, I fancy, engineered to make me feel guilty for arriving late, and I did, until I realised that I was still 15 minutes early.

'I've drawn the tools for you, but we are low on fire and steam, and the sandboxes need filling,' he said evenly enough, then, picking up the feeder, turned to carry on with the oiling.

'Dash it,' I thought, for I had wanted to investigate these things for myself, and mentally made a note to book on even earlier tomorrow.

Nothing more was said, and by working at the double I managed to complete all my tasks, even to the extent of adding limestone to the fire, in good time. We tested everything that could be tested before moving on to the table, and working strictly to the book I preceded him out of the shed and walked in the prescribed manner to the water column. Here, Percy left me to clean up while he went over to the amenity block to mash the tea before ringing off.

I thought that I had made a pretty good job of it, trimming the coal and neatly stowing our fire irons, apart from removing every trace of dust and soot from the footplate. However, when Percy returned, we still had to wait a further 5 minutes before departing, and during this time he was able to conduct a quick inspection that revealed an omission on my part. He did not say it in so many words, merely observing that he could not understand how enginemen could work with dirty cab windows and spectacle glasses. Ours were slightly smutty! I should not have allowed this to bother me, since it was generally understood that drivers cleaned their own, but in future I felt obliged to clean all glasses at the first opportunity.

Having collected our guard we duly arrived at Bromford after a trip that was notable for the higher than normal speeds that were usually attained by a light engine on the goods line.

The reader may recall that a Kingsbury trip involved nothing more than taking a train of empties from Bromford to Kingsbury Colliery and returning to Washwood Heath with a loaded coal train. However, Percy managed to make it look like the most important job at Saltley, and took off from Bromford as if he was driving the up express, setting the couplings clanking and the rust flying with all the delicacy and finesse of a medieval battering ram.

Not that this bothered me much, for had I not just completed a year with the most energetic passenger driver on the Region? But driving loose-coupled trains with 30 feet of slack between the engine and the brake-van requires an entirely different approach, and my sensitive soul felt every snatch and bump transmitted to that poor, long-suffering guard. Moreover, I rightly deduced that pointing this out to a man of Percy's character would only have incited him to go the opposite way and be more violent than ever. In fact, I soon learned that he was an ideal subject upon which to apply reversed psychology, and with practice found that he could be made quite pliant within certain limits - but all this took time, of course.

In common with most trip jobs we had a lot of free time on our hands and Percy, never an idle man, lost no time in plumbing the extent of my railway knowledge both practical and theoretical and, needless to say, soon exposed some extensive gaps. There was no question that he knew his stuff, for I never did meet his equal in terms of engine matters, but it was the manner in which he delivered his lectures that left so much to be desired, and I could readily appreciate why so many of his firemen took umbrage and promptly requested a transfer. It was common knowledge that he went through more firemen in the course of a year than any other driver at Saltley, but I was determined to retain my sangfroid no matter what malediction was hurled at me.

Nevertheless, my self-control was sorely tried on numerous occasions in those early days, and more than once I came very near to beaning him with the coalpick in thought, even if not in action. And so commenced a most memorable year, which, despite starting out on a somewhat shaky and strained footing, developed to become not only one in which I learned more about engines than in the previous six, but one that proved both exciting and enjoyable.

Once I had become used to Percy's congenital peculiarities, and learned to deal with them, I found I was not only able to live with him, but actually derived pleasure from his company. It may possibly be cruel to laugh at other people's weaknesses, but Percy's fiery temper, the arguments he inevitably became embroiled in, and the histrionic attitudes he struck while so doing, provided me with endless hours of entertainment, and after all, who could fail to be amused at the sight of a 57-year-old, 16-stone driver, purple in the face and frothing at the mouth, hopping up

and down in a temper tantrum like a brat in a kindergarten.

I might well be accused at this point of only describing Percy Trotter's worst features, but this was the side of his character one noticed on first acquaintance. His more endearing qualities and, let there be no mistake, he possessed a great many, were deeper beneath the surface and only came to light after a longer and more intimate association. Over the course of the next few months he proved not only to be a vast fund of knowledge, but a meticulous if somewhat brutal teacher, and a loyal and good friend who would toil tirelessly for you if he found you to be worth your salt.

From that very first week he laid his cards firmly on the table, asking point-blank whether I intended to become a driver and, if so, was I willing to take instruction from him? Since my answer was in the affirmative my education was in his hands, and when he found that I was an attentive pupil, his enthusiasm to teach increased so that in a very short space of time the whole thing snowballed. No day passed without some aspect of engine management or section of the Rule Book being laid bare, and on frequent occasions my head swam with the effort of trying to grasp this enormous input of information.

Gradually Percy's attitude changed and a bond of mutual trust developed to the point where I felt he sometimes regarded me as a slightly wayward son, and I for my part looked upon him as a sort of father figure, at least as far as railway affairs were concerned. In keeping with most human relationships we had our ups and downs. For one thing he would never praise me to my face, no matter how well I had accomplished a task. On the contrary, he seemed to find faults everywhere, even in matters outside railway work. For example, he continually derided my love of motor cycling and the fact that I possessed such a powerful machine.

'You'll break your silly neck on that contraption,' he would say, and I sincerely believed that he meant it until one day I overheard him boasting to a crowd of chaps in the messroom. 'My mate has the fastest motor cycle there is, and he must be a marvellous rider to handle it at over 100 mph.' (Actually this rose to 120 mph before the ensuing argument finished.)

I could barely believe my ears, but I later discovered that this was Percy! He would spend all day being as provocatively uncomplimentary as possible to you, then the moment your back was turned he would praise you to the hilt, usually throwing in a few imagined and embarrassing extras for good measure, the exact opposite of how the majority of human beings behave, but in many ways, may I venture to presume, more preferable.

My sense of humour was the main problem on my side for he had no sense of humour at all. He took everything said at face value, a fact that I kept forgetting, and the worst instance of this caused quite a scene one night in the shed. On the whole, though, we worked far better as a team than I had at first imagined possible, and even then there were some very pleasant surprises in store for me.

In general, Group 1 jobs not unnaturally contained the cream of the work at Saltley. Each link within the group seemed to concentrate on a particular area, and in the case of Section D we mainly covered all points west as far as Gloucester. However, so that drivers could retain a fairly comprehensive route card, we also had two jobs to Derby and one to Burton, but the most interesting turn was the one that gave the link its name - 'The Long Marston'. This was unique at Saltley since it involved working over Great Western metals, and, of course, here Midland Region's pride was at stake, so that every effort was made not only to run to time, but to show the Western just what a clever lot of fellows we were.

As with all other links, it required 12 weeks to cover all the jobs, and it was when we came round to the Kingsbury trip turn again that I received a pleasant surprise. By now I had fallen into the habit of arriving just about as early as Percy, and on Monday morning I was more than a little staggered when he suddenly announced that we would swop places.

'You are the driver this week,' he said, 'so get oiling. I'll look after the fireman's work.'

I must admit that until then I had considered him to be the last person at Saltley willing to take up a shovel, but there it was, and the opportunity was too good to miss. Right from the start he made it quite clear that I was not to do any of the fireman's jobs, and unless a crisis developed he did not expect to have to do any of mine. Fortunately, being more slender and agile than he, I was able to get through the oiling in good time, even though I lubricated every moving part in sight. Of course, that wasn't quite good enough for Percy, for I had put too much on here and not enough there, but all in all he wasn't hypercritical, being far too occupied with the, for him, strenuous firing duties. These he performed well enough for me to compliment him on his expertise, and I confirmed that I was prepared to take him anywhere with me!

It was grand to feel the response of an engine beneath my hands again, and although I had hardly touched a regulator for a year, by the time we had reached Bromford driving had become instinctive once more. Stan Jones, our little cockney guard, came up and advised Percy of our load just before we departed.

'Tell him,' said Percy, airily waving a hand in my direction. 'He's the driver.'

Stan, who closely resembled a cheeky budgerigar, and who tolerated the violence of Percy's driving with resigned good humour, stared incredulously for a moment, uttered the single word 'Strewth!', then hopped away. His expression left me with the impression that while he did not exactly approve, at least he thought that I could not possibly be much worse than Percy.

On receiving the 'right away', I eased gently out of the siding. The memories of hours of shunting at Water Orton came flooding back, and I was pleased to find that I was able to get the brake moving with hardly a judder.

'You don't have to be as gentle as that,' cried Percy derisively. 'They're not made of glass'.

At first my driving came in for a lot of criticism; I was always going either too slow or too fast, or shutting off too early, but gradually as the week wore on things improved to the point where only my starts were at fault.

As Percy was no doubt well aware, on joining an engine a fireman's prime task was to build up the firebed. In the interests of safety and cleanliness it was policy to use the inevitable spillage on the footplate first. The experienced fireman, though, would first close the cab doors, since when folded as shown they were a constant danger to his knuckles while swinging the shovel.

These, I am afraid, remained a bone of contention between us for as long as we were together, for my principal aim when driving was to give the guard as smooth a ride as possible. The more he tried to make me liven these up, the more gentle I became, and the guards highlighted this difference in our styles on jobs when we drove on alternate days. Most of them, out of sheer devilment, liked to rile Percy on every conceivable occasion, and a typical ploy would be to ask who was driving that day.

'He is,' he would say, as gullible as ever.

'Oh in that case,' replied the guard, 'it will be safe to make my tea now.'

This brought forth the desired reaction from Percy, who would invariably swell up, turn purple, spit profanities at them until out of earshot, then give them a hell of a ride the next day. However, they must have thought it well worthwhile, although for my part I dearly wished they would desist, because as may well be imagined, he vented his temper on the only person close at hand - yours truly.

As my confidence grew I was allowed to drive for longer distances on the less demanding road jobs such as the Class B freight to Burton, and the pick-up to Droitwich. However, fitted freights, particularly the westbound ones, were more than Percy could physically cope with, although he did on occasions let me take over for a short stretch while he indulged his appetite. Life therefore became very pleasantly interesting despite his being such an exacting task-master, and my all-round knowledge and skill developed apace under his guidance.

After a few weeks two unusual features of his character became very apparent. One was that he could not tolerate overtime at any price, and his whole time while on duty was dedicated to finishing as early as possible. He would do battle with both the yard staff and the Control to achieve this end, and drive like the wind to obtain and keep in an earlier path if at all feasible. Fortunately for him, the Control staff knew that he would not delay a more important following train, and frequently agreed to an unofficial rearrangement of the working timetable.

The other feature was that he was never happier than when he had a spanner in his hand, and I often wondered if his true vocation was really that of a fitter. He simply loved to take things apart and repair them, and rarely a day passed without some item on the engine not functioning to his satisfaction was stripped down. Not that he always effected an improvement; on the contrary, occasionally he made matters a good deal worse, because no matter how many times one takes down and reassembles a defective part, it still remains defective. However, I never failed to be amazed at the magnitude of some of the jobs he tackled, armed with no more equipment than the four regulation spanners, a coalpick, a few odd pieces of wire and his own pair of pliers. During the year I was with him, he accomplished while on the road just about every repair imaginable short of a major refit, but sometimes his enthusiasm had its embarrassing consequences.

I well recall one instance when working a Class B to Burton. I was driving that day and as was often the case we were backed into the loop at Wilncote out of the way of some faster traffic. We had a '4F' and the regulator handle was a very loose fit on its spindle, making delicate control difficult because of the excessive amount of free play.

'Right,' said Percy as we came to a standstill in the loop, 'we won't move until after the two fitteds and the slow, so that gives me half an hour to fix that dratted thing. I'll take the regulator off and make up a shim. Just sit there and watch.'

Perched up on the narrow driver's seat over the reversing screw, I watched him struggle with the securing nut, which over the years had lost its original hexagonal shape and was now virtually round. Eventually he succeeded, after much sweating and cursing, and he was hammering a large washer, procured from the vast collection of junk carried in his jacket pockets for just such an event, into a suitable shape for the shim, when the first fitted rattled past.

I had just wistfully watched it recede into the distance when I suddenly heard the familiar clunk of points being pulled over, followed by the clang of a signal arm. Looking out, I saw that we had indeed got the road and, by way of reflex, automatically kicked the taps shut, opened the small ejector and groped for the regulator handle. Not finding it in its usual place caused me to search around, then realisation dawned as I took in the boiler front bereft of that most important fitting; Percy of course, had only just removed it. With the distants now off as well, I regarded the regulator handle reposing peacefully across the fireman's seat.

'Percy, we've got to go now,' I called as gently as possible, since I did not wish to startle him too much.

'Eh?' he replied, not bothering to look round for he was enjoyably engrossed in belting the daylights out of that inoffensive washer with the coalpick, using the handbrake handle as an anvil.

'We've got to go now,' I repeated, more insistently this time. 'Can I have the regulator back please?'

He stared first at me, then at the signal, then back to me, his jowls wobbling, and visibly turning bright vermilion as he strove to find suitable words.

'We can't,' he stuttered. 'Only one fitted has gone. What does that bloody idiot think he's playing at?'

Crossing over to my side he hopped up and down, shaking his fist in the direction of the signal box as if by so doing he could reverse the course of events. In the meantime the bobby, obviously thinking that we had gone to sleep, started rattling the signal arm violently. Percy, finally realising that we now had no choice, slammed the regulator handle back on to its spindle, and as soon as it was in place I tried to open the valve. Unfortunately it was now so sloppy that at first I could gain no purchase, but with Percy's penknife acting as a temporary shim I managed to make a start that, unfortunately for the guard, was far from gentle. Some frantic spanner work over the next few hundred yards was called for, but with a clear road the crisis passed without further mishap. Needless to say, Percy never had a regulator handle off again while I was with him.

The real highlight of the link, though, was without doubt the Long Marston job. This was a Class A mixed freight turn which, because it was run over foreign metals, carried a prestige out of all proportion to the actual importance of the train. We were allocated a Class '8F', usually the best available, and ran from Washwood Heath Junction on to the Western via Bordesley Junction and through to Long Marston, the massive Ministry of Defence establishment, some 5 miles south-west of Stratford-upon-Avon. The route was a picturesque but precipitous one and, since we were mixed in with the Great Western vacuum trains, we had to really go, for there was hell to pay if one should happen to be delayed. As it happened, Percy had made his mark on the Western in much the same way as he had on his own native Region, and frequently we were turned out in front of their fitteds, since it was generally recognised that they were more likely to stop us than we would stop them. The Western men called him 'Peggy', which of course was a corruption of 'Piggy', but all the signalmen knew when he was driving, and had no hesitation in providing a path, no matter how slim the timings. From my own point of view, further interest was added because the route passed right by the house in which I was born, and travelling over the very rails upon which I had seen my first locomotive provided an enormous thrill.

In deference to my lack of knowledge of the road and also because we had only been together for four weeks, Percy did not drive with his customary enterprise the first time we worked the job, but on the second occasion he really cut loose. On the Friday of that week it was quite a memorable trip. We had No 8669, and although she had just about lost her post-shopping sheen, that crisp, taut feeling of newness was still there. The engine had been prepared for us, but as usual we booked on early enough to give it a thorough check and clean before leaving the shed. Our initial favourable impression was confirmed during the quick romp down to Washwood Heath, and when we backed on to our train the guard advised us that we had 20 load of coal next to the engine, and a further 28 wagons and vans behind that.

Everything else waited until the Long Marston had been got away, and within minutes we were being called out of the siding. As the week had progressed Percy's driving had become more inspired, and on this particular day, as if sensing the quality and eagerness of our steed, he set off in his best 'Scotch Express' style. I suppose on the engine we were already doing something like 10 or 15 mph when the brake-van jerked into motion, and with a clear road we were soon snorting past the pilot sidings, whistling for a banker as we did so. Although only travelling under Class A lights, the Long Marston was treated like a crack fitted, and Percy took full advantage of the situation as the distants came off in front of us.

I felt sorry for the poor pilot, though; he had to go like a dingbat to even catch up at Duddeston Road, and with 50 per cent cut-off at full first valve, we went past the loco making enough racket to cause a good many of our colleagues to stand and stare. Percy had meant to take a charge at the bank, and charge it he did. At Landor Street Junction the regulator was right across and we simply galloped up the section from St Andrews, barely noticing the 1 in 62. Shutting off at the Coventry Road overbridge, he allowed our impetus to carry us into Bordesley, where fortuitously the signal was off, for I am quite certain we would never have stopped had it not been.

A quick clanking snake through the sidings, then out on to the slow, where, with distants off, he opened up again. I always found this stretch a little tricky because, with six parallel roads, sidings at either side, and criss-crossed by numerous tracks, the signalling system on first acquaintance seemed rather complex and confusing. However, I always enjoyed passing under the Golden Hillock Road bridge at Small Heath, since it brought back nostalgic memories of spending many happy, if somewhat windswept, hours standing on that very bridge watching the pride of the Western go by.

From here we had to take things fairly gently, for after progressive signal checks we were brought to a halt at Tyseley South Junction, but I normally used this stretch to build up the fire for the 7-mile haul up to Earlswood Lakes, and today was no exception. A local passenger train was the culprit, but as soon as this had cleared we had the 'back 'uns' (distants) and Percy, begrudging the 3 minutes lost time, attacked the ensuing 1 in 200 with more than customary vigour. Full first valve and 60 per cent cut-off sufficed to get us nicely on the move, then, as the gradient eased to 1 in 502, so he wound back the screw to 45 per cent. Keeping her at this we fairly hammered up through Hall Green station, then on to the level stretch of line that ran near to the house where I was born. Here I always made a practice of crossing over to Percy's side to see the old homestead and wave to a small group of boys who inevitably gathered at the lineside fence there. It was hard to believe that some twenty years earlier our positions had been reversed and it was then I who was waving to the engine crews.

Over this short level section our speed built up impressively, but almost immediately the bank rose again at 1 in 500, steepening to 1 in 159 at Yardley Wood station, and this not unnaturally checked our pace. However, Percy was in no mood to allow No 8669 to find her own speed, and promptly compensated by lengthening the cut-off. Following a short level stretch approaching Shirley the gradient is less severe at 1 in 264, but still sufficient to keep me very busy indeed with the shovel.

Having now left Birmingham's suburbs behind, the scenery progressively improved and, as we climbed higher, opened out to give some really splendid views of extensive verdant woods, highlighted by the strong summer sunshine. At Whitlocks End Halt, which consisted only of a few well-weathered planks standing on rather rickety looking piles at the side of the track, I was able to take things a little easier, for with only 2 miles to the Lake's summit, I could now gradually run down the fire in anticipation of the 10-mile-long descent to Bearley West Junction.

No 8669 was steaming so well that despite a very spirited attack on the final 1 in 230 section, we rolled over the top with rather more steam and water in the boiler than I had intended, but now I was able to enjoy a lengthy rest with a well-earned lid of tea and a

cigarette. The descent commences at 1 in 281, soon increasing to 1 in 181, then from the short (176 yards) Wood End Tunnel there follows an uninterrupted 4½-mile drop of 1 in 150. Obviously with a loose-coupled train of this size a good deal of heavy braking was called for, and it was customary to apply the brakes on both the tender and brake-van and leave them thus for most of the way. With well-nigh perfect visibility, Percy let them run somewhat more than usual and we were soon rattling along as fast as any fitted. This had me a little worried at times, since apart from the fact that I considered we were sailing a bit close to the wind if ever we were required to stop, the wildly cavorting footplate kept spilling my tea.

Looking along the train during that hectic descent was fascinating - and for the guard I would have thought a frightening spectacle. A great fog of dust streamed aft from the rapidly moving vehicles, completely obscuring the brake-van at times. Had there been a hot axlebox, and this was a not infrequent occurrence when Percy was at the helm, neither I nor the guard would ever have known, while the wagons themselves were swaying and bucking so much that half the train appeared to be using the up line.

The distant for Henley-in-Arden being on, a full application of the steam brake was needed for the best part of a mile, and indicated that we had caught something up. We were in fact checked over the next 4 miles

The Long Marston link also enjoyed a number of freight turns to Gloucester, but because Percy never liked overtime he tended to run loose-coupled trains at rather higher speeds than the timetable compilers had envisaged. With most '4Fs' this often resulted in both me and the engine being a little short of breath at times. Built at Horwich in 1928, No 44466 is seen passing through Ashchurch station on a Washwood Heath to Barnwood Class B freight in 1957. *Pat Webb*

to Bearley West Junction, where once more the road cleared. Aggrieved at being delayed, Percy blasted No 8669 up the short bank to Wilmcote station where he was obliged to shut off for the sharp 1 in 75 drop down towards Stratford-upon-Avon East. Care had to be taken on the approach here over the switchback-like curved humps, but then, with the distants off, he absolutely ripped down the 1 in 92 descent into Stratford station at a higher speed than ever before.

The station is built on quite a severe right-hand curve, and taking 20 well-filled coal wagons through at that pace caused the inevitable to happen. Centrifugal force momentarily overcame gravity, and about 2 tons of best cobbles were suddenly strewn in an untidy trail along the full length of the platform. We were often called upon to supply unofficially our much-prized hard coal to Western stations and signal boxes, since their own native Welsh coal was difficult to burn in ordinary fires, but this unintended display of generosity was quite ludicrous.

Completely unaware of the commotion we had caused, Percy tore on over the Evesham Road Crossing, past the racecourse and out to our destination, now only some 5 miles distant. Just beyond the racecourse and right alongside the up track there was a platelayers hut, and as we roared by half a dozen of those 'stalwarts of the length' gave us a friendly wave and indicated by simple sign-language that they would be much obliged if we dropped them some coal. However, such was our speed then that it was quite impossible, but Percy, by dint of equally simple sign-language, made it clear that we would do so on our return trip.

'It pays to keep in with the natives,' he declared. 'Might want a favour some time.'

No wonder he had plenty of friends on the Western, for he went out of his way to 'butter up' signalmen with these gifts of black manna every day.

Once our train was safely deposited at Long Marston, we had to turn our '8F', and this was effected by running down to the triangle at Honeybourne, a round trip of about 8 miles. On occasions this operation took an inordinately long time, but Percy never

seemed to mind too much, providing that we departed with our train of empty wagons on schedule. Today we were fortunate and accomplished the exercise quickly enough to enjoy a relaxing hour over our lunch, but all too soon it was time to prepare for the much tougher ordeal of the return trip. Although it involved considerably more physical effort on my part, I enjoyed this latter half of the turn better than the outward run, mainly, I think, because of the challenge presented by 16 miles of virtually continuous uphill slogging. It paid handsomely to ensure that everything was in good order before leaving, and I always made a practice of going into the tender to break up coal and drag it forward if necessary.

We had quite a lot of slack and fines in that day's mixture and I wanted to extricate as many lumps as possible so as to first build up a hand-picked firebed. I had nearly completed this task to my satisfaction when I discovered an enormous lump as big as a medium-sized coffin and weighing fully 2 hundredweights. With some difficulty I dragged it down on to the footplate with the intention of breaking it up and using the fragments to complete my preparations. With the coalpick poised above my head, Percy stopped the downward swing in the nick of time.

'Don't smash it up mate, that's just the thing for those platelayers by the racecourse.'

It was of course logical and practical to deposit our gift in one large piece rather than a shower of small ones, which bounced and ran all over the place and took a devil of a job to find.

'OK, Percy,' I replied, 'but you will have to tell me when - it's as much as I can do to move the bally thing, let alone see the platelayers hut from the middle of the cab.'

With more optimism than I felt was appropriate Percy continued, 'We'll drop it 15 yards from the hut on the approach side - there's a clear patch there. The other side is too grassy, and in any case the embankment is steeper.'

With the details thus arranged, I finished off building up the fire, then gave the footplate a good clean down, working over and around that great ebony monster.

Shortly afterwards we departed and over

the easy gradients from Long Marston we soon had our train of 50 empty wagons rattling along at a good pace with only a whiff of steam and 25 per cent cut-off. I used this 5-mile stretch of light working to allow the fire to burn through thoroughly and get everything warmed up before the real hard slog started the other side of Stratford.

I suppose we were doing something between 30 and 40 mph when the racecourse came into view, and I decided it was high time that I moved the huge lump of coal into position for a quick heave over the side. It was far too heavy to slide on its side out between the uprights, and I therefore poised it on one end so that merely a light push at the top would suffice to send it toppling into space. In good time I checked clearances and found that it would just pass between the handrails with about a quarter of an inch to spare. With the hut just in sight I heaved the great lump upright and by a wiggling action manoeuvred it right up to the edge of the gyrating fallplate where with a struggle I just managed to balance it.

'Are you ready?' shouted Percy when the rapidly approaching hut was about 100 yards away.

'When you say the word,' I bellowed in reply, trying to keep my eye on the target over his shoulder and at the same time inching the lump even nearer the edge. As the point of release came up I experimentally pushed the 'coffin' between the uprights to make sure that it would fall cleanly when the time arrived. To my horror it stuck solid when halfway through - the left-hand curve we were now on had caused the tender and engine handrails to close just that fraction of an inch, trapping the lump firmly between them. Desperately I pushed and heaved, but to no avail - the thing was absolutely immovable. With all the aplomb of an RAF bomb-aimer, Percy began his countdown.

'Stand by.'

I pushed and heaved harder than ever, the coal groaning and chaffing in its grip of steel.

'Ready. . . go!'

It was all very well Percy doing his 'bombs away' routine, but the damned thing gave all the appearance of becoming a permanent fixture on No 8669. Percy sensed that something was amiss and looked round.

'Go on then, push it off!' he shrieked, his voice rising a couple of octaves as he absorbed my predicament. Whether it was Percy's excitement or just my normal mental processes eliminating other possibilities, but inspiration suddenly struck and, holding on to the waterscoop handle for balance, I delivered a flying kick to the top of the lump Kung Fu-fashion. With a loud crack of splintering coal, the massive chunk disappeared over the side with me very nearly following it.

Anxious to see what happened to the missile, I leaped to the side and was just in time to observe its leading end strike a patch of gravel 5 yards in front of the hut. In a cloud of flying debris, it took off again, and following a low parabolic trajectory very reminiscent of one of Dr Barnes Wallis's bouncing bombs of 'Dam Busters' fame, its torpedo-like end struck the front wall of the shack about 3 feet above ground level.

A solid 2-hundredweight lump of coal travelling at some 50 feet per second has a fair bit of energy, and it penetrated those stout timbers with the ease of a cannon ball and a resounding crash that could be clearly heard above the rumpus on the footplate. Fifty years of accumulated soot and dirt were suddenly shaken free from that aged building and its outline became momentarily obscured by a black haze. By now we had travelled to the far end of the building and were therefore nicely positioned to witness the door, torn from its hinges, burst outwards and go cartwheeling down the embankment. This was quickly followed by the still intact lump of coal, wearing the mangled remains of what a few seconds before must have been a smart, deal mess table.

There was a stunned silence on the footplate for a moment, then Percy threw an apoplectic fit, already feeling the hangman's noose tightening around his throat. Luckily 200 yards further on we spotted the gang of platelayers, and Percy, now somewhat red in the face, indicated to them that we had dropped off the coal as requested.

With grateful waves they disappeared into the distance, but whether they would be quite so happy when they revisited the scene of demolition was a matter of some conjecture. Funnily enough, although we expected to be called upon to answer for our sins, we never heard any more of the incident nor, for that matter, of the deposition of coal on Stratford station's down platform. Perhaps the Western men were too grateful for the fuel thus supplied, or maybe they just put it down to the peculiar ways of the mad Midlanders.

At Stratford, with this little piece of excitement now behind us, we concentrated on the task ahead, but having built up an immense fire, and with No 8669 steaming so well, I was confident that we would put up a good showing. Fifty empty wagons take a surprising amount of effort to hump up a bank of 1 in 75, particularly in the strong cross-wind that was now blowing. The wind gets into the wagons and causes a lot of drag, but full first valve and 50 per cent cut-off had us thumping up to Wilmcote in grand style at a speed more appropriate to a fully fitted. Unfortunately we were unable to take advantage of the momentum imparted on the descent to Bearley, for once again we were checked by signals at the junction.

However, this caused little hardship, since speed was quickly restored over the 2 miles of falling gradients to the point where the bank up to Earlswood Lakes commenced some three-quarters of a mile from Wootton Wawen. This was where Percy liked to demonstrate just what we could do, and we thundered through the station with a wide open regulator and 40 per cent, but as the distant for Henley-in-Arden came into sight we noticed that it was at caution.

'Damn their eyes!' he yelled, showing his displeasure by giving the brake valve handle a swift clout with the palm of his hand. 'We've caught up one of their blasted trains!'

He eased back the regulator and the gradient rapidly reduced our speed, but as this fell to around 10 mph so both the home and starter signals came off. He immediately slammed the regulator up to the horizontal and dropped the gear pretty well right down the rack. No 8669's exhaust exploded like a thunderclap, shooting up a great column of black smoke and, despite being on a 1 in 150

incline, started to accelerate most impressively. Leaving her blasting away in this ferocious manner, he came over to my side of the cab, then spotted what he was looking for. There, parked on the down line, was a Western fitted hauled by one of their 'Grange' Class. Its blower was wide open and the fireman hard at work with the pricker. Obviously it was short of steam and had been shunted across the road out of our way for a blow-up.

Being thus distracted for the moment, our own safety valve lifted, but before I could put the injector on Percy stopped me.

'Let it blow off for a bit, mate!' he cried jubilantly. 'That'll show 'em we've got plenty of steam to spare.'

He was as pleased as a dog with two tails, and waved derisively at the Western crew, who by their hang-dog looks seemed to appreciate that having to shunt a prize vacuum train out of the way of a Midland empty wagon Class B was rather letting the side down.

This little piece of one-upmanship seemed to put Percy into excellent spirits and inspire him to achieve one of the most sparkling performances I have ever seen with a Class '8F'. For the next 7 miles he thrashed her up that 1 in 150 bank in a manner closely following the traditions of Tommy Charles, keeping the regulator wide open and the cut-off at around 40 per cent. Our little 4 ft 8½ in driving wheels were turning so rapidly that we sounded more like an express than a nondescript freight, and for that matter it felt like it, because at that speed the cab was heaving about like a rowing boat on a rough sea. Despite this merciless treatment and low-grade fuel she steamed beautifully, although of course I was forced to fire almost continuously all the way, and towards the top the needle did fall back slightly.

Past Earlswood Lakes and starting to rattle down the falling gradients that now faced us for the next 6 miles, a still exuberant Percy suddenly got up and came over to me.

'See if you can take her down to Tyseley without losing any time, mate,' he said, with a facial expression that was the nearest thing he could manage to a broad smile. This offer took me aback somewhat, for he had never before allowed me to handle the Long Marston, but I gratefully accepted and enjoyed the added pleasure of actually driving past my old home for the first time. Instead of losing time I fell into the spirit of our exceptional run, and nearly overdid things when I had to stop at the junction. I had a few worrying moments, but Percy seemed to think it was just good judgement and said nothing when he took over for the rest of the trip.

We were over an hour early at Landor Street, but were nevertheless relieved by a spare Control crew. The men scheduled for this turn had not even booked on by the time we were off the premises, but then Percy liked it this way.

We had our moments of excitement, we had our ups and downs, but as a team we generally worked well and, if I may say so, efficiently together, each trusting in the other's competence. He still had his daily arguments, his tantrums, and hourly rages. This was the nature of the man and I learned to take no notice. However, one night towards the end of our spell together, when we really should have known each other's ways too well for it to have happened, Percy flew into just about the most violent rage of his life, and I was the target.

We were working a through freight to Gloucester, which departed from the West End at 11.20 pm, and because we were booked to travel home by passenger train the following morning, we prepared our own engine. This was a '4F' and, as was our habit, we always arrived in good time to make a thorough job of it.

Percy had not forgiven me for a little prank I played on him the previous night, when he got a trifle confused over engine numbers and prepared 44404 instead of 44004, which was lying on the opposite side of the shed. It was a pardonable error that many enginemen had made in the past and, when having gone to the correct engine, and then spotted him oiling the other, I at first thought that it was I who had made the mistake. However, after checking the train board again and confirming this with the shed foreman, a little spark of devilment urged me to say nothing at this juncture. After all, I had plenty of time to do both jobs and no harm would be done provided that we rang off at the right time. So, taking great care not to be seen by Percy, I set to work on 44004.

He meanwhile, not only oiled the other engine but loyally did my work as well, thinking that for some reason I had been delayed. We finished our work at roughly the same moment, and timing it to a nicety, I confronted him just outside the oil stores, holding an empty oil bottle in my hand as if about to go through the motions of drawing more lubrication.

'Good heavens, Percy,' said I in a tone of mock censure, 'wherever have you been? We're due out in ten minutes!'

I waited for the explosion, which true to form came right on time.

'Where have I been? Where have I been?' he screeched, eyes popping and wobbling jowls turning bright purple. 'Where have you been, more likely? I've only prepared the engine all by myself, and done your bloody job as well! I was just going to the lobby to see about getting another fireman.'

As he paused for breath I seized my chance.

'Don't quite see how you could have done that, Percy, because I've just prepared our engine and I've oiled it as well,' I replied with deliberately exaggerated serenity. 'As a matter of fact, I was just going to get the table.'

He visibly dilated to even greater proportions so that I thought his eyes were going to pop out of his head, then, when almost at the point of detonation, his expression suddenly relaxed into a sarcastic grin.

'What's the number of the engine you've prepared then?' he asked, the apparent explanation germinating in his mind.

'44004, the one on the board,' I replied as calmly as before.

'Ha!' he smirked, 'you've prepared the wrong one. 44404 is ours. Come and look.'

As was usually the case when Percy was having an argument, a small crowd of interested enginemen had gathered around and, with the promise of further good entertainment, they followed us to the engine board just like spectators do in Laurel & Hardy films.

'There you are,' he said, then stopped dead as the awful realisation dawned that it was he who had made the mistake. 'Somebody must have altered it since I first looked,' he exploded, trying to seek some excuse for his error. This tantrum would probably have continued for another half an hour, but fortunately Mr Evans, the Senior Foreman, arrived on the scene and quickly absorbed the gist of what had happened.

'Go on, Percy,' he chided 'it's been that number for hours. What you need is some new glasses.'

The happy band of spectators had had their money's worth and, to the sound of their laughter, I and a deflated Percy went about our business. He did not, however, speak to me for the first part of the shift, and gave the engine and myself the very devil of a rollicking all the way to Gloucester.

Although 24 hours had elapsed since that episode, the embarrassment still rankled and, while we now conversed again, I sensed that the mere act of preparing our engine brought back unpleasant memories that pained and worried his very being, like the exposed nerve of a bad tooth. I, for my part, had practically forgotten the incident, and was doing my level best to be the essence of good-natured geniality. Things were going very well indeed, and I was quite advanced with my side of the business, when I decided to check the sandboxes and tighten up the smokebox door en route.

He, meanwhile, was endeavouring to oil the big-ends. Unfortunately the engine was not set in quite the ideal position, but since it was on a short pit and hard up against the stop plates, there was little he could do about it. Now the reader may have deduced from my original description that he possessed a body that fell far short of the ideal shape to go climbing up the narrow gap between big-ends and firebox throat-plate. He could, under

normal circumstances, just about make it, but with one big-end set back slightly further than desirable, he met trouble. With much heaving and struggling, he had managed to wiggle his ample and wobbly corporation up past the offending hunk of metal, but now that he wanted to slide down again, that self-same hunk of metal squashed the resilient flesh up to form a ring around his equator like a spare tyre, thus effectively plugging the gap.

Percy was, therefore, firmly and uncomfortably supported by nothing other than his paunch, and to compound the problem his overall jacket on its downward slither had become rucked up and was now inextricably entangled with oil cups, set pins and strap nuts that had been cleverly distributed in that area to ensnare the unwary. In my usual manner, I had departed from the port side of the cab, trotted round the framing, tightened the smokebox door, and having made the pleasant discovery that all sandboxes were full, was just about to re-enter via the starboard side when I heard his voice, albeit somewhat muffled and distorted.

'Hey, mate! I'm stuck!' he gasped. 'Give me a hand, will you?'

Now, ever since I had first joined the railway, the time-worn joke of portly drivers being stuck in the motion had been bandied about, and the stock answer to such a situation was, 'Hang on mate, I'll move her back a bit.'

Everyone knew it, for it was as old as steam engines themselves. My honest intention was to climb underneath and assess the situation with a view to releasing him from his predicament, but, without thinking, that old stock answer slipped off my tongue: 'Hang on, I'll move her back a bit.'

Any other driver would have laughed wryly and retorted, 'Come on mate, stop mucking about and get me out of this.'

But not Percy, who, devoid of any sense of humour, took everything said as Gospel. To make matters worse, as I entered the cab the heavy spanner I had been holding slipped from my grasp and fell with a loud clatter to the footboards. This was the last straw: he evidently thought that I was about to put intention into practice, for a loud, hysterical scream rent the air, followed by the sound of tearing cloth and a thud.

Seconds later a hideous and terrible form emerged from the dark depths of the pit trembling with fright and rage. Holding a feeder in one hand and an oil torch in the other, it glared balefully around seeking its tormentor. Slowly it moved into the light and I could now see the extent of the disaster.

His overall jacket had suffered considerably, for the left half had been completely ripped away and was now trailing by a thread behind its erstwhile owner, that is to say except for the sleeve which was still incongruously in its original position. The

right sleeve, together with the sleeve of the shirt beneath, were conspicuous by their absence, while the area from midriff to matted hair was plastered with streaks of black oil and grease.

On numerous occasions over the past months I had managed successfully to control my mirth over the escapades and incidents Percy became involved in, but the sight of this caricature was too much for me this time. I let out a howl of laughter that could be heard all over No 2 shed; I then realised that it was the worst thing I could possibly do, but the more I tried to desist, the more I laughed, and the more I laughed the more that malevolent red glow that had begun to emanate from Percy grew in intensity.

'You bloody young lunatic!' he shrieked. 'You could have crushed me!'

I was unable to speak for laughing and tears rolled down my face.

'So you think it's funny?' he roared. 'I'll - I'll bloody well show you how funny it is. I'll bloody murder you!'

So saying, he let out a howl and, waving both oil feeder and torch about his head in a menacing fashion, charged straight for me. I took the only option now left open, and diving round the back of our tender set off NNW as fast as my legs could carry me. That was the problem, though - the dashed things would not carry me very fast at all. I imagine that everyone at some time in their life has dreamed of being chased by a monster or demon or some such equally terrifying apparition, and although one desperately wants to leg it as fast as possible out of the immediate vicinity, one's feet appear to be transformed into lead and will barely move. Well, that was the situation I now found myself in. Nothing saps one's strength more than being convulsed with uncontrollable laughter, and I was convulsed, so instead of achieving the desired sprint, all I could do was to stumble along at a very indifferent pace.

On the other hand, rage and a determination to get his hands on what he now looked upon as the cause of his near assassination fired Percy with a speed and energy hitherto quite unimaginable. This, then, was the equaliser, for an 11-stone 23-year-old in prime condition should have had no trouble whatsoever in getting away from a 16-stone, overweight 57-year-old driver with weak ankles.

After about two laps round the inside of No 2 shed it was all too evident that Percy was slowly gaining on me, and had he not been expending so much energy on shrieking profanities at the top of his voice, I would have been by now doubtless nursing a sore head. By lap three I could almost feel his hot breath breathing down my neck, and unfortunately for me every time I glanced over my shoulder the sight of a blackened and tattered Percy frothing at the mouth and galloping along with all the grace and elegance of a hammer-toed rhinoceros with advanced footrot was just too much, and a renewed outburst of laughter impaired my performance even more.

Two circuits later age began to tell, and Percy started to fall inexorably further behind despite quite a crowd of enginemen cheering encouragement from just outside the lobby. This sizeable mob had grown lap by lap from a small knot of chaps initially fascinated by the unusual spectacle of an hysterical top link fireman being hotly pursued by a ragged, demented driver waving a feeder and a flaming torch about his head, screaming blue murder. I do not know whether anyone actually made a book on it, but both Percy and I had our respective band of supporters going wild with excitement.

By lap eight, the penultimate one, the scene was reminiscent of the Grand National on race day, all quite happy to stay and witness the conclusion despite the distinct possibility of a late start. Percy was now puffing like a grampus, and realising that he was losing the race, made one last desperate effort with his remaining strength and hurled both feeder and torch at my rapidly retreating figure.

The former, spraying its slippery contents over all and sundry, went very much wide of its intended target and caught the portly figure of Mr Evans right on the tummy button just as he stepped from the lobby to see what all the rumpus was about, leaving a mark on his impeccable cow gown that never did wash out. The latter, whirling and weaving a fiery trail like a tracer shell, missed my left ear by only a whisker and plunged spluttering into a nearby pit beneath the bowels of a Class '2P' 4-4-0.

Mr Evans, always the soul of reason and toleration, quietly called us together.

'You two really seem to have it in for each other this week, don't you? I would have thought,' he said, turning to me with an imperious gesture like a headmaster lecturing a naughty schoolboy, 'that you would have had more respect for your driver than to go playing silly pranks on him. As for you, Percy, I am surprised to see a man of your age behaving like a young hooligan. Now put a stop to this skylarking and get on with your work. You're late!'

Neither of us had breath left to argue and we meekly returned to our engine under this imposed truce. Eventually when I was able to explain things and apologise, Percy took it in surprisingly good part, although his wife nagged him for months over the amount of sewing he had created for her that night.

The following few weeks sufficed to heal the rift, and when May came along once more, we parted as good friends, both of us having benefited from the partnership. There was no doubt that I had learned more of the practical side of being an engine driver from him than from the rest of my mates put together. He had insisted on perfection in all things right from the beginning, and both my firing and driving techniques had benefited enormously. I was also grateful for the amount of driving he had allowed me to do, despite the strictness of his tuition, and although I did not know it at the time, this practice was to prove most fortuitous, bearing in mind the attitude of my driver in the next link. Percy had also sparked off a growing interest in the theory of railway operations and the rules and regulations necessary to put this into practice, and again, in view of the exacting and responsible work over the next two years, it could not have come at a better time.

5
THE LITTLE SHEFFIELD LINK

My year in this link turned out to be the happiest and most carefree of my railway career, and this was due partly to the fact that I spent nearly half of the time driving, and partly to my daily contact with that delightful gentleman who brought this about.

Although I knew Freddie Burrows by sight, I knew nothing of his ways, but right from the start we took an instant liking to each other, a liking which grew as the year progressed. Fred was the exact opposite of my previous mate in every respect. At 56 he was still a handsome man, standing some 5 ft 10 in tall, of medium build, lean and active, and carried his years so lightly that at first sight he might well have been still in his 40s. The expression worn on his well-chiselled features was that of good-natured tranquillity, while his blue-grey eyes regarded the world with honesty and humour. The only thing belying his age was a thick crop of almost white hair, which even then only lent a certain reverent dignity to his overall countenance.

While physically Percy and Fred were poles apart, the difference in their respective dispositions was equally well defined. Fred was affability itself, for a more even-tempered person was hard to imagine, and during the 12 months I was with him never a cross word passed his lips. His easygoing, calm outlook on life rubbed off on all he came in contact with, and he never became embroiled in arguments no matter how provocative the situation.

Fred's only vice, if indeed it could be called a vice, was a liking for a daily flutter on the horses, but since this involved only a few pence it was done mainly for entertainment value rather than any monetary gain.

Admittedly he enjoyed the odd cigarette, but seemed far happier with a cup of tea than a pint of ale, and even then only indulged on a hot and thirsty day when nothing else was available. This tranquil mode of living thus protected him from many of the everyday stresses of life and, coupled with a generous helping of exercise derived from firing on alternate days, did much to preserve his youthful appearance.

Unlike Percy he was happy to work as much overtime as providence meted out, and consequently he never flogged an engine in an effort to avoid excessive hours. On the contrary, in keeping with most other top link drivers, Fred used the minimum of steam necessary to run to time and, because starting and stopping were the great wasters of energy, he aimed at keeping the train in motion for as long as possible. There was little sense in dashing up to a signal, then waiting for 5 minutes for it to clear, when by shutting off early and coasting gently along a complete halt could be avoided. The miles of running we achieved with the regulator closed were a real revelation after my previous two mates, and much appreciated on the longer freight runs when the going was frequently far from easy.

Our first job together turned out to be one of my favourites in the link. This was the 8.00 pm Lawley Street to Leeds semi-fitted, which we worked as far as Derby. On arrival there, we walked up to Derby North relief cabin and waited for the fish train from Hull, then worked this semi-fitted back to Washwood Heath. Although we were due to take over at around 11.30 pm, delays were not infrequent and many happy hours were spent with congenial company in that cosy little cabin. Even when running to schedule we made a little overtime, which of course pleased Fred, and on occasions we were hard put to catch our job for the following day.

During that first week we had plenty of opportunity to explore each other's working methods, knowledge, capabilities and general characteristics, and I was also able to discover what turns our link encompassed. We principally covered the northern runs, going as far afield as Sheffield, which in itself was a unique experience for me since not only was it to be the first time I had worked a freight job to that famous steel centre, but it also involved lodging there, and so far I had never been on a lodging turn. Apart from the seemingly inevitable Bordesley tripper, we also had a couple of westbound jobs that occasionally took us to Gloucester, although we were officially booked relief at Bromsgrove. By Saturday I was already quite convinced that I was going to enjoy working with Fred, but at that stage I still had no inkling of the joys to come.

The following week we booked on at the very pleasant hour of 8.30 am - made even more pleasant by the fact that our engine was already prepared - in order to work the 9.20 am Class B to Gloucester. Because of the considerable amount of passenger and fitted freight traffic at that time of day, we rarely got past Bromsgrove, but on about four occasions during the ensuing year we did manage to run to time and made Gloucester.

On Monday we were allocated Class '4F' 0-6-0 No 4108 and, after the usual check and clean-up session, we tootled gently down to Washwood Heath Junction to collect our train. This proved to be a fairly substantial one of some 40 wagons, equal in weight to 44 of mineral, with approximately two-thirds of those loaded coal wagons. However, No 4108 was a strong and efficient engine and, dispensing with the pilot at Camp Hill, we ultimately arrived at Blackwell far too late to entertain any ideas of working through.

I always took a great interest in drivers' techniques when descending Lickey and, after receiving the signal to draw ahead, I carefully watched Fred's every move. Both our guard and the brakesman must have been feeling full of beans, for initially they were rather over-zealous in pinning down the brakes and nearly dragged us to a standstill. This always boded ill, since they then had to desist for a while until the train had picked up sufficient speed

'Jubilee' No 45589 *Gwalior* on the down 'Devonian' running past Bromsgrove South signal box having just descended the 2 miles of Lickey Incline in September 1951. *Gwalior* was an outstanding performer during the early 'fifties, and was often seen on the more demanding duties.

Freight trains aimed to stop at the water column in front of the signal box, no easy task for non-fitted trains relying on only the engine brake and a number of pinned-down wagon brakes over which the driver had no control whatever.

to keep it in motion. The pre-calculated distribution of braking effort was therefore upset, thus leaving it very much more to chance whether a runaway would occur.

No doubt something of this nature happened, for although Fred initially appeared to have the train under control, by the time we were halfway down the bank the engine was being given a full brake application, and there it remained. We ran past the column with some 20 wagons before finally juddering to a standstill, and Fred observed, like so many other drivers I had worked with, that one could never really be sure of stopping at the other side of the column, let alone in the correct position for filling the tank.

After the brakes had been picked up and we had set back, I casually mentioned that I thought we would run past soon after commencing the descent.

'Have you ever driven one down?' asked Fred.

'Not yet,' I replied a trifle wistfully.

'Well I think it's about time you had a bit of practice,' said he. 'In fact, you can take her tomorrow!'

I was both surprised and delighted to say the least, because I had no foreknowledge that Fred was prepared to indulge in firing turns and of course no idea at all that he would carry this to the length of firing on alternate days over the routes I knew on just about every job in the link. As it turned out, even when I didn't know the road he soon made sure that I did, so that in time the only duties I did not drive on were the Sheffield lodging turn, which was routed over the Erewash Valley, and our one Sunday night express passenger job to Derby. In both instances the work was too rigorous for Fred to cope with, and in any case I never did fully learn the Erewash Valley in the time available. Even so, 11 weeks out of 12 at the regulator was beyond my wildest dreams, particularly when half of those were semi- or fully-fitted.

Needless to say, with the prospect of my first drive down Lickey in the offing I found it difficult to sleep soundly, and just could not get to work soon enough. Consequently I arrived a good half-hour early and was delighted to discover that we had been allocated a Class '8F'. This I found was not an infrequent practice when the Traffic Department notified the Motive Power that a heavier than normal train was waiting.

By the time Fred arrived I had thoroughly checked No 8420, added a few extra spots of oil to places Percy would not have neglected, and had virtually filled the firebox with hand-picked lumps of surprisingly good-quality coal.

Unlike Percy, Fred never regarded any assistance I offered in the way of firing as interference, nor looked upon it as a doubt aimed at his firing ability. On the contrary, we cleared up this point very early in our association. Feeling extremely grateful for the chance to drive, I told Fred quite bluntly that I would enjoy a greater peace of mind if he would allow me at least to build up the fire before the start of a run, thus saving him some of the hardest work. Fred with equal frankness retorted that while he quite liked a spot of exercise, he was not that addicted as to want to have it all to himself and that I should feel free to pick up the shovel any time I so desired provided that it did not detract from my driving duties. I therefore made a habit of filling the box for him whenever possible, and also firing in safe situations such as when slowly climbing a bank, since at that time I could bale in 20 hundredweights of coal in half that number of minutes without raising more than the odd bead of perspiration.

Fred I think was quietly amused at my eagerness to get going, for I even volunteered to mash the tea, but in fact I was trying to cover up my emotions with activity, for I readily admit to having felt more than a few butterflies fluttering around in my stomach.

Backing on to the train at Washwood Heath, we found that we had the expected full load of 50 wagons, which added a little more spice to the great occasion. No 8420 was in good condition and, since the braking power of a Class '8' matched its hauling capacity, it had a distinct advantage over a '4F' despite the heavier train. I was therefore a trifle more confident as we slowly drew out of the sidings than I would have been had we been equipped with one of those ubiquitous 0-6-0s.

The haul up to Duddeston Road was the usual protracted affair, involving the use of only a partially opened first valve, and just about full gear, but I did have the added pleasure of exchanging a few words with my former mate in the Pilots as we chugged past. We had to wait some 20 minutes before being allowed to tackle the bank, and while Fred sorted out his winners for the day I prepared a magnificent fire for him. At last the signals came off and, after giving a prolonged 'crow' whistle, during which time Fred released the hand brake, I eased open the regulator.

In near ideal conditions No 8420 was able to transmit her full torque to the wheels without fear of slipping, and as soon as we were nicely on the move I opened up to full first regulator. By Landor Street box I linked up to 60 per cent cut-off and, since our safety valves were lifting, decided not to waste the steam being generated and promptly heaved the regulator wide open.

It is a tremendously exhilarating sensation to feel the vibrant power of a large locomotive working hard, and as we hammered under the bridge at Brickyard Crossing I would not have exchanged places with anyone in the world. Once off the 1 in 62 section I eased back on to the first valve again, and still at 60 per cent cut-off we pounded steadily up to Camp Hill where, after consulting with Fred, we dispensed with the pilot. Over the 1 in 280 stretch to Brighton Road I reduced the cut-off by small increments to 40 per cent, which sufficed to build up enough momentum to give us a good run at the 1 in 100 climb through Moseley Tunnel. However, the distant at Kings Heath was at caution and we rightly concluded that a tripper was still performing at Hazelwell.

Following Fred's example I shut off early and kept the train in motion without actually coming to a standstill, then, as the signals cleared, I was able to open up gently and continue to Kings Norton. Here, as expected, we were turned up the goods line, receiving a green flag at the box to indicate that at least one train was preceding us.

We clanked steadily along to Halesowen Junction without actually sighting the other train's brake-van, before waiting a further 30 minutes for the road to clear. At Halesowen Junction the permissive section ends and the goods line is thereafter officially designated the slow. There then follows a block of some 2½ miles up to Barnt Green, involving a steady pull at 1 in 301 for most of the way but, with little need to hurry, No 8420 was allowed to amble along on a breath of steam and 45 per cent cut-off.

This time we were halted for no more than 5 minutes, and since the fast and slow lines converged to but one track from there until Bromsgrove, we were obliged to move a trifle more briskly, but not for long. As anticipated, our train was turned into the loop at Blackwell where we enjoyed our lunch amid those verdant surroundings, while a number of passengers and fitteds hurtled by.

At last the signal came off and with it realisation that my moment of trial was close at hand. Easing out on to the main line I experienced a momentary twinge of apprehension, but this soon disappeared as I became immersed in my work, and keeping the train well under control, rolled gently down the 1 in 291 gradient to come to a standstill just in advance of the brakeman's hut.

Over the last few years I had viewed the incline from this self-same spot on many occasions and in all sorts of conditions, but never had it appeared quite so long and so steep as it now did on this bright sunny afternoon. Despite a slight heat shimmer from the track, one could see quite clearly right to the bottom, and during that seemingly interminable wait for the brakesman and guard, it resembled a gigantic ski-jump more than ever.

Eventually they arrived, advising me of their readiness, and since the signal was already off I applied the steam brake so that Fred could release his hand brake. Trying to act as unconcerned as if I was merely moving an engine in the shed, I closed the taps and eased open the regulator.

Having watched many different drivers start off on innumerable occasions, I had already evolved my own theories on how it should be done, and consequently realised the importance of keeping the train moving at a steady pace while the brakes were being pinned down. Many factors were of course involved, since as more of the train ran on to the 1 in 37 gradient there was a tendency to accelerate, while, on the other hand, as each wagon brake was applied, so the resistance and drag increased. It was therefore very necessary to be extremely sensitive to these varying forces, and quickly compensate by small changes of the regulator opening in order to keep the train taut and moving steadily at about 4 mph.

As a matter of fact, I found this relatively easy, although it did demand a high degree of concentration and continual juggling with the regulator. At last I spotted the guard's waving arm indicating that he was now in his van and, after giving an answering hoot on the whistle, turned round to view the 2-mile descent ahead. There is a certain critical speed with any train in this situation, which must not be exceeded if one is to retain control, and, since it is a complicated formula full of variables, the driver has to rely ultimately on experience and a sort of sixth sense of what is actually happening at any given moment. I had no previous driving experience of the Lickey Incline to fall back on, but I had carefully studied cause and effect as a fireman. This had developed my sensitivity to a considerable degree so that the feeling of what was right or wrong now came very naturally.

After an initial application of the steam brake had enabled Fred to wind the hand brake hard on, I found that the train was already quite well under control, the guard and brakesman having done an excellent job in this respect. Even short applications had an

instant effect in reducing speed, and I considered myself very lucky to have so much in reserve. I was therefore able to experiment and gradually allow our speed to increase, for if one ran off the 1 in 37 section on to the 1 in 186 too slowly, the uncontrolled braking effect of the wagons would bring the train to a standstill far short of the water column at Bromsgrove South. Momentum had to be judged very finely indeed on the latter part of the descent to achieve this desired result.

Halfway down the bank we could clearly see the distant signal was off, showing that we were being routed over the fast line, and once again I thanked my lucky stars, for this meant that the column would be on my side and that I could keep it in view all the time during the final approach.

As the roadbridge at Bromsgrove station loomed ahead I permitted our pace to build up by letting the train run free and, as we thundered through the platforms, I waited for the inevitable rapid deceleration that would occur as all the wagons came on to the less severe gradient. Anticipating this by a split second, I gave a gentle touch on the brake to eliminate the possibility of a snatch, then made a series of applications to get the feel of the train again.

The column was now only 100 yards ahead and, although I sensed that I had more than an even chance of stopping in about the right position, I realised that every single yard would demand my full concentration. I had originally intended to play it safe and try and stop just short of the column, but with only 20

'8F' No 8420, later 48420, in LMS days. One of the 14 '8Fs' stabled at Saltley during the mid-'fifties, she was in fine fettle when I drove her for the first time down Lickey, and even obliged in stopping perfectly positioned at the water column at Bromsgrove South.

yards to go and everything seemingly fine, I decided to attempt to stop exactly right for water. That would be an achievement to write home about if it came off.

Ten yards, 5 yards, 3 yards, and with a final light rub of the brake we came to a halt right opposite the marker. I made a great effort to retain my outward calm, and with the air of someone who pulls off such a feat every day of his life, I climbed on to the back of the tender and put the bag in.

Whether Fred considered this a shining example of beautifully judged driving, or merely a fluke stemming from beginner's luck, I do no know, for he passed no comment, nor had he done so during the entire descent of the bank, and for that I was extremely grateful. Only the man holding the brake handle has the real feel of the train, and unless an obvious error is being made any advice or interference can only make matters worse.

The following day we had another '8F' on a similarly loaded train, and to my delighted surprise Fred once more gave me the engine. I was this time somewhat more confident, and right from the start aimed to reproduce the previous day's performance. This, I am happy to relate, I managed to do, at any rate within a foot of the exact spot, which was near enough for watering purposes, and I was led to conclude that descending Lickey was easier than I had supposed.

On Thursday we were allocated a '4F' and by the time we reached Blackwell I realised that I was faced with a somewhat tougher proposition, for in terms of brake power to weight ratio the '4F' was noticeably inferior to the Class '8s'. We set off from the top well enough, but by the halfway mark I was having to make prolonged brake applications in order to keep below the critical runaway speed, and for the last part of the descent the brake was on continuously. Moreover, it was raining fairly steadily and this threw in another variable to contend with. When passing through the station I was quite certain that we would over-run, but then we decelerated so suddenly that with some 50 yards to go it became apparent that we would stop short. I therefore eased open the regulator, intending to drag the train right up to the column, for I wanted to make it a hat-trick if at all possible. Shutting off at what I judged to be the correct point, everything seemed nicely under control over the last couple of yards as I made the final brake application.

I was just about to congratulate myself on another perfect stop when a powerful surge from behind suddenly pushed us past the column, locked wheels and all, by some three wagon lengths or so. Despite a vigorous attempt to set back, I was still a wagon length away when we had to call it a day. Whether the guard had noticed us dragging the train forward and released his brake I do not know, but the surge was so unexpected that it took me completely by surprise and I could have kicked myself for not settling for a stop on the correct side of the column. The disappointment must have shown in my face, for Fred, with a sympathetic grin, remarked, 'We all try to be just a little bit too precise to start with. If you can stop a few yards short you've done well enough.'

I remembered that Syd Lloyd had said more or less the same thing a few years ago, and decided in future to err on the short side.

The next day we again had a '4F', and bearing in mind the embarrassment of the previous trip I came down a little too cautiously and ground to a halt 10 yards from the column; however, it was then but an easy matter to uncouple and run forward for water, so no harm was done.

We finished the week with a Class '8', and since the train was somewhat lighter and very well braked, I found it relatively simple to stop right on the marker. With only one failure, I had come through the baptism much better than expected and, although Fred still passed no comment, he must have considered that I showed some promise, for from now on he allowed me to drive on alternate days over the routes with which I was familiar.

After my first week of handling trains down the Lickey Incline I became even more convinced that whether one stopped or not at the water column depended to a considerable degree on just how well one started from Blackwell. Maximum concentration over those first vital yards gave both the guard and brakeman a chance to exercise the skills upon which so much depended, and any lapse on the driver's part preventing the proper implementation of those skills was usually paid for at Bromsgrove South.

Our next turn also proved to be a great favourite of mine once I had learned the road. This was the 7.5 pm Water Orton to Toton, which ran under Class A lights. Outward-bound it was a very cushy number - the loadings were normally so minimal that I concluded that the principal reason for running the job was to return the Toton engine to its native depot. The most we ever had on was 18 vans, and on one occasion as few as six. The return trip, however, more than made up for this, being always a fully laden coal train destined for Washwood Heath.

The first time round Fred drove all week, for while I knew the road to Derby reasonably well, I had never been over the section from Stenson Junction to Toton and, of course, I had to learn this before being allowed to handle the regulator. We were generally allocated an '8F' for the job in both directions, and usually a pretty rattly, run-down one at that, but on the Thursday to my great delight we found on the engine board none other than No 92018, one of the new BR Standard Class '9Fs'.

I had been most impressed on first seeing one of these magnificent locomotives at Saltley shed the previous year. It gave the appearance of tremendous power, and looked the very essence of what a heavy freight engine should be. Percy Trotter, always conservative at heart, was with me at the time and, after we had given it a perfunctory examination, passed the comment, 'Bloody great thing, all boiler and wheels.' Although intended as derisory, it was nevertheless an accurate description.

Ever since that day I had been dying to get my hands on one, but although with every passing week they became a more familiar sight, until now no opportunity had arisen. Other than Garratts, neither Fred nor I had fired a wide firebox before, so this initial acquaintance was to become a protracted experiment for both of us. The general cab layout was very similar to that of a BR Class '5' except that the boiler was noticeably more

massive and the firebox sloped outwards at its base. Looking through the oval firehole at the wide grate made me wonder how difficult it would be to keep the back corners filled, but as with so many other things experience and practice soon showed the way.

While still on the shed I manhandled a quantity of large lumps into the firebox and poked these across to the rear corners so as to form a bed on which to build. Over the rest of the 40.2 sq ft of grate area I spread a fairly thin saucer-shaped layer of coal, somewhat thicker in the corners and under the door. In the course of time I found that Class '9s' were not at all sensitive to the manner in which they were fired. The shallow firebox precluded an unduly thick firebed but, this apart, they did not seem to mind if they were fired heavily or lightly, haycock or saucer-shaped, and such was their vast steaming ability that they were the only engine I have ever known to perform normal work with actual holes or dead areas in the fire.

Our old friend Les Suffield was the guard and, having given him my armchair to repose on, we tootled off light engine to Water Orton. None of us had been on the footplate of a '9' in motion before, and those next 6 miles, mostly on the main line, served as a real revelation. Judging by the dirt and grime ingrained on her broad boiler, No 92018 had travelled a fair mileage since leaving the paint shops, but she felt just like a new engine. The ride was uncannily stable, with no rolling or pitching, no lateral oscillations and very little vertical movement.

Admittedly Fred was only using a breath of steam, but the complete absence of any bangs, rattles and knocks was nothing short of staggering, considering that our speed rose to something approaching 50 mph through Castle Bromwich, and even here the most obtrusive sound was an intermittent buzz from the open cab ventilator as we passed over some of the less well-aligned rail joints. Until then I had considered these engines as purely for heavy freight, sort of super Class '8s', suitable only for slow-speed work, but now this impression of very free running plus a rock-steady ride made me consider far wider possibilities. I was not on my own by any means in this thinking, for it is now past history that these 2-10-0s soon found themselves working crack fitteds and eventually express passenger trains, when they caused some embarrassment to the hierarchy by running at speeds of up to 90 mph.

It would be fair to say that no one at that time fully appreciated just what a wonderful machine had been created in the '9F'. With an axle loading of only 15½ tons on each of its driving wheels (the BR Standard Class '3' 2-6-0 was 16½ tons), route availability was as wide as engines of half their power, and what other locomotive was equally happy and efficient on either heavy minerals or express passenger trains? The other point that became obvious on our brief run to Water Orton was the colossal reserve capacity of the boiler even when compared to '8Fs'. On arrival the water level seemed hardly lower than when we had departed from the shed, and although the fire was by no means properly burned through and the firedoors left wide open, pressure had remained constant at 245 lbs per sq in.

After backing on to our train, it was only a matter of minutes before Les returned and stated that we had but 16 vans, and since the five next to our engine were fitted, would we like them piped up? Fred immediately agreed to this because any additional brake power was always welcome, and with nearly a third of the total under direct control we would in this respect be equivalent to a semi-fitted.

Although designated Class A we were timed quite briskly, but with only 16 vans behind the tender, No 92018 hardly noticed them. With just a whiff of steam on, Fred quickly had her linked up to 15 per cent cut-off, and at this she travelled so swiftly that we soon caught up the preceding train. I had a very easy time of it since we ran for miles without requiring either coal or water and, because I was so unoccupied with firing, I was able to concentrate my attention on just how the fire burned over the whole grate area, damper settings and injector delivery rates.

The favourable gradients from Tamworth to Burton of course assisted our effortless progress, but even the rise of 1 in 454 to Repton & Willington station passed unnoticed and soon we were at Stenson

Junction. I did not know the road from here on, but one advantage of changing links in May is that the lengthening days permit a much more detailed study to be made of any new route, which in turn is naturally conducive to its rapid learning. When only viewed at night it takes considerably longer to acquire the necessary knowledge, particularly of gradients and scenic landmarks.

From Stenson Junction the road falls at 1 in 226 for a mile then travels through flat, uninteresting country for the following 2 miles, when there are some small undulations up to Chellaston Junction. Fred pointed out that from Stenson there were seven overbridges before sighting the distant signal at Chellaston, and these should be noted to determine one's position on a dark night.

There is a slight rise of 1 in 440 up to Weston-on-Trent station, then the road drops for the next mile at 1 in 220. This is the fastest stretch on the section, since the gradients continue to be favourable through Castle Donnington right down to the approach of Lock Lane Crossing some 4 miles distant. Here a short rise of 1 in 330 is useful in checking one's pace if so desired, before dropping again at the same inclination to the Crossing itself, which is but three-quarters of a mile from Sheet Stores Junction. We were usually brought to a halt before joining the Derby line, which then took us down to the complex of Trent, and after running round the back of this island station we were generally held until relieved by a Toton crew.

Having no other means of transport, we stayed on the footplate for the short 2-mile run through Long Eaton to Toton itself, where we left our colleagues and walked over to the loco sheds for a spot of supper before collecting our engine for the return working. Obviously it was not in our interest to be late since it ate into our rest period, but on the run back to Washwood Heath with the coal train there was no such sense of urgency, and Fred never complained of the resultant overtime as long as we were not too late to catch our job for the following day. I soon learned the stretch from Stenson Junction to Toton and, 12 weeks later, after an initial refresher run, Fred let me take over.

From then on I drove on alternate days and, since a Class '9' was usually provided, enjoyed myself enormously, particularly outward-bound when I was able to let rip. Fred generally gave me full freedom to drive in my own style, although with such a lightly loaded Class '9' it was so easy to travel rather too swiftly, and on these occasions he did restrain my over-exuberance.

As the year progressed so did Fred's confidence in my ability increase, and I well recall a magnificent run to Toton that stands head and shoulders above all the others and serves to illustrate one aspect of Class '9' capabilities. It occurred in November, when after six months of driving with Fred I was really beginning to get the feel of things. We were now having Class '9s' every trip and, although darkness prevailed over the whole distance, by the end of the week I had fully acclimatised to the change in conditions.

Examining the engine board on Saturday evening I saw that we had a high-numbered Class '9', so it was no great surprise to find that No 92137 was in mint condition; not so much as a single stain blemished her gleaming paintwork when we climbed aboard. She had obviously just been run in, and this was probably her first true road job, for even the leather seat coverings had that distinctive smell of newness.

After the usual checks had been accomplished, I built up the fire and swilled down the footplate while Fred went off to make our first can of tea prior to ringing out. He returned with our guard, Les Suffield, who, after bidding me good evening in his usual courteous manner, remarked on the weather.

'Chilly tonight, chaps. Almost cold enough for snow I would say.'

We both agreed, since it was one of those raw, damp nights that despite heavy cloud cover gave one the feeling that the temperature could very quickly get down to freezing point.

'You'll soon be all right Les, when you get in that cosy little caboose of yours,' chided Fred.

'Well, you're not too bad on these, are you?' the latter replied, indicating the wide oval firehole that even now was radiating a comforting warmth to our three posteriors as we stood in front of it.

'Not as long as you can keep the doors open,' admitted Fred, 'but then when you're firing it's too damned hot.'

This latter statement was only too true, for I had soon discovered that the large oval firehole permitted a far greater amount of heat to be radiated out into the cab than on engines equipped with the standard circular hole. When the fire was white hot under normal working conditions even a brief exposure at close proximity caused one's overalls to smoke in a most disconcerting fashion, and any flesh coming into contact with the hot material suffered accordingly. With 40 sq ft of grate area to cover, the fireman generally applied more coal at any one session and spent that much longer doing it, so the problem was compounded. Furthermore, to reach the back corners the shovel had to be virtually thrust inside the furnace, bringing one's hands very close to the flames. Substantial gloves were to my mind a necessity when firing a Class '9', and this was another reason why I built up as large a fire as was practical for Fred's benefit when he was firing.

Later I discovered a little dodge that greatly helped to reduce this emission of unwelcome heat. Before starting a round of firing I always dropped two or three shovelsful just inside the firehole so that a small hump of dead coal was formed. This not only blanketed off much of the radiation, but also acted as a deflector, since by bouncing the shovel blade against this hump at the correct angle, coal could be shot into the back corners with the minimum of effort and without the need to get too near.

Having thus briefly debated the relative comforts provided by our respective charges, the shed signal came off and the yard foreman shouted across to us that we could go. Leaving the taps open to blow out the condensation that would have accumulated in such a cold atmosphere, I eased open the regulator and, amid much hissing and great clouds of steam, we rolled smoothly off the shed and over Duddeston Road bridge. We were turned out on to the main line and by the time we were passing Bromford it was obvious that even for a '9', No 92137 was exceptional. I have already extolled the virtues of the class, but this one was truly remarkable, for with no more than 40 lbs per sq in showing on the steam chest pressure gauge and 15 per cent cut-off, we were already going like a racehorse. Furthermore, there was not the slightest whimper of steam, trace of vibration nor rattle coming from anywhere; in fact, the only noticeable sound was the click of passing rail joints, and had it not been for this one might have easily imagined that we were not running on wheels at all but merely floating just above the tracks. All the controls were incredibly smooth and light to operate, giving one the immediate impression of being in full command, and I particularly relished the tautness of the regulator, since this allowed for adjustments as fine as 5 lbs per sq in to be made on the steam chest pressure gauge.

In a remarkably short space of time we arrived at Water Orton, neither Fred nor Les having conceived the slightest notion of how swiftly we had travelled, since they had been deep in conversation while toasting themselves in front of the now bright fire.

After backing on to our train, I dropped down to change the headlamps and have a quick feel at the wheel bearings to make sure that all was well, for new engines sometimes ran warm until a certain mileage had been logged. I had just completed this inspection when I was surprised to meet Les at the end of the tender.

'Shouldn't give you much trouble tonight, Terry,' he said brightly. 'We've only got six. They're all fitted and so is the brake. Shall we pipe them up?'

'Might as well,' I replied with a tingle of excitement beginning to form within me. 'It will give you a better ride and me a bit more stopping power if I get the chance to run 'em.'

So with Les illuminating the scene with his handlamp, I ducked under the buffers and wrestled with icy couplings and stiff hoses until all were screwed up as tight as I could manage. When the brake-van was finally connected I joined Les in the 6-foot, and for the first time noticed that the van also appeared to be just out of the shops.

'Oh, so you've got a new one too,' I remarked, indicating the spotless tail-end appendage, the stovepipe of which was already topped with a healthy red glow from the roaring fire beneath.

'Yes,' smiled Les, 'it's a North Eastern one, so I should be all right, and some kind soul lit the fire for me as well.'

I had often discussed the riding qualities of different types of brake-vans with Les and other guards in the past, for this too had to be borne in mind if the occupants were to be treated with consideration, and, as previously mentioned, when driving I made a particular point of giving them as good a ride as possible. It was generally agreed that for fast travel a North Eastern brake could not be bettered. Next to these came the standard BR variety that were closely styled on the Eastern pattern, followed by the LMS, SR and GWR brakes, in that order. I personally liked travelling in Great Western brakes, but this was only because they were more commodious, and the full-length lockers enabled tired passengers to lie upon them in comfort while catching up on their lost sleep.

Returning to the engine, since we still had time to spare I set about building up a really massive fire for Fred. With this engine and such a light load I calculated that if I filled the firebox to its practical limit we should make Stenson Junction without need of much further attention.

At last we were called out and, with the signal set for the fast, we left Water Orton in our correct path. With only six vans No 92137 required very little more steam than when moving as a light engine, and by the time we reached Kingsbury Junction we were fairly romping along at less than 15 per cent cut-off and 50 lbs per sq in steam chest pressure. By Wilnecote the distants were beginning to appear at caution and, since there was no point in coming to a standstill, I reduced the regulator opening even more. With the firedoors wide open and the rear damper just cracked off its face, she was steaming so well that Fred had filled the boiler up out of sight in an effort to prevent blowing off, but with working so lightly there was little possibility of priming. This was about the only effort Fred was put to, though, for with his feet resting on the damper control wheels, reclining comfortably on his padded seat and listening to the soporific clickety-click of wheels over rail joints, while all the time bathed with the warm radiance from the fire, he was having a job to keep his eyes open.

Despite being brought to a halt in Burton station, we were slightly ahead of schedule at Stenson Junction, thanks to the rapid and effortless acceleration at my disposal, and possibly because of this we had a clear run across on to the Trent line. While standing at Burton I had quickly fired a dozen shovelsful, filling in the odd spots where it was a trifle thin and generally levelling the firebed, so again there was no need for Fred to disturb his repose.

Once clear of the junction we normally enjoyed an uninterrupted run, and banking on the probability of having nothing ahead to block our way, I gradually eased open the regulator. With 60 lbs per sq in now showing on the steam chest pressure gauge, and the cut-off at 15 per cent, our pace began to quicken. At night this stretch of line is as black as the ace of spades since there are no towns nearby to cause a glow in the sky, and being overcast not even the stars were present to help one distinguish between ground and sky. Peering out of my open side window I could see nothing of the cutting nor the leafless trees that I knew grew in abundance atop its banks, and save for the fleeting glimpse of a passing telegraph pole as it was briefly illuminated by a shaft of light from the fire, the whole world seemed to be enveloped in inky blackness.

How fortuitous was the existence of those seven bridges, for without them acting as regular markers I would not have had a clue as to where we were. By the sixth bridge it was obvious from the click of the rail joints that we were travelling faster now than we had at any previous point of our run, but otherwise there was nothing at all to signify this. Still the same silent, turbine-like smoothness prevailed, while the ride was so steady that not even the lid of tea I was resting on the brake pedestal showed more than a ripple or two on its surface. That a 140-ton locomotive could travel in excess of 50 mph with no more commotion than a well-oiled sewing machine was surely a wonderful tribute to the near

perfect engineering attained in this Class '9F'. Suddenly remembering Les, I glanced back towards the brake and was reassured to see his side light still there, although I must admit it was bucking about more than somewhat, then, with the approach of the last bridge, I concentrated my attention on seeking the distant for Chellaston Junction.

Our speed was by now higher than it should have been, but with all wheels except our pony truck braked, I decided to keep her going, for although the night was dark, I should be able to pick out the signal in good time. Fred had been literally nodding off up to this point, which I thought was a considerable show of confidence in my driving prowess, but I was surprised to see him rouse up at the seventh bridge, stare ahead until satisfied that the distant was clear, then drop off again. He was so familiar with the road that he must have been subconsciously counting the bridges. The expression 'he could do it with his eyes closed' had more than a ring of truth in this instance.

With the short rising gradient of 1 in 440 up to Weston-on-Trent just ahead and Fred once more with his eyes closed, I gently inched open the regulator so that 70 lbs per sq in appeared on the gauge. Even on the incline a slight increase in pace was perceptible, but having surmounted the hump and falling at 1 in 220 we really started to go. I could still see nothing of the trackside, but the click of the wheels - one pause, five pause, three pause - rang out more rapidly than ever.

Feeling that this was now an ideal moment to experiment with gear settings, I reduced the cut-off to just under 10 per cent and increased the steam chest pressure to 80 lbs per sq in. No 92137 was as smooth and as quiet as ever as we hurtled over the falling gradients down to Castle Donnington, where the red aircraft warning lights on the power station chimneys and cooling towers stood out clearly against the jet black backcloth.

Goodness knows at what speed we were travelling when we reached our peak about 2 miles from Sheet Stores Junction but, the click from the last tender wheel was followed almost immediately by that of the pony truck striking the next joint. Even so, not a sway or a tremor disturbed Fred's peaceful slumbers, and I can honestly say that no other class of tender engine I ever worked on approached this '9' in terms of riding quality. Unfortunately this incredibly smooth, silent, effortless progression was extremely deceptive, particularly when no landmarks were visible, and no sooner had I shut off on spotting the distant for Sheet Stores than I became aware that it was swimming towards me at an alarming rate. In keeping with other BR Standard types, the Class '9' was equipped with an independent steam brake and, not wishing to alarm Fred by making a heavy and noisy application of the vacuum brake, I grasped the handle, yanking it back to the limit of its ratchet.

Very little appeared to happen at first and I became conscious of a slight pang of anxiety as the yellow light continued to approach at a seemingly undiminished pace. I still did not want to disturb Fred, but quickly concluded that he would be infinitely more disturbed if I over-ran the home signal, so as the distant loomed up I started making gentle applications with the vacuum brake.

The distinctive hiss of this soon roused Fred, who stared out in an effort to orientate himself. Meanwhile the lights at Sheet Stores and beyond were now visible, as was indeed the home signal, and I was now able to calculate stopping distances with a useful amount of visual aid. The answer came out in about two-fifths of a second that I would have to kill our speed pretty quickly if we were to stop at all, so instead of taking out some 10 inches of vacuum, I started knocking the needle down to zero for quite a lengthy period. I sensed Fred's tension as he stared ahead, also working out speeds and distances, and I smiled wryly to myself when I thought of how much more he would have tensioned had he known that the steam brake had been hard on for the last half-mile or so. However, his only observation was, 'It's on, you know!'

'OK, I've got it, Fred,' I replied more calmly than I felt, at the same time making another prolonged full application. Suddenly our speed fell away in that unaccountable manner so typical of vacuum-braked trains, and for the last hundred yards I barely had to check our pace, even though I had by now released the steam brake. Before we actually came to a standstill the signal dropped and I chuffed gently down to Trent station, where we were brought to a halt.

Presuming that we were being detained pending the arrival of our relief crew, I crossed over to Fred's side and joined him at the bucket for a quick swill. Moments later voices raised in earnest discussion could be heard approaching, then the dazzling beam of an electric torch flashed across the cab side from down below. Voice A, a deep bass, suddenly exclaimed in astonishment 'Bloody hellfire!' You're right mate, it is her!'

To this forthright statement voice B, a light tenor, made the reply, 'I thought she looked a new 'un as she passed the end of the platform.'

The bass, now directed his voice at us and endeavoured to attract our attention.

'Ay up! We're after you.'

Trent Station South Junction signal box, looking south. The main lines from Derby and Castle Donnington merge with the London main line alongside Trent's island platform.

I pulled open the cab door and, after a bit of puffing and blowing, voice A materialised through it in the form of a portly Toton driver who was obviously a trifle short of steam.

'Christ Almighty,' he continued, pulling out a pocket watch. 'What have you done, come over the fields? Do you know, you were supposed to be passing Stenson 15 minutes ago? Bloody Control, don't know what they're doing half the time; haven't even had time to mash our flaming tea yet!'

This old driver was not in a very good mood, thinking that the Control was to blame for him having to dash around, and it would have been imprudent of me to say otherwise. Fred, who was only just beginning to realise how early we were, also said nothing except to remark how inclement the weather was for this time of the year.

Ten minutes later Fred and I bade them farewell outside the loco as we made our way over the numerous tracks towards the ancient but nevertheless cosy messroom, feeling just as sprightly as when we had started out. With the possible exception of a diesel or an electric, I do not think any other locomotive could have brought us there with so little effort or fatigue as did that Class '9'.

We had just finished our sandwiches and Fred had joined in a game of dominoes while I was enjoying a quiet smoke when Les bowled in. As usual he had had to stay with the train until it was stabled, but now he was free to relax for an hour or so with us. With his customary friendly smile he seated himself next to me and got out his supper. As he did so I asked my inevitable question.

'How was the ride, Les? Hope I didn't rattle you around too much, only we seemed to be getting quite a lick on through Donnington.'

'Ah!' he replied, looking a trifle uncomfortable. 'I hope no one looks at my journal too closely. I've had to book 15 minutes from Stenson to Sheet Stores, and that was stretching it a bit. They'll think I was drunk unless they check with the bobby's, then Fred will be asked some embarrassing questions.'

I fervently hoped that a check would not be made, but I was on tenterhooks for the next two weeks. Fortunately nothing came of the matter, and Fred never did know that we had covered 12½ miles in 15 minutes, rather faster than a Class A is permitted to travel. Les did admit, though, that the Eastern brake-van had given him an impeccable ride, although at times he thought that some of our six vans had spent as much of their time on the down line as they did on the up.

'Mind you, I have been faster than that once,' he said, 'working the "Pines Express" down through Eckington!'

Our lodging job to Sheffield also followed this same route through Toton and up the Erewash Valley, rather than the more direct one via Derby, and even in summer we always traversed this section in darkness. The 21 miles from Toton to Clay Cross was a difficult road in many respects, and I found it the very devil of a job to learn during the time available. By the end of the year I had only managed to grasp essentials from the firing point of view, and would have required a much longer acquaintanceship to drive competently over it at night.

On the Sheffield we were booked a Class '4F' 0-6-0 and usually hauled a full load under 'Maltese' lights. By the time we arrived at Toton the fire was already past its prime, and from here on there is a steady 18-mile pull right up to Morton Sidings, with the gradient as steep as 1 in 150 over the section between Pye Bridge Junction and Coats Park North. The stretch contained no fewer than 28 blocks, which meant of course an almost unbroken chain of signals, and this was made twice as complicated because there were four tracks. Furthermore, numerous sidings lay strewn on either side and, since much of the area was subject to severe mining subsidence, speed restrictions, both permanent and temporary, abounded. To make matters worse there was a pronounced tendency for mist to develop along the course of the valley, and when this became well mixed with the heavy smoke pall coming from the many collieries and industrial plants that were dotted along the line, real old-fashioned pea-soupers occasionally blanketed the scene for days at a time.

Bearing in mind the above facts, and with the whole of my attention concentrated on

Sheffield Grimesthorpe MPD. Coaling plants came in all shapes and sizes, but invariably they were noisy and dirty structures. When I visited this depot on my first lodging turn, I felt that it was aptly named. Certainly the coaling plant did not look out of place, for the surrounding area matched it perfectly. Note the electrically powered capstan and rope (left foreground) by means of which wagons were positioned on the lift for loading into the hopper.

providing enough steam to run efficiently, I had little time available for road learning. When I did look out of the cab and my eyes had adjusted to the darkness, I found that one lot of signals appeared very much the same as the next. Only by constantly asking Fred and making continual references to a route card that I had previously made out, was I able to pin-point our position and gradually learn the correct block sequence. However, it was all very interesting and instructive and the knowledge came in extremely useful a year later when I was working the Carlisles, which on Saturdays followed this route.

From Morton Sidings it was far easier, since we were able to coast for 7 miles right down to Tapton Junction, where the roads to Sheffield and Masboro parted company. I always made use of this downhill stretch and built up the fire for the 5-mile slog at 1 in 100 up to Bradway Tunnel. It was quite a drag and with combustion efficiency deteriorating we were very hard put to maintain time. I was therefore always well pleased to see those grimy stone portals loom up because they signified the end of my ordeal. At slow speed, though, it did seem to take a dickens of a long time to pass through those 2,027 yards of dripping, noxious brickwork, but at least outward-bound we were coasting. In fact, the road fell at 1 in 100 for the 6 miles to our destination, Queens Road Depot, so apart from cleaning both the footplate and myself, I was able to sit down and watch the view.

After depositing our train we ran the 3 miles or só down to Grimesthorpe where we left our engine for the shed staff to deal with. Grimesthorpe shed was well named, for Saltley seemed by comparison like a luxury hotel. On the other hand nearby Brightside, where the Company Lodge was situated, appeared to be a bit of a misnomer, since it was

just as filthy as the rest of the area. However, the lodge itself was quite presentable on the inside, with adequate if unappetising food, clean and reasonably comfortable beds, and just sufficient warmth if the weather did not happen to be too inclement. Unfortunately, a shunting spur ran just beneath the bedrooms and the local Sheffield lads seemed to spend half the day with the noisiest Class '3F' on the system trying to knock the buffers off a rake of rusty wagons with their brakes pinned down. With this fearful racket going on outside, sleep, after the first couple of hours became rather fitful; indeed, it was sometimes a profound relief when the call came to get up.

The return journey was somewhat easier since most of the hard work was done during the earlier stages when both I and the fire were fresh, although the 8-mile haul from Grimesthorpe to Bradway Tunnel could prove something of a problem with a cold engine. Six miles of unrelieved 1 in 100 had those old '4Fs' extended to the limit, and it required all one's skill, together with a little bit of luck, to maintain sufficient pressure. Needless to say the tunnel itself seemed twice as long when pounding up through it, but once out into clean air again one could practically coast the next 5 miles all the way to Tapton Junction. From there it was admittedly a fair pull up to Morton Sidings, but on as far as Trent it was easy running over favourable gradients, and I did much better at learning the route from its northern end than from the other direction. This lodging turn came round every six weeks, since it required two crews to cover one week's work, and it provided a pleasant introduction into such duties and was to prove an excellent grounding for the Carlisles later.

As mentioned at the beginning of this chapter, one of my favourite turns was the 8.00 pm Lawley Street to Leeds, returning with the Hull semi-fitted. On this job I discovered a method to eliminate the snatch problem over one tricky little section of the run. Quite early on in the year, when our fish train was cancelled, we had to travel home from Derby as passengers in the brake-van of another semi-fitted. Approaching Burton station I decided to help myself to a lid of tea, and since we had so far enjoyed a smooth ride I was very surprised when a sudden snatch slopped half of it down my shirt. After I had uttered a derogatory comment about the driver, Les Suffield, who was also travelling with us, explained that on all loose-coupled trains, including semi-fitteds, one invariably experienced a snatch at that point.

Intrigued, I asked him why, and from the ensuing discussion it appeared that there was a slight hump in the track there. Because of the speed limit through Burton station, and also because the signals were difficult to sight, drivers shut off somewhere around Wetmore Sidings, then coasted down to the station. However, the hump caused the train to buffer up quite tightly, but once over it the forward part ran away, making the couplings feel taught to the driver when he opened the regulator. A snatch would occur in any case even if the engine was not opened up, but this act, no matter how gently performed, only seemed to accentuate the snatch.

Having thus been presented with the bones of the problem I thereupon decided to try and devise a cure. Analysing what was happening through the length of the train, it soon became obvious that if the engine was kept pulling, even if very lightly, then the wagons would not buffer up. The trouble was, though, that speed had to be held down approaching the station. On the other hand, if one slowed too early time would be lost, and in any case this slowing in itself would cause an unwanted surge. The only answer seemed to lay in gradually easing the regulator some distance from the station so that there was a breath of steam on over the hump. Everything would have to be very finely judged in case the signals at Burton Station South were on, but I resolved to give it a try at the next opportunity.

This occurred the following night since it was my turn to drive. Our train was some 30 minutes late arriving, but at last we climbed aboard the usual 'Crab' and learned that we had 48 vehicles behind the tender, 18 of which were fitted. After driving gently forward so that Les could relieve the guard, I replied to his hand signal and set off steadily down the goods line towards Derby station. Here we ran round the back of the platforms, and since we were usually held a short while before being turned out main line, it was advisable to proceed with caution.

As it happened on this occasion the road was clear, so opening up on to full first valve we pounded off towards Melbourn Junction in that distinctive wiggly way of those engines. 'Crabs' have a relatively weak first valve and any really hard work requires the regulator to be pushed well over, but they coped so effectively with these fitteds that the first valve sufficed to accelerate our lengthy train up the 1 in 435 gradient to Melbourn. From there, with the road virtually level, we soon started to rattle along at a handsome pace on no more than 20 per cent cut-off, and by the time we reached Stenson I was obliged to ease the regulator slightly.

These 'Crabs' were really magnificent engines on such duties, for although we were hauling 48 vans at something like 45-50 mph, she was only fractionally extended. Under such light working Fred had a fairly easy time

During their lifetime 'Crabs' did their fair share of passenger duties, but by the late 'fifties they had been largely relegated to what was to prove their ideal niche - middle-distance fully or semi-fitted freights. I learned to respect these efficient locomotives from both sides of the footplate when working the heavy Hull-Birmingham fish trains from Derby North Junction. No 2903 is seen entering Saltley station on the down main with an evening local on 5 July 1947. Part of the Metropolitan Cammell Carriage & Wagon Works can be seen on the right beyond the up and

keeping her steaming like an old kettle, seemingly tossing only the odd shovelful of coal into the firebox every few miles or so. Although the distants were off, in accordance with my predetermined plan I started easing the regulator still further at Clay Mills, which was some 2 miles out from Burton station. Gradually our speed began to fall on the level road, but by Wetmore Sidings I had to make further reductions since our pace was rather higher than desirable.

At North Stafford Junction my nerve nearly failed because we still seemed to be going fairly fast, and as yet I could not see if the road was clear to Leicester Junction. Concentrating ten-tenths, I tapped down the regulator handle so that it was just cracked open and even wound back the gear lever to give less than 15 per cent cut-off. It was very tricky at this stage, balancing things to give just sufficient delivery of steam to keep the couplings taught while at the same time keeping speed down so that we could stop in case the signals were on.

Then all of a sudden we were into the station and I could see that the road was clear. A quick assessment of our speed showed that we could have indeed stopped in time had the necessity arisen, and I realised that with the

brake power of a semi-fitted I could use this technique with confidence in the future. It only remained to be seen if by keeping steam on in this manner a snatch had been avoided, and I could hardly wait until we got to Washwood Heath to find out. After detaching our train we were sent off light engine to the shed, but we always waited a few minutes while Les and any other passengers who had travelled home in the brake walked up to us.

I was just fixing our tail lamp when he arrived. Les, always the gentleman, invariably thanked me for a pleasant ride, provided of course I had given him one, and having passed this complimentary comment, I quickly asked if he had noticed the usual snatch at Burton.

'Now that you come to mention it,' he said with slow deliberation, 'I don't believe that I did.'

I went on to explain that I was experimenting with a different technique to try and eliminate the snatch and that I would be very grateful if he would take particular note at that point and let me know of the results.

Two nights later he was able to confirm that the brake-van had traversed the hump as smooth as silk, and from then on I was able to develop my method to a fine art with confidence. As with everything else, practice makes perfect, so as time went on judgement of speed and where and how much to ease off became second nature.

The reward for the concentration put into this exercise came about one winter's night late in the year. Widespread fog blanketed most of the northern counties resulting in many delayed and cancelled trains. Although conditions were reasonable between Derby and Birmingham, our own train was over an hour late and a number of Saltley crews waiting in the cabin at Derby North had scant prospect of finishing without excessive overtime unless they travelled home with us. Strangely enough one of the drivers faced with this problem was my old mate Percy Trotter. Never keen on overtime, 'Piggy' had been chomping at the bit since we arrived, and after making repeated vociferous requests to the Control, finally obtained permission, along with two other sets of men, to return to Saltley in our brake.

Since visibility was too poor to see the brake lights I had to judge the length of the train, then give them a minute or two to climb aboard, but having started off we found the distants were in our favour. The fog was just sufficiently thick to keep me on my toes without actually proving too much of a problem, although the run up to Burton Station with steam on did cause some tense moments. However, everything went as planned and being aware that my colleagues at the rear end would be passing judgement on my driving, I pressed on as fast as I dared and with as much delicacy as I could muster.

We arrived at Washwood Heath without incident, and with a very crowded footplate slowly travelled through somewhat murkier conditions the odd mile to Saltley loco. Only Les had as usual passed comment on the smoothness of the ride. Later as we cycled home together he broke into conversation.

'Were your ears burning tonight?'

'That,' I replied, recalling eyebrows and hair encrusted with frost collected as a result of being forced to keep my head stuck out in a slipstream of freezing fog, 'was the last thing I was likely to have.'

'Well, you see,' he went on, 'I just happened to say as we were approaching Burton that you were the only driver to go through there without giving a snatch, and in fact you were so gentle that the main problem was keeping awake. Percy then started singing your praises saying that it was he who had taught you all you knew. Whereupon Horace [another driver who was almost as garrulous as Piggy] said that whatever Percy might have taught you, it certainly wasn't gentleness and everyone knew how he drove and most still bore the scars to prove it. Well, you can just imagine it after that - they were at each other's throats all the way back to Washwood Heath, so nobody got any sleep. Still, it was a very nice ride all the same.'

Knowing Percy so well I could readily picture the near riot that would have taken place, and no doubt the finer points of my efforts had passed unnoticed, but at least Les appreciated them, and that after all had been the original object of the exercise.

Early in January an amusing little interlude took place that serves to illustrate the erroneous impression even a railway enthusiast has of what it is like to ride on the footplate. Derek Bayley, an old school friend of mine who was then working as a chemist in the laboratories of Fort Dunlop, had for some time been badgering me to arrange a trip for him on an engine. His departmental chief had invited him to write an article for the work's magazine, and since railway topics were still of great interest to many people, he thought that a first-hand description of footplate life would be rather unique and gain wide acceptance.

Unfortunately, official footplate passes were so hard to come by that he did not even bother to apply, therefore I was duly approached in order to devise some clandestine scheme. The problem was of course that such a ruse would have to take place under cover of darkness, since for all our sakes we must avoid detection. All our regular turns involved long and uncertain hours coupled with the inevitability of frequent exposure to many grades of staff. However, we did have one job in the link that was absolutely made-to-measure.

This was our solitary passenger duty, which came round only on one Sunday night every

'Jubilee' No 45660 *Rooke*. This locomotive gained fame during special test runs including the Settle to Carlisle section in October 1937 when it is reputed to have developed extremely high indicated horsepower figures in excess of 1,800. When I fired it from Birmingham New Street to Derby one Sunday evening 20 years later it was so rough that I would have been prepared to believe that it had not been shopped since then.

12 weeks. It could not have been better since we departed from Birmingham at 7.45 pm, invariably with a 'Jubilee', and arrived at Derby 1 hour later. After uncoupling, the engine was then left for the disposal men on Derby loco, and after walking back to the station we relieved the 9.20 express that terminated at New Street. This meant that we were back at our starting point only 2 hours 35 minutes after setting out, and in ample time for my friend to catch his bus home. Just in case some prying eyes should spot a third man on the footplate we arranged for Derek to be disguised as a Traffic Inspector by clothing him in my macintosh and a felt hat, the official uniform of one of those gentlemen.

The night in question found Fred and I standing at the end of No 7 platform while Derek was trying to make his languorous 6 ft 4 in frame inconspicuous by lurking in the shadow of a supporting pillar. At 7.40 pm a filthy looking 'Jubilee', which turned out to be *Rooke*, trundled in with much clanking of side rods and juddered to a halt halfway under the bridge.

'She's a bit run-down,' commented the Bristol driver as we exchanged places, then as he disappeared from sight I ushered Derek to my side of the cab.

'Just stand behind my seat, old lad,' I said. 'You'll be out of the way there while I put a bit on.'

Having flashed a dozen shovelsful round the box, I just had time to point out the principal controls and gauges before the guard's whistle blew. Answering with a raucous hoot, I then crossed to Fred's side to see the train out.

As I came near to him I spoke softly in his ear. 'Pull her well up mate - after all, we want to give Derek something to write about.' (It may be recalled that a rough engine always knocked more violently when run on a short cut-off.)

With 13 coaches behind the tender Fred was obliged to take a fairly hefty handful of regulator, and on New Street's perpetually greasy rails *Rooke* slipped. The cacophony this created startled even me, so you can well imagine the wonders it did for Derek. The term 'panic-stricken' might be a shade too strong, but in the glare of an already white fire I saw him grab the nearest handrail with both hands while he glanced fearfully around with an expression registering shock and alarm.

This initial slip and the subsequent thunderous gallop down through the tunnels left us in no doubt of what was to come. Poor old *Rooke* was just about as run-down as any locomotive I had had the misfortune to work on, and was obviously at the upper mileage limit and more than ready for a major overhaul. In fact, by the time we reached Derby I was quite prepared to believe that the last one had been missed and she was going round for the second time.

She rocked, she rolled, she waggled and she oscillated in a most spectacular and uncomfortable manner, while the excessive play in the big-end bearings caused three tremendous crashes to shake her from stem to stern at every revolution of the driving wheels. Sitting down was out of the question and Fred, instead of linking her well up to make her knock, ran with the longest practical cut-off in an effort to subdue this defect. Derek in his naivety had intended to make notes of our progress, but as far as I can recall he never relaxed his grip on the handrail for the entire journey, not even when we came to a standstill in Burton station for our brief halt.

I must admit that I had my work cut out firing her at speed, and this particular feat seemed to fascinate Derek above all else.

'I cannot understand,' he said afterwards, 'how you manage to fire coal through the mouthpiece, let alone place it accurately on the grate when the firehole has moved to an entirely different position in space by the end of your swing from that when you started it - quite incredible.'

His scientific brain had tried to work out a regular pattern of motion for he felt sure that I could not have done it without being able to predict the various movements. However, *Rooke*'s wildly cavorting footplate followed no set formula and, as I explained, success was due to nothing more than years of practice, a feeling of what was happening being transmitted through the feet, and split-second reflexes.

We could not have given Derek a worse first ride if we had planned it, and after suffering an hour of that treatment we were all heartily glad to drop *Rooke* on Derby shed.

I did nearly walk away with the exhaust injector steam valve control wheel as a souvenir, though. The banging and crashing had caused many cab fittings to become loose and one of these was the aforesaid control wheel. The bally thing kept shaking off its spindle and rolling around the footboards. Having become thoroughly tired of playing 'hunt the slipper' every time I wished to operate the injector, I took to keeping it in my jacket pocket, hence the near oversight.

Despite the fact that the 'Black Five' was also below average, our return journey was a much smoother affair by comparison and both Fred and Derek were able to sit down for most of the way. We arrived back at New Street practically on time and a somewhat deaf and numbed but infinitely wiser Derek, looking like a cross between Al Jolson and one of the Harlem Globe Trotters, tottered off into the night. His article, when it came into print, made footplate life seem like some fiendish, perpetual torture, but then he did have a very rough ride.

The happy periods in one's life pass all too quickly, and that glorious year with Fred was no exception. May came round again and once more I was torn between wishing to stay on with him and wanting to progress to higher things. Since these higher things included the prospect of working the much venerated Carlisles, which had been my burning ambition since first signing on as a cleaner, I found our eventual parting less painful than I formerly imagined. As it turned out I went into the Bradford link, which contained four weeks of Carlisle jobs, and when the notices were duly posted I suddenly realised that at last I was one of the elite. I did not know my future driver Les Field, but Fred assured me that as far as the Carlisles were concerned I could not be with a better mate.

'You will not expend an ounce more energy than is strictly necessary with Les,' was his parting shot.

It was ironical that I was to expend more energy with him over a concentrated period than at any other time of my life, but I could not have even guessed at the circumstances then, and therefore suitably reassured I joined the Bradford link with a happy confidence.

The year with Fred had enabled me to considerably extend my road knowledge, but even this was but a cock stride compared to the marathon Carlisle run. However, my driving experience had given me a much greater appreciation of the problems and ideals to aim for when working steam locomotives, and this was to prove a great benefit during the coming year.

6
THUNDER OVER AIS GILL

At Saltley the Carlisle turns were surrounded with a certain awe and reverence in no way even approached by any other duty. The sheer magnitude of the job in terms of mileage alone was a daunting prospect to driver and fireman alike, for there were no booked stops at which to take a rest. Indeed, if all went well and the train ran to schedule, it meant seven hours of undivided concentration for the driver, and an equal amount of time with a shovel in his hands for the fireman. When not infrequent delays occurred, this ordeal could well extend to ten hours or more, and, on the outward-bound trip at any rate, this fearsome task was made all the more difficult by the fact that the really hard work started at Skipton, more than 5 hours after booking on, and some 140 miles from Water Orton. Here, already tired, with a fire well past its best and the coal at the back of the tender, one had to gird one's loins to tackle just about the most demanding 87-mile mountainous stretch on British Railways over the Settle and Carlisle line. It was little wonder then that on many occasions even healthy young giants of firemen had to be literally carried from the footplate at the end of such herculean labours, rigid with exhaustion.

Much has already been written about how the Settle and Carlisle line came into being. Suffice to say that it was born out of blood and sweat in an era of unparalleled human endeavour, hacked out of some of the most wild and barren moorland to be found in England, at great expense and cost in human lives. That it was all worthwhile lives on in the gifts to posterity offered by such superb constructions as Ribblehead and Dent Head Viaducts, and Blea Moor and Rise Hill Tunnels, fittingly set amid the grim grandeur of the Pennine Peaks. The challenge of that stupendous climb up to Ais Gill was exciting enough, but added to this was the barren isolation of unpopulated mountains, which the weather lashed in quickly changing moods with a fury that I have never experienced anywhere else. Every trip was a unique adventure and no two runs were ever the same. So many variables could come into play over such a long journey, and even the climate was totally different up in the fells 180 miles north of our starting point.

This paramount job had a long and regal lineage, for the development of the Birmingham-Carlisle service came about during the reign of Victoria in the year of her Golden Jubilee, when the 4.30 pm loose-coupled express freight train from Lawley Street to Derby was extended through to Leeds, conveying important North and Scotch traffic from Birmingham and district. The train was given the unofficial title of 'The Jubilee' by railwaymen having dealings with it, and was referred to as such for many years.

In 1931 Scotch traffic had grown considerably and the decision was taken to run a semi-fitted Class D freight at 4.30 pm from Lawley Street through to Carlisle, for Scotch traffic only, followed at 4.40 pm by 'The Jubilee', running from Lawley Street to Leeds as an express freight. Special authority was given in the Classification and Marshalling of Freight Trains circular for the 4.30 pm train to be double-headed when required to convey a maximum of 60 vehicles, and the train ran under this authority on

A general view of Skipton station. When the Birmingham-Carlisles arrived here they had already covered 140 miles. With the fire getting dirty and the coal well back on the tender, a tired fireman had to gird his loins in preparation for the long and formidable climb up to Ais Gill.

many occasions, especially during the very heavy fruit season, with vans emanating from Evesham. A subsequent development of this arrangement was for a train to be booked through from Evesham to Glasgow during the main fruit period.

In 1936, to enable better connecting services to be given, a more intensive marshalling programme was introduced with these northbound and other trains, and experience showed that this extended marshalling could be undertaken with much greater facility at Water Orton Sidings. This resulted in a re-arrangement of the connecting services into the trains. These trains then commenced their journey to the North from Water Orton at 4.40 pm to Carlisle and 4.50 pm to Leeds.

The demands for express freight services grew, so that by 1946 a 3.50 am semi-fitted freight from Water Orton to Carlisle was introduced to give a speedy transit to traffic that had accumulated during the night period in Water Orton, and to avoid such traffic having to wait for the afternoon services. A further improvement was introduced in 1952 by the running of the 4.45 pm Water Orton to Glasgow, which, in addition to Glasgow traffic, took wagons for Edinburgh (Lothian Road) and Dumfries perishable traffic.

Even in the early 1950s occasionally a

'Crab' found itself heading this crack train, and sometimes a Class '4F' 0-6-0 has been known to take over from Leeds in the event of an engine failure, but happily while I was in the link a 'Black Five' or '9F' was always rostered.

From my earliest days in the Shed link I had listened to many tales of exciting exploits on the Carlisles. They were like folklore, handed down to succeeding generations, and I tended to regard them as such, for some were so far-fetched as to be hardly creditable. Most of these stories concerned the ferocity of the weather over the Settle to Carlisle stretch and, although no doubt somewhat embroidered with each subsequent telling, I later discovered at first hand that little exaggeration had crept in over the years.

Who could imagine a train being blown to a complete standstill by the force of the wind at Ribblehead? Or snow so deep as to bury telegraph poles? Or cold so intense that injectors froze solid? I personally did not believe that large lumps of coal could be stripped from the tops of tenders like so much dust, or that securely roped wagon sheets could be blown away as if they were tissue paper. The story of the guard who was left clinging desperately to his hand brake wheel after the very fabric of his van had disintegrated around him sounded to me very much like the inventions of an over-fertile imagination. However, seeing is believing and I duly came to experience some of these wild conditions before the year was out.

When I joined the link the limit of my knowledge was Sheffield, a mere 90 miles away, and although I was confident that I could work at full effort for up to two hours, how would I cope over a journey of 226 miles, involving maybe eight or ten hours of continuous labour? It was something of a relief, then, to find that I had three weeks with Les before our initial run to Carlisle came up, and I used this time to prepare myself for the task. Providentially our first job together was nothing more exacting than a local tripper, which gave us plenty of opportunity to discuss what I honestly considered were the only important turns in the link.

Les Field was of medium height and build, neither fat nor thin, and he dropped nicely into the classification so commonly termed 'average'. He looked his 57 years and had the usual thickening around his middle for a man of that age. He always wore a cloth cap that was long overdue for an oil-change and often a tweed sports jacket that likewise had seen better days, believing that these items of apparel gave him a more respectable appearance when popping into 'the local' to lay the dust after a run. Les liked his pint and also got through a fair quantity of Capstan Extra Strong cigarettes, but never allowed either habit to interfere with his job.

As a driver he was superb and, from the point of view of technique and route knowledge, undoubtedly the best I ever rode with. He never used an ounce more steam than was absolutely necessary, having the happy knack of using regulator openings and cut-offs to keep the engine always running at optimum efficiency. Les Field's driving was the model of consistency, which made firing for him a real pleasure, for one was never caught out by a sudden change of mood or display of temper. He could, however, drive as hard and as fast as anyone if the occasion demanded, and on the Carlisles this was sometimes necessary to gain or retain a favourable path.

As a companion, however, he had certain shortcomings. His reticence to hold a conversation meant that I had to pump every piece of information from him, and at times this was both discouraging and also hard work. He was not a very happy soul either, rationing himself to about one laugh, two chuckles and three smiles per week. If something cropped up that really amused him, and as a result he used up his quota on the very first day, then the remaining six were very dry indeed. In addition Les never offered to take up the shovel, but then I for my part had far too much to learn about the roads north of Sheffield to entertain any ideas of driving.

In order to familiarise myself with this unknown marathon, I obtained from Les a list of all the principal places, mileages and ruling gradients for the whole route to Carlisle. I laboriously wrote these out during the first week with the idea that I could consult this chart during the run and quickly obtain some notion of my whereabouts and what to expect. It did in fact prove very useful in as much that I could plan out in advance when I should require a heavier fire, when I could expect to be busy and for how long, when I could get coal forward and when I could reasonably snatch the odd sandwich.

Therefore by the time that first trip to Carlisle came along I had a little knowledge of what to expect, and Les fortunately supplemented this with some practical advice. For example, he suggested that I carried double rations of food and drink, for one never knew what was going to happen over such a distance. He also recommended that I select a new firing shovel, run it in on other jobs then put my name on the handle, so that it could be kept in the stores for my exclusive use. Furthermore, he pointed out that it was a good idea to carry a second shovel, two coalpicks and twice the normal complement of fire irons, then if by accident I lost or broke some item of equipment we would not be in trouble.

It was an undeniable fact that everyone at Saltley leaned over backwards to help when they knew that you were working the Carlisles, and the storemen were no exception. These fine fellows guarded new equipment as devotedly as if they had paid for it out of their own pockets. When I asked for a new shovel to break in for the Carlisles, I was immediately invited into that holy of holies and told to pick one out from a row of brand new 'Bulldogs'. After working my way through a dozen or so, I found one that possessed just the right balance and feel, and thereafter it was kept for my own exclusive use.

New shovels are not particularly pleasant to work with, since both blade and handle are rough and unpolished. A lot more effort is required to throw coal any specified distance, while the handle drags in the hand, making it difficult to execute those little twirls and flicks that were part of the virtuoso's repertoire.

However, after a few weeks of work I had the blade gleaming like stainless steel, while the handle was as smooth as a test match cricket bat. Admittedly I helped things along with a sheet of emery cloth and a drop of linseed oil, but the shovel turned out to be a real beauty and was at its best when I finally left British Railways.

For our first week's work on the 4.45 pm Glasgow we were required to book on at 3.55 pm on Monday, work up to Carlisle, then return on the 4.03 pm, which was scheduled to arrive at Washwood Heath No 2 at 11.33 pm Tuesday night. Wednesday was a rest day, and on Thursday and Friday the whole performance was repeated once more. We were paid on a mileage basis and, although we only actually worked four days, it was the equal in terms of pounds, shilling and pence to a full week of nights, but in terms of

concentration and sheer physical effort it was the equal to just about any other two weeks' work in the link.

My preparations for that first momentous day were as thorough as I could conceivably make them. I arrived at the shed a full hour before I was due to book on, and to my delight discovered that we had No 5265, then one of the best 'Black Fives' at Saltley. She was standing on the back departure road, coupled to the locomotives for the Carlisle and Leeds, both of which accompanied us to Water Orton. The shed men had made, as always, an excellent job of preparing her. A mountain of best-quality coal rose high above the cab roof, making a mockery of the 9-ton nominal load, while the firebox already contained a well-built-up fire, just nicely alight. The cab had been hosed down, and even the windows had been cleaned.

I next examined the tools and fire irons, and, finding them all satisfactory, set off to obtain a second coalpick, a bent dart and a long clinker shovel to supplement those already on board. Having done this, I collected my own firing shovel from the stores and was just sweeping all traces of sand and char from the framing when Les arrived. As usual he did not have much to say except that he was glad to see that we had a good engine and, after stowing his belongings, carried out a thorough examination of all and sundry, including testing the sanding gear. While he was there I operated both injectors, making

No 45265 was one of the best 'Black Fives' at Saltley in June 1958 when I fired her on my first ever trip to Carlisle. Whenever possible only the finest engines were allocated to this marathon 226-mile run. Built by Armstrong-Whitworth in 1936, No 5265 is shown at Gloucester two years later. Note the crosshead-driven vacuum pump that was subsequently removed, and the code '5P5F' below the cabside windows.

use of the water supplied by the exhaust one to hose down the over-filled tender. When all this was completed, we still had 10 minutes or so before ringing out, so Les went off to mash our first can of tea. He told me that this would have to last until Skipton South Junction, where we were booked for examination and water at 9.00 pm.

The tea Les brewed was strong enough to start with, so that by the time it had stewed for five hours on the drip-tray, it was positively vitriolic, quite capable of burning holes in the footboards, in fact. I therefore only partook of one lidful at Water Orton while it was still fresh and, even then, I was forced to dilute it with milk from my own supply. For the remainder of the run I satisfied my thirst with orange juice or water, leaving the tea for Les and his own cast-iron innards that were, after all, far more used to it than mine.

Dead on time the shed signal dropped and, with our guard as passenger, all three engines chugged over Duddeston Road bridge amid much hissing of steam from open cylinder cocks and the respectful stares from colleagues who always gathered to watch the most important departure of the day. This was a proud moment for me, one I had waited eight long years for, and now that it had arrived I was finding difficulty in realising that it was not just another job. Here I was, about to embark on the longest run I could ever hope to make, and so far it felt just the same as dozens of others, but no doubt before the day was out the right impression would make itself felt.

Our quick run down to Water Orton proved that No 5265 was in fine shape, but the oscillations incurred by our speed shook down an awful lot of coal from that overfilled tender, so by the time we backed into the sidings the footplate was knee-deep in cobbles. It had been my intention to fire the engine as lightly as possible, for I had already discovered how consistent Les was in his driving methods, but with so much debris lying on the footboards I was obliged to fill the box in the interests of tidiness.

With the headlamps correctly set and everything else in perfect order, we awaited our guard to advise us of the load, which happily on this first run turned out to be a fairly light one - no more than 29, equal to 32, in fact well within our limit. 4.45 pm came and, after being called out, we drew down to Water Orton station to await our signal. At precisely 4.50 pm it dropped, and with no more than a faint beat from our chimney we rolled gently into motion and headed out over the fast towards our far-off destination.

With Les there were no spectacular displays of pyrotechnics in getting away, just slight, almost imperceptible, increases in the regulator opening, coupled with an appropriately progressive shortening of the cut-off. Without any apparent effort we quickly accelerated our train so that by the time Kingsbury was passed we were rattling along at a good 50 mph. With so little steam being used I had a relatively easy time and was consequently able to enjoy the excellent ride provided by No 5265. The weather was also near perfect, being pleasantly mild and with clear visibility. By the time we stopped for water at Sheffield some two hours later, the coal was still falling down on to the shovelling plate, which was a good indication of how little we had used so far. Moreover, I felt in excellent spirits, but from now on I would be travelling over strange territory and would have to rely on Les for details of the road ahead.

I do not intend to detail the first trip since a fuller description of the route will follow, together with exact timings, of a memorable run with No 92137. Suffice it to say that we arrived at Skipton on time at 9.00 pm after an uneventful but nevertheless interesting journey. Here we were booked for examination and water, and while the tank was filling I walked over to the nearby cabin and made a can of coffee. By now I felt as though I had come a fair distance, but excitement kept fatigue at bay and I was really looking forward to the assault upon Ais Gill, which from all accounts was the best part of the run.

On returning to the engine I found that Les had cleared the fire from the back set of bars and he advised me to pull out any clinker to be found there. With 33 miles of virtually unbroken uphill work ahead I thereafter always made a practice of so doing. With rocking grate engines it was of course no problem, and in any case I kept these relatively clean by frequent use of the intermediate rocking position.

Before departing at 9.17 pm I was able to pull some coal down, but there was still no necessity to keep the tender doors open all the time. In fact, it was not until we were approaching Ribblehead that I was forced to continually go into the tender.

The 14 miles from Settle to Blea Moor has a ruling gradient of 1 in 100, and even with only 29 vans in tow, Les had to give her a fair amount of stick. However, I do not recall many details of actually firing the engine at all; I was far too interested in absorbing the new panorama that unfolded at every bend in the track.

I have often recounted the benefits of changing links in May, but never was this more apparent than on the Carlisle run. As one progresses north and west in summer, so the actual time of sunset becomes later. I was therefore able to enjoy the glories of a magnificent sunset right up into the northern fells.

Seeing those great grey peaks and heather-covered moors for the first time, softened with continually changing shades of pinks and golds, was a sight I shall never forget. Then again, looking down from the top of Ribblehead Viaduct to the moor 169 feet below reminded me of all that I had read about the problems of its construction. As I was admiring this superb feat of engineering Les told me that this was the point where a westerly gale was most felt. The valley formed a funnel with its widest end opening out right on to the Irish Sea, and as the wind entered this its velocity increased until the full force was concentrated over the viaduct. It was hard to imagine such conditions on this calm summer's evening, but I was to find out for myself the terrible fury the elements could unleash later in the year. He also told me that a payment of 10 shillings was formerly given by the company to the local inhabitants for recovering wagon sheets blown away by such storms, a sure indication of the frequency and seriousness of this problem.

Blea Moor Tunnel, too, was a welcome sight, partly because this, at 2,629 yards, was the longest tunnel I was to journey through, and partly because it represented the end of our hardest climb. We had, of course, another 10 miles to travel until the summit of Ais Gill was reached, but this was an undulating course and the stiffest gradient against us was a mere 1 in 165. Moreover, a drop at 1 in 440 through the tunnel enabled us to gain sufficient momentum to overcome these short rises without undue effort, and only the last mile up to the 1,167-foot summit appeared a drag.

The stone portals of Blea Moor Tunnel looked innocuous enough in the soft failing light, but Blea Moor took on a totally different aspect in the depths of winter and, although I am digressing, I vividly recall one night standing on the top of our tender while taking water during a return trip the following November. It was heavily overcast, and save for the glimmer of an oil lamp in the nearby signal box, the blackness was complete. Not a single outline could be distinguished - it was just like being shut up in a coal cellar - and the feeling of utter isolation from the rest of civilisation was hard to describe. Never have I visited a blacker spot than Blea Moor, and it was also here that I had the unusual experience of sighting strange lights in the sky that may well have been UFOs.

This occurred during that same week in November on the outward run. We were hammering up the section from Ribblehead to Blea Moor and because the fire was now being allowed to run down somewhat, I was leaning out of my window taking a breather and staring out into the impenetrable darkness. Thick cloud cover obscured the stars so that it was impossible to ascertain where the mountains ended and the sky began, and of course in that remote area there were no reflections of street lights on the clouds. Suddenly I became aware of five orange lights, each about twice the size and intensity of Venus at her brightest, at an elevation of around 45 degrees, apparently keeping pace with us and formed into a diamond shape. This pattern then changed to that of an arrowhead, then elongated into a straight line.

I watched these manoeuvres for a few moments wondering what they might be, and

Blea Moor signal box, seen here looking north, was always a welcome sight for the fireman in either direction. Travelling towards Carlisle it was the end of the most arduous climb on the run from Water Orton. Going south, 14 miles downhill with a ruling gradient of 1 in 100 enabled the fireman to take a well-earned breather after the long haul up to Ais Gill. On a dark winter's night the blackness was complete at this wild and remote spot. The signal box was subsequently removed to the opposite side of the tracks just south of the water tank.

frankly I was puzzled. As a frequent observer of the night sky I had never seen anything at all like it, and none of the usual explanations given for such sightings seemed to fit. They were certainly not stars, aircraft navigation lights, street lights, nor the reflection of car headlamps. In case they were in fact UFOs I called Les over to witness the spectacle, but he too could offer no valid explanation. I watched these fascinating lights until we plunged into Blea Moor Tunnel, but on emerging at the other end no trace of them could be seen. Thinking that someone else might also have made an observation, I scoured the papers next day and was disappointed to find no mention of any such sightings. I was therefore obliged to write it off as just another of those inexplicable happenings that come into everyone's life from time to time.

It was now becoming too dark to pick out features in detail, but I did manage to get an idea of the size of Dent Head Viaduct as we raced over its 200 yards length. On both sides of the line rose the vast black shapes of the fells, and I realised that I would have to wait until our return run before I could enjoy the scenery of this section.

Within minutes we were clattering into the 1,213-yard Rise Hill Tunnel, the exit from which provided a positive marker for dropping our water scoop into the famous Garsdale troughs, which, at an elevation of 1,100 feet, were the highest in the world. I was also very interested to see the well-known turntable at Hawes Junction around which, so the story goes, a stockade had been constructed to protect it from the violence of the wind in that area. I had been amused at this tale of a forlorn engine and an even more forlorn crew being given a protracted merry-go-round ride on a turntable that was apparently unstoppable until the wind force abated. Whether authentic or not, the fact remained that I managed to glimpse that unique circle of sturdy timbers as we roared past.

Then began our last 2-mile climb up through the short Moorcock and Shotlock Hill Tunnels to Ais Gill where, framed against the darkening western sky, could be seen the black brooding mass of Wild Boar Fell. We breasted the summit at about 10.40 pm and, having been continually active for the past six hours, I was thankful to hear Les say that I could now sit down and take it easy for the next 15 miles. This section from Ais Gill to Ormside was virtually all downhill at a ruling gradient of 1 in 100, so I took the opportunity thus afforded to finish off the rest of my sandwiches as we coasted down through the mountains at speeds up to 60 mph. Most of the wild beauty of this area passed unnoticed in the darkness, but I did manage to make out Mallerstang Edge rising to a height of 2,328 feet in the east and the dim lights of the village far below.

This brief respite enabled me to reflect on how effortlessly a 'Black Five' performed its allotted task on this long run. The previous year I had come to appreciate the suitability of

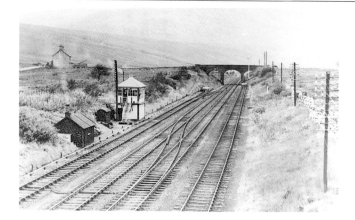

Ais Gill signal box. At 1,167 feet above sea level this famous summit was the highest point on the Settle to Carlisle line. It was a formidable obstacle to overcome with any train in either direction. Southbound it was nearly 50 miles out from Carlisle, the last 15 miles from Ormside, mainly at 1 in 100, was particularly demanding on both engine and fireman.

'Crabs' on medium-distance semi-fitteds, but in terms of all-round efficiency and comfort they could not be compared to a 'Black Five'.

No 5265 was still steaming beautifully and I do not suppose that at this stage I had fired more than five tons of coal. With a similar load few other engines could have accomplished the journey with such economy of fuel and effort, while at the same time giving us a tolerably comfortable ride.

From Ormside it was back to the shovel, which unaccountably now seemed much heavier, for the undulating climb up to just beyond Appleby. From there we still had some 30 miles to travel until our destination was reached, although the gradients were mainly in our favour for the next 15 miles down to Lazonby and I was able to cope without undue effort. The stiff 1-mile climb at 1 in 165 out of Lazonby called for a bit of extra steam, as did the final haul up to Low House Crossing, but once this hump was surmounted I was able to run the fire down during the 7-mile run at 1 in 132 down to Carlisle.

Three minutes early and with everything looking as spick and span as when we left Saltley, No 5265 rolled into Petteril Bridge where we were relieved by an awaiting Carlisle crew. I must admit that I felt much more spritely than I would have expected as we walked the short distance to 'The Barracks'. Perhaps the thoughts of a refreshing shower, a hot meal and a comfortable bed added a certain pep to my stride, for I found myself having to slow down a couple of times to enable Les to catch up as we climbed the steep slope to that very presentable establishment.

The lodge itself was large and modern, and in an entirely different class to the one at Sheffield. This perhaps was not surprising, since Carlisle was a natural relief point for the long-distance Anglo-Scottish traffic. The washroom was well equipped, having both baths and showers, while the canteen was designed on the self-service principle and provided a good selection of food right round the clock. The bedrooms, too, were a vast improvement upon what I had previously experienced, being relatively commodious, well soundproofed and having individual radiators. I also much appreciated the drying-room, since I frequently arrived at Carlisle soaked with perspiration, and without this facility I would have been obliged to don still wet clothing the following day.

After a satisfying meal and a congenial chat with crews from foreign parts, we retired to our respective rooms, where I for one slumbered soundly for a full eight hours.

One surprising point had arisen during the course of a conversation with a Camden fireman in the canteen. He was an old hand and several years senior to myself, but he had been quite sincere when stating that he did not envy us Saltley men on our run. When I asked why, since he had just fired a 'Duchess' over a considerably longer run, he pointed out the following facts.

The old LNWR route was for the most part much flatter, with Shap the only bank of any note. They worked the finest express engines in the country which, apart from giving a superbly comfortable ride, were equipped with coal pushers. This relieved them of the necessity of getting coal from the back of the tender - they only had to fire it. Furthermore, being an express passenger train they were virtually guaranteed the road, and in any case they were only on the footplate for five hours. We, on the other hand, travelled a route like a switchback with the formidable Settle to Carlisle section right at the end. Being only a fitted freight, our progress was much more subject to delays and we could be anything from seven to ten hours on the footplate of nothing better than a 'Black Five'. With no coal pushers and the need to clean the fire en route, it amounted in his eyes to a good deal of hard work.

'I think you're a lot of bloody heroes, mate,' said he as a parting shot, and before I closed my eyes I perhaps unjustifiably felt one.

While we rested, our engine was re-fettled and left at the near-derelict Durran Hill loco shed. This was now only used for stabling engines such as ours, because of its close proximity to our starting point, Durran Hill Sidings. The following afternoon we signed on, did the usual checks, then topped up our tank before leaving the depot. Although we were booked for water at Appleby, only 29 miles on, Les preferred to have the tank as full as possible in order to save precious minutes once our journey had commenced. He liked to gain time if possible on the off chance that we might be slipped into an earlier path, for the sooner we arrived home the better.

The first part of our run from Durran Hill was quite a taxing affair, for although we again had only a moderate load of 32 equal to 36, it entailed a 7-mile climb at 1 in 132 from a cold start. Departing at 4.3 pm on a pleasantly bright afternoon I was able to see all the details I had missed the previous night, and the run up through the picturesque Eden Valley fully lived up to what I had expected. Thick woodlands and luxuriant pastures were to be found in profusion on the fertile soil, and it contrasted strongly with the barren fells further on.

We spent some 5 minutes taking on water at Appleby, then with the fire well built up and thoroughly hot, we set about the attack

on Ais Gill. For the next 18 miles and 45 minutes the regulator was over on the second valve and, with the cut-off varying between 25 and 45 per cent, we hammered away in a most exhilarating fashion. At last I was able to see what had only been names on a route card and also obtain an idea of the gradients involved: 1 in 100 from Ormside to Griseburn Sidings, 1 in 166 to Crosby Garrett, 1 in 190 up to Kirkby Stephen, 1 in 100 to Mallerstang, then, after a half-mile stretch at 1 in 330, 1 in 100 all the way up to Ais Gill. Despite her exertions No 5265 was steaming beautifully and, with the exhaust reverberating around the mountains like a thunderstorm, I really enjoyed every moment of that truly wonderful 45-minute climb.

The run along the high fells to Blea Moor took but 16 minutes, and we topped our tank up over the troughs as a precaution. Then, with the prospect of a 14-mile descent mainly at 1 in 100 before me, I sat down to view all the places of interest I had missed while firing on the outward trip. As on the day before, we were booked for examination at Skipton, but, having only been on the road for three hours, I did not attempt to clean the fire. I normally did this at Rotherham, where we were again booked for water at 9.3 pm.

The return run differed in as much as we travelled via Rotherham, rejoining the main line again at Tapton Junction. This little diversion took us past the countless collieries in that area and, while aesthetically there was little to commend it, even on a bright summer evening the industrial activity was nevertheless interesting.

As the evening turned to dusk, familiar places and names began to slide past and I felt a sense of urgency in wanting to get home as soon as possible. It affected all of us, including No 5265, for she seemed to be now running better than ever. At 10.20 pm we passed Derby North, and it seemed incredible that only last year a trip to Derby represented a whole day's work. Having come all the way from Carlisle during the past 6 hours 20 minutes, this 40-mile run to Birmingham was now but the final lap.

Over the fast from Kingsbury I cleaned down the footplate and both Les and I washed

Carlisle men always made an excellent job of coaling Saltley engines with the best available for their return run. Understandably the lowest-mileage engines were allocated whenever possible in order to lighten the crew's burden somewhat over this very long haul. Standing at Durran Hill loco in June 1952, No 44966 has the look of a recent shopping as she awaits her crew for the 4.3 pm Carlisle to Washwood Heath. *Pat Webb*

away the traces of 226 miles of toil, so by the time we were relieved at Washwood Heath we looked clean and fresh, and even the appearance of the fire belied the fact that it had just burned five tons of coal.

Relieving the Carlisle at Washwood Heath may seem extravagant in the use of men, since we normally rode on the footplate to the shed in any case, but occasionally the Camp Hill loop was blocked and it was quicker to walk. Not wishing to delay our booking off any longer than necessary was, therefore, a further indication of the 'Red Carpet' treatment offered to the Carlisle crews.

Soon after I joined the link Class '9s' were substituted for the more usual 'Black Fives' as they became more readily available. Like many of the other drivers, Les was a little

conservative in his attitude towards them and somewhat apprehensive about having his favourite engines usurped on this prime duty. However, as their finer points became better appreciated, the moans gradually died away and the fact that they always gave a superb ride while handling even the heaviest trains with consummate ease soon won the acceptance of all who worked them.

Generally speaking I found that on light and medium loads somewhat more coal was used than with a good 'Black Five', but this may have been partly due to Les not initially working them at their most economical settings. With further experience he discovered that a '9' could be effectively operated at shorter cut-offs than a 'Black Five', but this took time.

Kirkby Stephen station in Midland Railway days in 1905. It had changed little 50 years later when I thundered through with the Birmingham-Carlisle fitted freights. The section southbound from Crosby Garrett to Kirkby Stephen was somewhat easier at 1 in 190, but then up to Mallerstang it was 1 in 100, and following this, except for the half-mile stretch of 1 in 330, it was 1 in 100 all the way to Ais Gill summit, still some 7 miles distant.

With heavier trains the '9s' were undoubtedly less troubled and this showed up in the coal consumed. It was noticeable, however, that if we were delayed and the time in steam considerably extended, a disproportionate amount of fuel was burned. This was not really surprising, however, when one considers the relative grate areas involved - 40.2 sq ft as to 28.65 sq ft for the 'Black Five'.

While on the subject of coal consumption, I well recall two occasions with Class '9s' when it was touch and go whether we made it to Saltley. Both were what we termed the 'morning job', which was scheduled to depart from Durran Hill at 11.45 pm, arriving Washwood Heath at 6.55 am. Unfortunately, this turn was more subject to delays than the others, particularly in winter, and on the first instance we arrived at the shed with no more than 2 hundredweights of dust in the tender. On the second occasion we cut it even more fine and, after a 10½-hour run I fired the last of our coal approaching Water Orton. Knowing that we had sufficient reserve in our boiler and firebed to get us to the loco, provided we did not encounter more undue delays, I brushed out and hosed down the tender so that it presented the appearance of a big, shiny empty bin. Doug Pinkerton and a young passed cleaner relieved us at Washwood Heath. It was not the first time that Doug had done so, and as he climbed on board and glanced approvingly around the spotless footplate he stated in his usual loud manner

that he had just been telling his mate what a pleasure it was to relieve us.

'That's the way to bring 'em in, young feller,' he declared. 'Not a speck of coal lying about and the fire so clean you can see the bars.'

'There's not a speck of coal in there either, Doug,' I retorted, nodding towards the tender doors. He drew them aside, then reeled back in surprise as he surveyed the gleaming cavern thus exposed.

'Good grief,' he gasped, 'you have had a rough trip.'

His mate also goggled in awe, looking first at the empty tender, then at the shovel, and finally at me. His expression indicated how his mental processes were working. If this is what firing in the top link meant, he wanted none of it.

We were always allocated Class '9s' fitted with tenders capable of carrying 9 tons of coal and 4,725 gallons of water, the 7-ton variety being inadequate for the Carlisle run. Since they were invariably over-coaled, we went out with something like 10 tons on board, and because 5 tons of this had to be shovelled forward en route, I suppose I had shifted something like 15 tons of coal during the course of this run. Taking into account breaking up innumerable lumps in addition to one's other duties, it added up to a fair night's work.

Despite these strenuous labours I never felt particularly exhausted and must have

While the 4.3 pm Carlisle-Washwood Heath usually ran on time throughout its journey, the 11.45 pm seemed far more subject to delays. Freight traffic was at its most dense during the early hours, and it only required one struggling mineral to displace a fitted from its correct path. When this happened things usually went from bad to worse - instead of arriving at 6.55 am it could be 10.00 am, which naturally resulted in a much higher coal consumption. On two such occasions with Class '9Fs' I completely emptied the tenders. Passing Burton loco some three hours late is Saltley 'Black Five' No 44805. *Pat Webb*

appeared quite fresh since, on more than one occasion after such a run, colleagues in the lobby would ask whether I was booking on or off. While some firemen seemed to relish looking as if they had been down a coalmine for eight hours, I took the opposite view and tried to preserve a clean, smart appearance at all times.

Having proved their ability, Class '9s' were used more frequently on the Carlisle runs, and I accurately logged one journey I made in late July with No 92137. The run was quite typical in many respects, and shows how competently both Les and the engine handled a heavy load, although the weather proved to be exceptional in the form of violent thunderstorms, but then something different always seemed to take place on the Carlisles. This, apart from its arduous duration, made the turn so interesting - one never knew what was going to happen next.

After a week of unusually high temperatures and unbroken sunshine, I arrived at Saltley just after 3.00 pm. With the thermometer once again in the high 80s I was already perspiring profusely despite having cycled at quite a leisurely pace, and as I walked across to No 92137 standing on the back departure road, not a breath of air stirred the layer of coal dust covering the yard in that area. Such smoke that came from the engines' chimneys coiled lazily up into the heavy atmosphere and any steam emitted evaporated almost immediately.

Struggling on board I became aware of an all-pervading sullen silence; human and animal activity seemed to be at a minimum and even the birds found it too hot to sing. The heat in the confines of the cab was absolutely stifling, and after depositing my kit I slowly went through the check routine. Every movement brought fresh rivers of sweat streaming from my brow, and I looked forward to the time when we could get into motion so as to generate a cooling air flow.

I had just finished trimming the coal when Les arrived looking a trifle like a boiled lobster just out of the pot.

'Christ, its bloody close today,' he gasped by way of a greeting. 'Won't be right until we have a good storm I reckon,' he continued.

'Looks as though we might get one too before the day's out.'

Les nodded towards the north where in the far distance I could discern not a few towering masses of cumulonimbus already building in an ominous fashion. I agreed with his observations, adding that if he thought it was close while standing on the ground, wait until he parked himself on the footplate. Having completed our preparations we sat in the shade of our engine, chatting to the other crews of our little group who likewise found conditions in their respective cabs intolerable. I had already downed a can of water when at last, and with great relief, we left the shed.

Although No 92137 had been out in service for some time now, she was still in excellent condition, and even the short sprint down to Water Orton proved this beyond all shadow of doubt. It also proved that at 50 mph sufficient wind force could be generated to revive a wilting form, providing that the head was stuck well out into the slipstream. This did not help the rest of the body very much, though, but I soon found that by holding a gaping sleeve out of the window and aligning my arms so as to remove any kinks, a forced flow of cooling air could be ducted up the right sleeve and around the torso, exiting via the left sleeve. During the following seven hours this simple technique did much to keep me in a reasonable state of efficiency.

Just when we could have done with a light train to keep physical effort to a minimum, we found on arrival at Water Orton that no fewer than 48, equal to 52, awaited us. This was just about the heaviest train I can recall taking to Carlisle, and while it may make good reading for the record, it made me shovel an extra ton or two of coal at a time when I could have well done without the exercise.

Building up the fire while static in that heat was bad enough, too much in fact for Les to remain on the footplate in front of the open fire. However, this was nothing compared to the agonies I endured later when exposed to the wide area of searing white heat revealed by those huge firedoors, and engulfed in a flow of hot air coming off the boiler casing - air, by the way, that had started out in the mid-80s. When actually firing, a thermometer in my overall pocket would probably have registered at least 140°F, and 226 miles of this had a more than somewhat debilitating effect on the system.

Despite everyone's obvious lethargy, we departed from Water Orton dead on time, accelerating rapidly over the fast on full first valve and 25 per cent cut-off. It was a sure indication of the high ambient air temperature that no steam was noticeable from our chimney, only a light haze of smoke. As can be seen from the table on page 122, although checking our speed for the 15 mph permanent way restriction at Branston we were exactly on schedule at Burton station. Here we encountered a series of signal checks all the way to Derby, but such was the reserve power of a Class '9' that we were only a minute adrift at Derby North.

By this time Les was driving in shirt-sleeve order, but because of the furnace radiation I was obliged to wear my overalls; however, these were now soaked right through, and were providing some cooling effect when exposed to a flow of air.

The steady climb from Derby North to Ambergate was accomplished in the scheduled 14 minutes, but over the more arduous drag up to Stretton an extra 5 per cent cut-off gained us 3 minutes, and the following quick dash down to Clay Cross added a similar amount. We therefore had no less than 6 minutes in hand when halted by signals. Unfortunately the London passenger train was running late, and we did not get under way again until 6.20 pm. Even then we were dogged by signal checks all the way up to Dronfield Colliery Sidings, and consequently No 92137 was not able to show off her climbing ability on the 1 in 100 bank. Moreover, no lost time was recovered on the descent into Sheffield, where we arrived for water 6 minutes late.

It seemed to be hotter than ever, but whether this was due to the atmosphere getting heavier and more electric or my physical exertions I know not. However, while our tank was filling I dived into the staff room on the end of the platform, quaffed a quick pint or two of water, then filled both my cans with this cool refreshing liquid. We set

off from Sheffield at 7.00 pm and, after rattling down to Wincobank in the prescribed 8 minutes, Les opened up with sufficient purpose not only to pull back our deficiency, but also to gain a further 2 minutes over the rising gradients to Cudworth.

This was the beauty of a Class '9', for with so much power in reserve, even with a heavy load over adverse gradients it was so totally in command of the situation that time could be gained with no apparent effort. Normanton was passed dead on time, and here we noticed that an ominous coppery glow had spread across the northern skyline, silhouetting great dark grey masses of clouds that were piling up and thickening all the time.

A further series of signal checks from Stourton Junction to Wortley Junction pushed us 2 minutes behind schedule, but some spirited running then gave us 2 minutes in hand passing Shipley Leeds Junction. We had now run under the vast blanket of black clouds and it became so dark that I was obliged to light the gauge lamp. In this premature night at Keighley I saw in the distance the first flash of lightning reflected off the clouds. This was the precursor of what was to prove the longest and most spectacular thunderstorm, or rather series of thunderstorms, that I have ever witnessed in this country, and a fascinating spectacle it turned out to be.

Signal checks at Snaygill delayed us somewhat, so we arrived for examination and water at Skipton South Junction 5 minutes late. While the tank was filling I gave the fire a quick rattle, before nipping off to the relief cabin to make a can of coffee and obtain more drinking water. Once away from the engine I could clearly hear heavy and almost continuous thunderclaps rolling down from the hills, indicating that the storm could be no further away than Hellifield.

Les had lighted the headlamps during my absence, and in near night conditions we departed at 9.19 pm only to be halted at Skipton North to pick up a linesman. He told us that a violent storm had been raging in the hills for some time and that he was being sent to Garsdale where lightning had damaged the block signalling apparatus. Les set off at a cracking pace, covering the 10 miles of mainly

4.45 pm Water Orton to Glasgow College fully fitted freight
Engine: Class '9F' No 92137
Load: 48 (=52) wagons

	Booked time	Actual time	Remarks
Water Orton Station Junc	4.50	4.50	
Kingsbury Station Junc	4.55	4.55	
Tamworth	5.03	5.03	
Wichnor	5.13	5.12	
Leicester Junction	5.20	5.20	15 mph PW restriction (Branston)
Burton station	5.21	5.21	Signal check
Repton	5.27	5.29	Signal check
Stenson Junction	5.30	5.33	Signal check
Melbourne Junction	5.35	5.37	Signal check
Derby London Road	5.39	5.40	Signal check
Derby Midland	5.40	5.41	
Derby North Junction	5.41	5.42	
Ambergate	5.55	5.56	
Stretton	6.08	6.06	Signal check
Clay Cross	6.18	6.12-20	Signal check
Horns Bridge	6.24	6.27	Signal check
Chesterfield Midland	6.25	6.28	Signal check
Tapton Junction	6.26	6.29	Signal check
Bronfield Coll'y Sidings	6.36	6.41-42	Signal check
Sheffield Midland	Arr 6.48	6.54	Water
	Dep 6.55	7.00	
Wincobank Station Junc	7.03	7.08	
Cudworth	7.36	7.34	
Normanton North Yard	7.54	7.54	
Altofts Junction	7.56	7.55	
Stourton Junction	8.06	8.08	Signal check
Engine Shed Junction	8.10	8.12	Signal check
Whitehall	8.20	8.13	Signal check
Wortley Junction	8.13	8.15	Signal check
Shipley Leeds Junction	8.32	8.30	
Keighley	8.43	8.45	Signal check
Snaygill	8.56	9.00	Signal check
Skipton South Junc	Arr 9.00	9.05	Examination and water
	Dep 9.17	9.19	Collected linesman - block failure at Garsdale
Hellifield	9.40	9.40	Violent thunderstorms
Settle	9.45	9.50	
Blea Moor	10.22	10.20	Violent thunderstorms
Ais Gill	10.41	10.40	Linesman set down at Garsdale
Kirkby Stephen West	10.49	10.50	20 mph PW restriction at Ormside
Appleby	11.01	11.10	Signal check
New Biggin	11.10	11.20	Signal check
Lazonby	11.21	11.29	
Carlisle Petteril	11.40	11.40	

4.03 pm Carlisle Durran Hill to Washwood Heath No 2 fully fitted freight
Engine: Class '9F' No 92137
Load: 45 (=48) wagons

	Booked time	Actual time	Remarks
Carlisle Durran Hill Depot	4.03	4.08	Thunderstorms
Lazonby	4.33	4.39	Block failure due to storm
New Biggin	4.48	4.53	
Appleby	Arr 5.03	5.02	Water
	Dep 5.08	5.08	
Kirkby Stephen West	5.36	5.20	Signals at Mallerstang due to woman being killed on line
Ais Gill	5.54	5.48	
Blea Moor	6.10	6.05	
Settle Junction	6.30	6.22	
Hellifield	6.35	6.28	
Skipton North	6.50	6.44	
Skipton	Arr 6.52	6.45	Exam and water
Dep	7.12	6.55	
Snaygill	7.15	7.00	
Keighley	7.27	7.12	Signal check
Shipley Leeds Junction	7.38	7.25	
Wortley Junction	7.54	7.43	
Whitehall Junction	7.56	7.45	
Engine Shed	7.57	7.49-51	Signal check
Stourton Junction	8.05	7.57	
Altofts Junction	8.17	8.07	
Normanton South Yard	8.19	8.09	
Cudworth Station	8.40	8.28	
Wath Road Junction	8.52	8.42	
Swinton Junction	8.54	8.44	
Rotherham Masboro'	Arr 9.03	8.55	Water
	Dep 9.10	9.03	
Masboro' South Sidings	9.14	9.05	
Beighton Junction	9.23	9.15	
Staveley	9.32	9.25	
Tapton Junction	9.37	9.30	
Chesterfield Midland	9.38	9.31	
Horns Bridge	9.39	9.32	
Clay Cross	9.46	9.38	20 mph PW restriction through tunnel
Stretton	9.53	9.43	
Crich Junction	10.02	9.52	
Ambergate	10.03	9.53	
Derby North Junction	10.21	10.09	Diverted to goods line to LNW Junc
Derby Midland	10.24	10.12	
Derby London Road Junc	10.25	10.14	
Melbourne Junction	10.28	10.17	
Stenson Junction	10.33	10.25	
Repton & Willington	10.36	10.28	
Burton station	10.42	10.32	15 mph PW restriction (Branston)
Leicester Junction	10.43	10.33	
Wichnor Junction	10.52	10.40	
Tamworth	11.05	11.00	Signal checks
Kingsbury Station Junc	11.13	11.10-11	Signal checks
Water Orton Station Junc	11.19	11.16	
Castle Bromwich Junc	11.23	11.20	
Washwood Heath Junc	11.28	11.23	
Washwood Heath No 2	11.33	11.25	

stiff adverse gradients up to Hellifield in 21 minutes. This, of course, kept me pretty busy, and the glare from the fire nearly polished off the poor linesman, who was already suffering some distress from the unaccustomed high temperatures in the cab.

Here we caught up with the storm. Jagged streaks of blinding fire, displaying all the colours of the spectrum, flashed and crackled all around at no more than 5-second intervals. In between these scintillating discharges the great black clouds intermittently blushed in a deep red glow as if trying to hide the electric violence raging within their interiors. Then came the rain - not cool and refreshing as rain usually is in this country, but an impenetrable deluge of warm steamy fluid that made one feel hotter than ever. It was like being hosed down with a slaking pipe.

Poor Les was soon as drenched as I, and, not being able to see much, lost 5 minutes in getting to Settle, but with the rain easing off as suddenly as it had started, we attacked the 14 miles of 1 in 100 up to Blea Moor with a display of pyrotechnics that would have been most spectacular had it not been for the far greater one raging overhead.

With having to drag coal forward between bouts of heavy firing, I was now continually busy and would have welcomed another deluge, but it did not come. However, I was able to snatch a few seconds now and again to gaze in awe at this fantastic electrical storm that grew in intensity as we proceeded. At Selside the flashes were almost continuous, for as one died away another occurred at a different point. Sometimes these enormous zigzag bursts of energy seemed to travel horizontally at almost eye level, entwining the hillsides in glorious webs of ethereal fire.

Approaching Ribblehead a full-grown pine tree was struck not 50 yards away, and suddenly exploded in a sheet of sparks and flame, while at such close range the accompanying thunderclap sounded and felt like the concussion from a 9.2 howitzer, and even in spite of the noise on the footplate it was loud enough to make all three of us nearly jump out of our skins.

For all the elemental distractions, No 92137 performed so vigorously that we arrived at Blea Moor 2 minutes ahead of time, and the long dark tunnel provided quite a contrast to the violence we had experienced during the past half-hour or so. At the other end we were met by torrential rain again, but Les battled on at such a pace through these unpleasant conditions that we breasted Ais Gill Summit a minute in front of schedule, even though we had stopped at Garsdale to put down the linesman. This was a tremendous effort considering our load and the foul weather.

Our long descent began, and although the lightning had abated somewhat, the rain still came down in sheets that obliterated visibility. Here Les was once more able to demonstrate his superb enginemanship and route knowledge, for at Kirby Stephen we were but one minute late. However, a 20 mph permanent way slack at Ormside and a stop for

Hellifield. Already 150 miles and five hours since commencing the run from Water Orton to Carlisle, the fireman had $3^1/_2$ miles of easy running to Settle in which to prepare for the 'Long Drag', $14^1/_2$ miles of virtually continuous 1 in 100 gradient up to Blea Moor Tunnel. Even then there was a further 10 miles to travel before reaching Ais Gill, with Carlisle still 59 miles away. *V. R. Anderson*

signals at Appleby put us back a further 8 minutes, but then with a clear road Les set about making up for lost time.

New Biggin to Lazonby took but 9 minutes, and from here Les really turned on the power. In the pitch-black conditions on that beautifully riding '9' I am sure that Les did not realise just how quickly we were travelling. The last 14½ miles from passing Lazonby to a dead stand at Carlisle Petteril Bridge took just 11 minutes, an average speed of 78 mph! So incredible did this seem when I came to analyse the timings that I double-checked with both Les and the guard, but all agreed that we arrived at 11.40 pm.

It will be recalled that the previous year, when driving this same engine, I had run at a very high speed between Stenson Junction and Trent using only 80 lbs per sq in in the steam chest and 10 per cent cut-off. Les on this occasion had used about 180 lbs per sq in and between 15 and 25 per cent cut-off, and furthermore the last 7 miles was down a gradient of 1 in 132, so perhaps we did attain the 90 mph necessary to achieve this average. Certainly it did not feel like it, but then No 92137 was an exceptionally fast and smooth-riding engine even for a Class '9'.

'Black Fives' always made the crew aware of the fact when travelling at over 70 mph, but '9s' were so deceptively smooth. I wonder just how many times fitteds have been near to derailment when pushed under circumstances similar to our exuberant dash.

Despite the thunder, which was still rolling continuously in the distance, and the lateness of the hour, the temperature had dropped very little. Every stitch of clothing I possessed was drenched with perspiration and, although I enjoyed a refreshing shower, I was obliged to dine in uncomfortably wet garments. Fortunately the drying-room was functioning and most of my outer clothes were nicely aired by the following day.

Once again the early afternoon heat was oppressive and we were not entirely surprised when another thunderstorm broke soon after we arrived at the shed. This gradually grew in intensity so that by the time we departed from Durran Hill 5 minutes in arrears, it was just as violent as on the previous night. A block

failure due to the storm between Armathwaite and Lazonby delayed us further, but although we hauled a load only slightly lighter than that of the outward trip, 45-48, we arrived at Appleby 1 minute ahead of schedule.

Departing from there dead on time, Les used the power of the Class '9' to such effect on the 1 in 100 that we had gained no less than 16 minutes at Kirkby Stephen. Regrettably a woman had been killed on the line at Mallerstang, and we were halted by signals to be advised of this. Even so we reached Ais Gill with 6 minutes in hand, and, in spite of a signal check at Hawes Junction, passed Blea Moor 5 minutes early.

Even coasting, a further 3 minutes were gained during the descent to Settle and, despite the intervening 5-mile climb up to Otterburn, we arrived at Skipton still 7 minutes ahead of schedule. Slick work here gave us an added advantage so that Snaygill was passed 15 minutes to the good, and although checked by signals at Keighley we arrived at Leeds 8 minutes before time.

We ran some 10 minutes in front of time all the way to Derby North, where we were diverted on to a goods line as far as LNW Junction. Fortunately this was clear and did not delay us unduly, so that the 10 minutes' advantage was maintained. Severe signal checks at both Tamworth and Kingsbury did, however, cut this down to but 2 minutes, but some spirited work over the last 9 miles gained a further 6 minutes, so we finally arrived at Washwood Heath Number Two at 11.25 pm instead of the booked 11.33 pm; not a bad effort for an engine and crew that had already travelled well over 200 miles.

This run was typical of the fine performances Class '9s' could achieve. Apart from power, their main advantage over a 'Black Five' on longer runs was that the much larger grate area seemed to suffer far less from the build-up of ash and clinker. In other words, they were never short of steam, even at the end of a journey when large quantities of inferior-grade fuel had been consumed. Admittedly, a diligent fireman would make full use of the rocker grate equipment, but then this facility was also available on a number of later 'Black Fives'.

7
THE SUMMIT

Towards the end of the year quite a furore was created by the arrival at Saltley of No 92165, the first of three Class '9s' specially modified and fitted with American Berkeley mechanical stokers. These had, of course, been successfully used for many years by foreign railways on engines usually with firegrate areas of over 50 sq ft when firing rates in excess of the physical capability of a single fireman were demanded. In this particular instance the experiment was instituted in order to explore what increased output was attainable on a Class '9' by this means, although mechanical stoking for a grate area of only 40.2 sq ft was generally thought to be unnecessary in this country because of the relatively short journeys involved.

However, the Birmingham to Carlisle diagrams were the most arduous freight runs in the land, and we were therefore presented with the task of testing these engines on the road in normal service. That insufficient preparation had been done to provide suitable coal was not the fault of the design, since their diet was intended to contain nothing larger than small cobbles.

I for one was most enthusiastic at the possibilities offered by mechanical stoking. It was not so much the reduction of physical effort as the prospect of having more time available for road learning that appeared so attractive. Apart from the great length of the Carlisle run, there were some very complex sections, and when firing on the 'little and often' principle necessary to keep a clean fire, continuous observation of the road was just not possible.

The arrangement was robust and simple, consisting of a main conveyor screw lying in a trough at the bottom of the tender coal space, driven by a small, infinitely variable and reversible engine mounted on the tender front drag box. The screw, working on the Archimedean principle, looked very much like a king-size mincing machine, and forced coal through a crushing grid that broke down larger lumps to a usable size. A secondary screw, known as the raiser screw, delivered the crushed coal to a distributor plate set just inside the firehole. Four separately controllable steam jets fitted below the distributor plate were arranged to direct fuel to the front and back of the left- and right-hand sides of the firegrate respectively. The controls to these steam jets were mounted on a panel in front of the fireman, and the valves for the stoker engine somewhat lower, at seat level. Below the main steam pressure gauge, three others showed the engine and jet pressures; black hands indicated the pressures to the back corners, while red hands showed the pressures to the front corners.

A standard-size firehole was fitted above the raiser screw housing, and access was gained by butterfly-type firedoors. This arrangement permitted normal manual firing, although in practice hand-firing was rendered extremely difficult for three reasons. Firstly, the firehole was much higher than normal, secondly the raiser screw housing obstructed the fireman's usual stance, and finally, because of a 'safety' barrier, coal did not drop on to the shovelling plate, but had to be extracted from the tender.

The other departure from standard on these three engines was by way of improved draughting and the fitting of double chimneys. Subsequent testing at Rugby showed that no greater evaporation rate proved possible than with hand-firing, for at 29,000 lbs of water per hour, 6,000 lbs of coal was being consumed by the stoker in place of 4,750 lbs with hand-firing. This discrepancy was due to the production of fines by the crushing grid, and the jets had to deal with both dust and cobbles up to 4 cm. The dust, of course, tended to be carried out through the chimney unburned, and just how this worked out in service I was soon to learn.

Quite out of the blue we were told to book on the following Monday morning for special training with the mechanical stoker. This was the first intimation we received that such an engine had arrived at Saltley, and when we learned that three Class '9s' equipped with these devices were to be used on the Carlisle runs, there was much speculation amongst the men involved.

It was arranged that these engines would be first used on Bordesley trippers for the dual function of running in and training the crews, or rather the firemen, in the use of this new equipment. Since Les and I were due for the afternoon Carlisle the following week, it was planned that we would work the initial run, and therefore we took the first turn on the training programme.

Mr Wood, the firing instructor, being in charge of tuition, was already on board No

92165 when we joined her in the shed yard. Apart from sporting a double chimney, there was little to distinguish her from a normal Class '9' externally. However, on gaining the footplate the modifications were very obvious. During the half-hour or so before we rang off the shed, Mr Wood ran through the theory of mechanical stoking and pointed out the various components and their respective functions. It was all very interesting, for I had never seen a mechanical stoker before, nor had I ever considered the possibility of its application to British locomotives.

He explained that, pending the arrival of special fuel at Saltley, we would use passenger coal from the hopper. Since this contained larger lumps than was desirable, it would be dropped into the tender in small amounts and each layer would be broken up by a gang of cleaners acquired for the purpose. However, to eliminate the possibility of blockages during the training period, the tender would be only partially coaled and, if a jam did occur, this could be cleared by the means of an inching bar used as a sort of poker. This latter was a massive steel rod about 2 inches in diameter and some 5 feet in length, weighing the best part of 100 lbs. Needless to say, trying to clear a blockage with this mighty implement involved the expenditure of more effort and was far more tiring than firing half a ton of coal. He did go to considerable lengths, though, to point out that the bar must not be used with the stoker engine operating, since should it become caught in the conveyor screw, no end of damage might result. The fact that one's foot might also be caught in the screw was not mentioned, but some small measure of protection was offered by a 3-inch-high transverse steel strip attached to the shovelling plate just below the tender doors. This was supposed to serve as a reminder that something quite nasty lurked on the other side of it. In actual fact, no problem was

The fireman's view of the boiler fittings on No 92166. The battery of jet controls is within easy reach when seated, while their related gauges are arranged below the main steam pressure gauge. Note that the high butterfly-type firedoors leave no room for a drip-tray, hence the tea-can suspended from the gauge lamp bracket on the driver's side. *Author* experienced in stepping or, for that matter, tripping over the thing, but it did prove a confounded nuisance by preventing coal from even a well-filled tender falling down on to the shovelling plate.

Steam to the stoker engine was controlled by a valve wheel as previously described, and this was sufficiently sensitive to achieve a very fine range of speeds to the conveyor screw. I soon found that it could be set to deliver just a gentle trickle of fuel at the minimum setting, or a veritable avalanche when fully opened. Unfortunately, with the lumpy mixture of coal we had in the tender the conveyor screw was never consistently loaded, so that the feed to the delivery plate was usually intermittent. This negated to some extent the fine control obtainable from the stoker engine, but I soon learned to detect whether it was feeding satisfactorily by the sound it made. When conveying coal the screw omitted a quiet, muffled rumble accompanied by a graunching sound as the fuel was pulverised against the crushing grid. When starved by a blockage, the screw rotated at a greater speed, giving off a higher-pitched ringing noise, and there was no graunching. An inspection flap at the top of the raiser screw housing enabled a visual check to be made of the actual flow rates, and a small hole in the firedoors proved useful in keeping an eye on just where the fuel was going. All these techniques were acquired later in the day, after some hours of practical operation, but initially I had to rely entirely on Mr Wood's guidance.

Having digested the theory and familiarised myself with the position of the controls and their respective function, we came to the actual operation. Opening the butterfly firedoors, he bade me inspect the fire. There was very little of it, just a thin layer barely covering the bars and surrounding several patches of apparently dead ash.

'It's best to build a thin fire by hand first,' he said. 'Make sure that you have a reasonable amount in the back corners because they tend to be starved by the jets.'

During the next 10 minutes I discovered just how difficult and exhausting it was to fire one of these mechanical stoker '9s' manually. Picking up the shovel I looked around for coal but found none in the usual place, for it was all dammed up behind that benighted footguard.

'You'll have to open the tender doors I'm afraid,' said Mr Wood apologetically.

Having done this another problem presented itself, because there was no flat surface to shovel off. The coal had to be dragged and scraped forward over the retaining strip, and I could visualise that, even with a full tender, getting coal on to the shovelling plate would be a strenuous business. As it was, the tender was now less than half filled with lumps broken down to a nice size for manual firing on a conventional engine, but it took far longer than normal to get 2 hundredweight forward on to the shovelling plate. At last it was done, but then I found that I could not take up my usual firing stance because of the thick trunking rising up from the middle of the footplate. I was forced to scoop up a shovelful of coal, then, holding it chest high, shuffle round the trunking on the driver's side, since this was not obstructed by damper wheels. The coal had to be delivered by an ungainly thrusting action with the arms held at virtually full stretch, and this after a short time proved a great strain on both arms and back. I was glad that only a thin fire had to be built up in this way, for I felt the need to sit down more than if I had just cleaned the fire on a Garratt.

'Right,' said Mr Wood after the fire had brightened up under the influence of the blower and a fully opened rear damper. 'We'll try the stoker.'

He first opened the stoker engine valve and, with the firedoors wide open, I watched as a 'river' of coal slowly poured over the distributor plate. Satisfied that this was moving at the desired rate, he then turned on the jet's main valve so that the gauges showed about 40 lbs per sq in for the front and 30 for the rear. Mr Wood had previously set the individual jet controls, but we subsequently adjusted these from time to time during the day as working conditions demanded.

As the jets came into action, the stream of coal falling over the distributor plate broke up and flew to all corners of the firebox, but even at this early stage of the proceedings I noted that, quite logically, the smaller particles carried further than the larger ones. Together with the action of the blast these small particles tended to build up in a solid bank under the brick arch, thus artificially reducing the active grate area by no small degree. It was a problem that was never satisfactorily overcome while standard coal continued to be used, although experience obviously lessened the tendency for this to occur. Even so, on the Carlisle runs it was necessary to periodically drag this fiery slurry back over the grate with a rake.

The blast of steam coming from the jets flattened the flames in the box so that accurate observation of the shape and condition of the firebed could easily be made while they were in use. This was one bonus that was not available on standard engines and most providential in view of the sometimes unpredictable distribution of fuel.

A few minutes' use of the stoker produced the equivalent of a light round of manual firing and, with a healthy column of smoke belching skywards, our steam pressure increased quite rapidly.

By the time we rang off the shed I had acquired the hang of things, and was left to experiment during the run down to Washwood Heath. I soon found that because of the small size of coal delivered by the stoker, it burned away very quickly and it was necessary to fire in short, frequent bursts in order to maintain any sort of firebed at all.

After backing on to our train prior to departure, we encountered our first jam, caused by some larger lumps riding on top of the conveyor screw and preventing any small coal from dropping into the trough. I then experienced the agony of using the inching bar. After only 2 or 3 minutes of vigorous prodding, every muscle in my body was quivering with fatigue. Mr Wood, too, was reduced to a sweating, inarticulate hulk after just 1 minute of showing me how it should be done. Fortunately our exertions were not in vain because after running the screw in reverse for a few seconds, a full flow of fuel was once more achieved.

Being able to reverse the screw was extremely useful in helping to clear jams, since it tended to push the offending lumps back out of the way,

but the main problem was when coal interlocked to form a substantial arch over the trough. This then had to be broken down by levering and prodding, which was no easy matter when it was covered by several tons of coal, as I duly discovered on my first Carlisle run.

I was, of course, interested to see how she would steam when working hard up Camp Hill bank and, after the usual stop-go dawdle to Duddeston Road, we finally had a clear run. I think Les also wanted to see what would happen because he opened up rather more vigorously than strictly necessary with 50 loaded mineral wagons, and soon had her at full regulator and 60 per cent cut-off.

I set the stoker engine at about 50 lbs per sq in, which was sufficient to give a fair flow of fuel, and the jet gauges showed 40 lbs per sq in for the front and 30 for the rear. Immediately great black clouds of smoke erupted from the chimney indicating that the coal was being spread around to good effect, and this abated little even when the firedoors were opened two notches. Unfortunately, the test was somewhat spoiled by another blockage just beyond St Andrews, but by then we had sufficient reserve in the boiler to see us safely into Bordesley without too much loss of pressure. The shape of the firebed was quite a revelation, though, for a substantial bank of small, half-burned particles of coal had built up under the brick arch. On the other hand, the rear part of the grate contained very little fire, while the centre section was actually bare.

On engines fitted with front and rear dampers it was usual to open only the rear, but with the stoker '9s' I soon found it expedient to use a wide open front damper and keep the rear almost closed. This allowed more air to the forward section of the grate, which in turn helped to burn away the excess of fuel that found its way there. Also, when the engine was working normally it was possible to fire the box much more evenly by periodically varying the jet pressures. This was easily achieved by manipulating the main shut-off valve, and in fact the jets could be dispensed with altogether for short periods. By so doing, a mound of coal built up at the back of the grate; however, care had to be taken so as not to block the jets under the distributor plate, although this in itself was not serious if quickly cleared. Later on I frequently used this technique when building up the fire at the start of a run, for when a large hump had been produced beneath the firedoors, I merely reached in with the firing shovel and spread it into the back corners.

Our second trip up the bank was rather more encouraging from the firing point of view. For one thing we did not get a blockage at the crucial moment, and for another further continual experimentation enabled me to control the jet pressures more effectively. The one disturbing factor was the regularity of blockages over the conveyor screw caused by lumps too large to fall into the trough.

Even so by the end of the day I was extremely enthusiastic about the project, particularly when I received Mr Wood's assurance that closer attention would be paid to the breaking down of lumps to a more suitable size during coaling operations. I had visions that if the stoker would work reliably, I could devote a lot more time to road learning, together with the added bonus of arriving at destinations considerably less fatigued than normal.

Les on the other hand was far less convinced as to the supposed benefits of mechanical stoking. It appeared to him as an unnecessary complication that could go wrong and lead to a failure of the engine. He did not say much at the time, but took everything in, particularly our strenuous jam-clearing efforts, which he regarded with mild amusement and toleration. In the event his judgement was to prove correct, but not, as it turned out, for reasons of mechanical breakdown.

The following week, as promised, we were booked a stoker '9' and, being the initial trip, Mr Wood had arranged to accompany us as far as Leeds. By then No 92166 had arrived, and since No 92165 was still being used for training purposes, it was decided, rather unwisely as it happened, to provide this later engine. Being well aware of the coal problem and also because any bad blockages would reflect upon himself, Mr Wood had personally supervised the coaling operation most fastidiously, and when I inspected the tender it certainly appeared that an excellent job had been done. The top layer at least was nicely broken to a uniform size and I remember thinking at the time if what lay beneath was exactly the same, we would not experience any trouble.

No 92166 was positively gleaming, fit for a Royal Train in fact, and even the paintwork still retained quite a pungent tang. I quickly ran through the usual checks, then operated the stoker engine in both directions to make sure all was well. The coal fed through very satisfactorily and, having dumped a fair load under the firedoors, I spread this into the back corners with the firing shovel. Then, by manipulating the jet pressures, I built up the fire into a reasonable shape without resorting to manual means. Les duly arrived, displaying no emotion either way, but after conducting

Stoker-fitted '9F' No 92166 stands at Water Orton waiting to depart on its maiden trip with the 4.15 pm Glasgow fully fitted freight. The well-filled tender shows a surface of finely broken coal belying the problems that lay beneath. *Author*

his normal thorough inspection, returned to the footplate with a doubtful frown on his face.

'Doesn't seem to have done much mileage,' he muttered, half to himself. 'I'll have to check with Woody.'

The latter arrived soon after, complete with bowler hat and a small leather case containing his paraphernalia. Les wasted no time in broaching the subject of the engine's apparent nominal mileage, and Mr Wood had to admit that apart from running to Saltley, she had only worked for one day on a Bordesley. However, there had been no indication of undue tightness, since he personally had been in attendance all day. To these remarks Les rather scathingly pointed out that there was a slight difference between a Bordesley tripper and the Carlisle, when our first stop would be 90 miles away after running continuously at around 50 mph. It was therefore with a certain amount of doubt as to whether No 92166 would reach Carlisle without problems that we set off from the shed.

On arrival at Water Orton Les quickly dropped to the ground and felt all the bearings with the back of his hand.

'What do you think, Les?' enquired Mr Wood a trifle anxiously.

'Number 4 driver axlebox on my side seems a little warmer than the rest, but we will not really know until it's done some work,' he replied with a shrug.

After changing the lamps I examined the said axlebox, but could barely detect any difference from the others so, hoping for the best, I returned to the footplate to complete my preparation of the fire.

We departed dead on time with 36 equal to 40 behind the tender and set off over the fast, accelerating at a fairly leisurely pace since Les obviously did not wish to press her too hard. I carefully adjusted the stoker engine and jets to deliver a light spray of fuel and soon a healthy trail of smoke was billowing from our chimney. I was very conscious that the future of these stoker '9s' depended much on how successful they proved to be on these first trips, and I was determined to do my part and make them work. I therefore devoted my whole energy to achieving the most efficient

combustion possible and because I lacked practical experience at this stage I found it necessary to make frequent inspections of the firebed and adjustments to the controls.

Even so all went exceedingly well until Tamworth, when the screw 'ran dry'. This was the first of many blockages that spoiled what should have been an easy and comfortable journey.

In all fairness, Mr Wood immediately buckled down and did his share and with both of us prodding and poking, none of the jams proved too much of a problem. However, clearing them was very hard work and at times it was necessary to fire by hand, but the great thermal reserve in Class '9' boilers carried us over these difficulties.

We arrived at Sheffield more or less on schedule, and while we were taking on water Les hurriedly examined the engine. His face, on returning to the footplate, displayed concern.

'That number 4 axlebox is running very hot,' he exclaimed. 'We may have to fail her at Leeds.'

This was sad news indeed, for apart from the delays this action would incur, it was not the sort of start I had wished for on the initial run of the stoker '9'.

Departing therefore in an atmosphere of some anxiety, Les nursed the troubled engine as best he could and fortunately he was helped in this direction by a number of signal checks. Every time we actually came to a standstill, he would leap down to have a look at the offending axlebox, obviously trying to decide whether, and at what point, to telephone Control for a replacement engine. As luck would have it the easier going north of Sheffield allowed the bearing to cool somewhat, and by Altofts Junction he announced to my intense relief that it appeared to have loosened up. He thought that we might complete our run in safety.

Although we arrived at Leeds some 15 minutes late, Mr Wood seemed quite confident that I could now handle the stoker unit efficiently, and, wishing us luck, took his leave as planned. Fate, as fickle as ever, contrived to produce more jams on the second half of the run than when Mr Wood was in attendance, but since the coal was now somewhat depleted they were a little easier to clear. Even so, on balance I used just about as much energy as I would have done firing a standard engine manually.

At Skipton I gave the grate a good rattle and levelled the ridge that had built up under the brick arch so as to ensure maximum efficiency for the climb up to Blea Moor. This was the place to test the stoker on the sort of work it was designed for, namely continuous high output, so the 14 miles of 1 in 100 from Settle to Blea Moor should give us some idea of its worth. Fortunately with fuel feeding reliably into the screw I experienced only one or two minor starvation problems, and the stoker performed exceedingly well over the entire ascent. Les, sensing that I was in command of the situation, gave her a fair bit of stick and pulled back several minutes on the climb.

Despite the fact that the boiler provided all the steam that Les could use, I gained the distinct impression that the mechanical stoker '9s' did not steam quite as freely as did the standard engines. However, the ability to accomplish the hardest part of our journey without having to get off my seat convinced me that we were on to a good thing and, with the correct fuel and further experience, the units should prove to be a godsend in the future. It was up to us as firemen, then, to overcome these early problems so that they would gain universal acceptance.

The 20-minute dash across the mountains to Ais Gill should have proved easy going, but for me it was far more strenuous than the preceding 14 miles. A number of larger lumps of coal became wedged over the conveyor screw and in the darkness I had considerable difficulty in locating and clearing them. A spotlight in the tender would have been most useful; as it was, I had to rely entirely on my sense of touch, which with a 100 lb inching bar was far from sensitive. As a result we breasted Ais Gill with no more than 180 lbs per sq in showing on the pressure gauge and half a glass of water.

During the ensuing descent to Kirkby Stephen I took the precaution of building up the fire manually, and this insurance paid handsome dividends, for I experienced a bad patch of blockages right through to New Biggin. However, from then on the stoker worked perfectly all the way to Carlisle, where we arrived practically dead on time.

My conclusions, as I lay in bed reflecting on the day's run, were that the stoker unit in general performed reasonably well. At maximum effort the engine did not steam quite as freely as the standard locomotive, due in part, no doubt, to the fact that the firebed could not be maintained in the same perfect shape as with manual firing. Also, it was undeniably less efficient since we had burned considerably more coal than normal with a train of this weight. This could, however, be largely accounted for by the wastage of fuel passing out of the chimney as unburned fines and was one of the debits that had to be accepted with mechanical stoking.

As far as I was concerned the real nigger in the woodpile was the lack of reliability caused by the presence of lumps of coal of a larger size than could be accommodated by the conveyor screw. Starvation could, and did, occur at any time with painful regularity, and this completely upset one's carefully calculated firing programme. With the correct fuel a run to Carlisle should have been a veritable joyride, but with things as they were, firing was very much a hit-or-miss affair.

Our return journey the following day was a little better in this respect. The Carlisle lads had been more punctilious in breaking up the coal and also, with the previous day's experience behind me, I tended to run with a somewhat thicker firebed. Furthermore, I took the precaution of operating the stoker engine at frequent intervals even on downhill sections just to make sure that it was still feeding, but even so blockages seemed to occur all too often when they were least welcome.

Two days later we had No 92165 on these runs, and things followed roughly the same pattern. Consequently our report at the end of the week stressed that while the stoker unit performed satisfactorily on a diet of small cobbles, far too many large lumps were finding their way into the tender, causing feed problems.

Other crews experienced exactly the same troubles, and it was just one of those unfortunate oversights in planning that a supply of suitable coal was not provided before the engines arrived. In point of fact a number of weeks elapsed before some ideal fuel was obtained, but even then this was only delivered to Carlisle, not Saltley. It took the form of screened chips 1-2 inches in diameter, and was apparently the coal used by Heysham-Isle of Man steamers, which were also equipped with mechanical stokers.

The reader may recall that earlier I stated that everyone achieves a peak of performance in any form of endeavour which is never surpassed. My own particular peak in terms of continual physical effort came about quite unexpectedly on our next afternoon Carlisle duty. The winter storms were now setting in, but high winds, although contributing to the problems, were not the cause of my excessive labours. Ironically it was on No 92167, the third of the mechanical stoker '9s', that I performed my feat of endurance.

As usual I was delighted to find that we were booked a stoker '9' and, on gaining the footplate, the well-coaled tender seemed to have received the full attention of the cleaning gang. However, I had been deceived before by the appearance of a well-broken top layer, so I quickly checked that the diabolical inching bar was lying in the fire iron compartment. After ensuring that the stoker engine and jets worked satisfactorily, I gave the still gleaming cab a final polish while Les conducted his usual tests.

Right on time we departed from the loco and, during the ensuing run to Water Orton, I operated the stoker two or three times to keep a reasonable fire in the grate. It worked perfectly and, as far as one could judge over such a short distance, No 92167 seemed to be the best of the three stoker '9s'. I therefore felt pretty confident when we backed on to our train of 43 vans equal to 45, and looked forward to a good trip.

Five minutes before being called out of the sidings, I built up a good bed of fire at the back of the box and, with a full boiler and 245 lbs per sq in showing on the pressure gauge, I relaxed on my seat with a lid of tea, eyeing the gathering winter darkness with the benevolent gaze of one who is snug and warm and well protected from a bitter north-west wind.

At precisely 4.50 pm the signal came off

No 92167 passing Burton Station North signal box with the 4.45 pm Water Orton-Glasgow. I felt that this was the best of the three stoker '9Fs', and although later converted to manual firing, she survived until June 1968, thereby being the last of the class in service. *Pat Webb*

and, as Les pulled smartly out on to the main line, I instinctively opened the stoker engine valve. A healthy graunching sound could be heard by an ear cocked for the purpose and, thus satisfied, I stood behind Les watching for our brake-van lights to appear. Having ensured that the train was in good order, I crossed back to my seat and was just about to sit down when the graunching changed to the distinctive ring of an empty conveyor screw.

'Blast,' I said, loud enough to cause Les to turn his head, and, after resignedly closing the stoker engine valve, hauled the heavy inching bar from its compartment. The mere act of holding this implement was effort enough, so a few seconds of prodding and levering at an obstruction buried under several tons of coal soon brought beads of perspiration to my brow. A minute later I decided to give the engine another try but, on opening the valve, only a small trickle of chips fell over the distributor plate, then it ran dry. I reversed the screw since this was often effective in clearing jams, but on running it forward again no more than a hatful of coal came through.

Once more I grasped the bar and attacked the compact mass until my muscles ached and I was gasping for breath, but with no more success than on the first occasion. The trouble was that I could neither see nor really feel what was causing the blockage due to the great weight of coal in the over-filled tender, and it was very much a case of luck whether the bar penetrated to the critical spot. Twice again I carried out the same procedure, each time more frantically than before, until I finally sank back on my seat with knotted muscles shaking with fatigue.

Meanwhile our steam pressure had fallen to 165 lbs per sq in and there was only a third of a glass of water showing in the boiler. Les, who had been regarding my efforts with a pensive eye, was now forced to intervene.

'You had better get some coal on or we'll soon be in trouble,' he yelled unsympathetically.

He was quite right, of course; I had expended far too much time and energy in trying to get the stoker to operate. Dragging my still panting and exhausted body upright, I looked into the firebox and was dismayed to find great patches of ash surrounded by precious little live fire. No engine but a Class '9' would have travelled this far with the fire in such a state. Determined not to cause the engine to fail through lack of steam, I set about the laborious business of extracting coal from the tender before shovelling it, equally laboriously, into the firebox. Had she been a standard Class '9', to cover the firebars would have been the work of but a few minutes. As it was; because of that accursed guard strip and the obstruction caused by the raiser screw trunking, it seemed to take ages to fire even a couple of hundredweight over the grate.

The boiler had already been mortgaged pretty heavily but I was forced to let it go even further in the interests of retaining steam pressure. By energetic and diligent use of the rake I spread live fire over the whole area of the firebars as it lit up and finally the downward swing of the pressure gauge needle halted at 150 lbs per sq in. With the water just in sight at the bottom of the glass, it was now necessary to use the injector in short bursts, but despite this and the very thin firebed, pressure slowly began to recover.

Stoically I worked like an automaton, first pulling out coal from under the tender doors with pick, shovel or even by hand, then, when there was sufficient lying on the footplate, shovelling it up and thrusting it awkwardly into the firebox. After closing the firedoors, a quick burst with the injector then repeat the operation over again. All the time muscles and sinews burned with the fiery ache of excessive fatigue. I longed to relax for even a minute, but there was no respite. The whole process was so inefficient that it demanded every ounce of effort I was able to muster.

Very slowly at first, then with gaining momentum, both steam pressure and water level rose until by Derby North they were back to where they should be. However, after an hour of expending so much energy at such a high rate I felt absolutely shattered. With blood sugar at zero, I suddenly remembered the supply of glucose I carried and promptly munched a few of those large tablets, washing them down with half a pint of cold water.

The prospect of another 180 miles of this sort of caper was pretty daunting to say the least, so, after hanging my head in the cooling slipstream for a minute, I tried once more to clear the blockage. Despite a prolonged and frantic attempt, the result was frustratingly negative and, with holes once more appearing in the firebed, I resignedly returned to the old routine.

The following 70-minute run to Sheffield was sheer hell, for although my back and arms were quite capable of normal shovelling at the rate of 2 tons per hour for seven or eight hours at a stretch without showing the slightest sign of stiffness, they were now, because of the unaccustomed awkwardness of the operation, a blaze of excruciating pain.

A diet of glucose and water undoubtedly helped to keep me going, but even the brief stop for water offered no relief, since I was fully occupied dragging coal out on to the footplate while the tank was filling.

Fortunately this task of extracting fuel was made somewhat easier by the fact that, with the release of pressure from the back of the tender doors, I was now able to open them. Even so, the conveyor screw remained obstinately blocked and my many attempts to clear it ended fruitlessly. For a further hour I endured the purgatory of hand-firing No 92167 until at Altofts Junction Les could restrain himself no longer.

With growing concern he had been watching me flog myself to quite unacceptable levels of effort and I was now obviously showing signs of the severe strain imposed by these dreadful labours.

'I think we had better fail her at Leeds,' he yelled above the noise. 'You can't go on like this all the way to Carlisle.'

I made no reply, partly because I had no breath to spare for talking and partly because he had phrased it as half question and half statement. Since I did not wish to be personally responsible for failing the engine and the subsequent consequences this action might incur, I chose to regard his remarks as a statement of fact. His logic was undeniable, but I so much wanted to prove that these mechanical stokers were a viable proposition that I just would not admit defeat.

Grasping the inching bar, I plunged it into the coal above the conveyor screw with a fury born of desperation and disappointment. This time it penetrated deeper than on previous occasions and the tip seemed to lock under some solid object. I levered downwards with all my might and the object, whatever it was, moved upwards. Then a sudden jerk of the engine brought a small avalanche of coal down from the back of the tender, rendering further prodding impractical.

Half-heartedly I opened the stoker engine valve, then, wonder of wonders, I immediately heard the graunch of coal being broken on the crushing grid. Nor was it just the previous trickle, for on opening the inspection flap I perceived with great relief and immense satisfaction a full-blooded flow of fuel, falling over the distributor plate. Composing myself as much as one can compose a body shaking with exhaustion, I staggered over to Les and informed him that the stoker was once again operating and that I thought we could now manage.

'Well, it's up to you,' he said simply with a shrug of his shoulders, and immediately returned to his task of observing signals.

Always the opportunist, I grabbed a couple of sandwiches and greedily munched them while the jets were spraying in enough coal to cause the safety valves to lift from time to time. For 10 glorious minutes I was able to relax on my seat, allowing the stoker to actually build up the fire, then once more the screw ran dry. Coal, shaken down by the tender's oscillations, was again lying deep over the trough, so that no amount of prodding produced any worthwhile results. Reluctantly I gave up further attempts to get the stoker operating and returned to manual firing, having come to the cynical conclusion that the only mechanical stoker working that day was yours truly.

During that 10-minute break I had pondered the cause of our problems and it required no genius to conjecture that a pretty large lump of coal must be lying squarely over the conveyor screw, thus excluding the passage of the rest of the fuel as securely as a tailor-made lid. I would just have to be patient and wait until we had used up sufficient coal to expose it. Unfortunately we still had over an hour's run before we arrived at Skipton, and I now had doubts as to whether I could stand up to this murderous effort for very much longer. The hardest part of our journey started at Skipton, and if the stoker was not working by then, well, the prospect of hand-firing up the mountains to Blea Moor was too terrible to even contemplate.

In the event my worst fears were realised and the next hour proved a torture of endurance beyond anything I had previously experienced in my life. Despite several futile attempts, the stoker remained stubbornly inoperative and now, after four hours of incessant maximum activity, my whole body was racked with pain and fatigue. I hardly noticed our arrival at Skipton, and so distressed was my general condition that for the one and only time during our partnership, Les volunteered to go off and make a can of coffee while I attended to the watering. No doubt he did not wish to see me suffering, for the 15-minute halt was one of frantic activity.

Summoning up all my depleted reserves, I cleaned and levelled the fire, an exhausting enough task in itself when carried out in great haste. Then down to ground level to turn off the water, followed by a laborious scramble on to the top of the tender in order to extract the heavy hose. With my breath coming in rasping sobs, I made my way back to the footplate where, with failing strength, I desperately tried to dig out the obstruction. If only I could uncover the object I might stand a chance, and it was this driving thought that enabled me to extract, and fire, 5 or 6 hundredweight of coal before Les returned.

He regarded me quizzically for a moment in the firelight before asking the inevitable question.

'Is it alright now?'

I guessed that he meant the stoker engine and I shook my head, but quickly gasped that I had just started to uncover the obstruction. Hissing safety valves, a full boiler and a bright fire convinced Les that at least the engine was in good fettle and, after obtaining my nodding assurance that I was prepared to continue, he blew off the brakes.

As we drew out on the main line I automatically draped myself over the cab doors, watching to see that the train was complete while at the same time sucking in lungsful of cold refreshing air. Despite the fact that we were still in the shelter of a cutting, I could not help noticing how blustery the wind had become, for I was obliged to place a restraining hand on my cap before withdrawing inside again.

Although there was now a good body of fire on, Settle was only 15 miles distant, so the need to uncover that obstructing lump was most pressing. I therefore returned to the task without further ado. It is said that every black cloud has a silver lining, and on this occasion it took the form of the exposed end of that great slab of coal. The upper surface was smooth and flat and, despite the restrictions imposed by the confines of the tender, I had at last something suitable off which to shovel. Stupified with fatigue, my movements were slow and clumsy, but even so I was able to shovel coal out on to the footplate much faster than at any other time on the run so far. It was of course necessary to keep the footplate reasonably clear of coal, so the only place I could dump it was in the firebox.

Contrary to logic, therefore, considering my wretched state, I considerably over-fired the engine for the next few miles in a final attempt to expose the obstruction before my strength failed altogether. By Hellifield my mining operation had laid bare some 4 feet of the monster slab that was sitting so firmly over the trough, and I thereupon decided to shatter it in situ while I was still able to swing a pick. Staggering out on to the footplate, I collected the implement and on returning I was just about to commence the destruction of it when I realised that all was not as I had left it. Blinking unbelievingly through rivers of sweat, I saw in the reflected light of the fire that a fall of coal had almost completely covered the slab again.

I nearly wept with despair, for victory had seemed so near, and now it had been tantalisingly withdrawn at the last moment. Quickly this emotion changed to one of baleful resentment. To me, the successful application of mechanical stoking now appeared to be wholly hinged on the removal of this devilish obstruction, and I was not going to be beaten by a bally lump of coal. Once more I started shovelling with limbs now so weak that they would barely follow the brain's instructions. Had it not been for the years of built-in reflexes, they would doubtless have not worked at all.

Les was by this time thrashing the engine pretty hard for, apart from battling up the 1 in 100 gradient, we also had to overcome the force of a full-blown gale. Even so, No 92167 was still steaming beautifully; in fact, ever since the initial failure of the stoker, pressure had not dropped below 240 lbs per sq in, and because of my recent frantic efforts to use up fuel we had if anything an excess of it.

My little world inside the tender was now beginning to swim around in a most disconcerting manner and much to my annoyance I unaccountably kept losing my balance. Like all athletes, a top link fireman is the product of many long years of hard training. His strength and skills are acquired through thousands of repetitive exercises, while at the same time he learns to hold something back for the great effort when it is needed, rather like the finishing sprint of a long-distance runner. But so enormous were the physical demands this day that even my considerable reserves of stamina had been used up long since and for the past hour I had been running solely on that peculiar source of nervous energy that only the mind can produce, a mind so obsessed with the need to succeed that it totally refused to acknowledge the sad state of its body.

Gradually I cleared the area above the great slab again, but as I did so my angry frustration slowly diminished until eventually, unable to stand, I found myself working on my hands and knees, feebly pulling out pieces of coal with my fingers. I decided that this time I would try and lever the obstruction up and away from the trough, and taking a firm grasp heaved with all my remaining strength. Although it barely budged, the movement was sufficient to disturb the almost vertical wall of coal rising high above, and 2 hundredweights came crashing down from the top. It took me completely by surprise, and the first intimation I had that anything untoward had happened was the feeling that both hands had been suddenly amputated at the wrists, followed immediately by a violent blow on the forehead.

I reeled back as if kicked by a mule, the excruciating pain shooting up my arms and stinging my brain so acutely as to cause a myriad of coloured lights to whirl before my eyes. This was the last straw - if that blasted lump wanted to play it rough and have a fight then I would give it one. Gone was the cool, logical, efficient fireman, gone was the poor worn-out wreck of a labourer grovelling on all fours. A Hercules fired with the superhuman strength of the insane now stood with coalpick poised over the offending object. With the fury of a madman I unleashed a blow so violent that it might well have penetrated the very plating of the tender itself. The end of the lump disintegrated into a shower of fragments that ricocheted in all directions and cut into my face. I felt no pain, for the anger that possessed me did not permit distractions. Again and again the pick swung up and down. I did not so much break up the lump - I annihilated it. For a full minute the wild attack continued, until with a final shattering stroke, the last piece disappeared.

At once the blackness of the tender seemed to spread outwards and engulf me, and I felt myself falling down into a dark abyss; the sensation was not at all unpleasant, for a soft, relaxing peacefulness seemed to suffuse my whole body. I could hear the murmuring of water like that of a nearby brook, and it seemed that I was sleeping blissfully on the bank of some shady stream. Then I became aware of a vague rumbling that became more insistent and forceful with every passing second, and this I found was decidedly less pleasant.

A distant voice was calling my name. I opened my eyes and was puzzled to find myself looking up at an inky sky dotted with the brilliant pin-points of light from a thousand stars. The voice grew louder until the words began to register in my mind.

'Terry, are you alright, mate?'

I focused my gaze and saw the silhouette of Les standing out boldly against the white furnace light. With painful suddenness I snapped back to reality and with his help struggled to my feet. With the regaining of full consciousness came the awareness of agony, an agony that I had hitherto never experienced. Every part of my body hurt abominably and co-ordination of movement proved extremely difficult.

'It's OK, Les,' I heard myself say. 'I just over-balanced.'

A strong helping hand guided me firmly to my seat, where I slumped thankfully while fighting to regain my composure. I recognised Hawes Junction as it flashed past and realised that the sound I had heard a few moments ago must have been Les picking up water over the troughs. Of the long climb up to Blea Moor I could remember very little, but since fire, steam pressure and boiler level were all up to the mark, I concluded that I had somehow managed my duties.

If only my hands did not hurt so much, I thought, and with the idea of trying to relieve the pain, I began to gently ease off my gloves. I was surprised to see that they were badly torn and, as I pulled the tattered remnants free, I discovered why they had felt so soggy of late. The nail on the second finger of my right hand was missing, while long gashes ran very nearly the full length of my third and fourth fingers. My left hand had suffered slightly less but, even so, the skin across all four knuckles was split wide open. In keeping with my face, which sported a lump the size of a golfball in the centre of my forehead, both hands were a mass of congealed blood and coal dust.

Les, who was now looking closely at me, was aghast at the mess.

'Good God lad, whatever have you been doing? Just sit there for a minute until we're over the top.'

I needed no second bidding, and in a detached way I was also quite content to watch him top up the bucket with warm water from the slaking pipe and then, after obtaining a piece of towelling from his own haversack, bring them both over to me. Displaying a sympathy that belied his gruff exterior, he carefully bathed my face, cleaning coal dust out of the cuts with all the thoroughness of a trained nurse. In between quick bouts of looking out for signals and adjusting the brake, he also helped me to wash my hands and, when properly cleaned, dressed the wounds with makeshift bandages made up from two spare handkerchiefs.

'You know, you are a bloody young idiot,' he said quietly as he tied the final knot. 'You should have let me fail her at Leeds. I would not have come past Derby myself without the stoker working, and to be perfectly honest I've been expecting you to give up ever since.'

I thanked Les for his attentions, which had certainly made my hands feel a little easier, although of course they still throbbed and burned like the very dickens, and sought solace in a good drink of coffee and my first cigarette on the run. The combined effect of these stimulants, coupled with 10 minutes complete rest did much to make me feel human again.

With the stoker engine operational once more, the remaining 32 miles from Appleby to Carlisle proved relatively easy, which was just as well, for the mere act of holding the firing shovel proved both difficult and painful. Admittedly I did have to venture into the tender on several occasions in order to push coal into the conveyor screw trough, because with only about one ton of fuel left at the back of the coal space, it would not shake down by itself. Fortunately I was able to accomplish this by means of my feet rather than the more usual way with coalpick and shovel. I even found sufficient time to clean down the footplate, so that when we were relieved only some 2 minutes behind schedule, all was looking more or less as spick and span as ever.

As I dragged myself slowly up to the lodge I was comforted by the thought that I had managed to fire some 8 tons of coal into a mechanical stoker's firebox by hand, a performance equivalent in sheer effort to three or four times that amount on a standard Class '9'. However, I knew then that I would never again achieve such a high level, nor for that matter indeed attempt it. This was to be my peak, a peak that, apart from providing some personal satisfaction and extracting a surprising response from Les, turned out to be of little practical value in furthering the cause of mechanical stoking. On arrival at the lodge I showered and had my injuries properly dressed, but I felt too exhausted to tackle a square meal and therefore promptly tottered off to bed to sleep the clock round.

It would be dishonest to say that I awoke

feeling 100 per cent fit, for my back was abominably stiff and, apart from the cuts, my hands were black with bruises. Nevertheless, yesterday's marathon now seemed like a nightmare best forgotten, so when Les suggested that it might be prudent for me to return home as a passenger, I protested so strongly that he did not bring up the matter again. Fate produced another of its illogical quirks by providing only 18 vehicles for the homeward journey and, as if by way of compensation, I only had two or three minor blockages, which were easily cleared. After the best run yet with a stoker '9', I arrived back at Saltley feeling much perkier, although it took a few weeks for my hands to become normal once more.

Strangely enough we did not have another run on a stoker '9' after that. A number of problems developed that took one or other out of service just at a time when, ironically, the correct size fuel had been provided at Carlisle. This, as previously mentioned, took the form of small chips as used on the Isle of Man steamers, and a number of wagons had been sent to Durran Hill expressly for our use. It would have been ideal, of course, since this 1½-inch diameter coal 'flowed' rather like dry sand and jamming was impossible. Obviously it was equally unsuitable for standard engines, but since this coal had been provided exclusively for the Carlisle-Birmingham, the Carlisle-Birmingham had to use it.

We first discovered this problem on the next morning tour of duty. Winter had set in with a vengeance and, after several days of intermittent snow falls, a large high-pressure area over Scandinavia was bringing arctic winds down over all the country. As was often the case with the morning turn, we had a 'Black Five', and departing from Water Orton at 3.50 am the frost was just about at its most severe. Under a setting moon, the snow-covered countryside looked superb, but even with the effort of firing I was none too warm.

Surprisingly, the further north we travelled the thinner the snow became, until by Derby it petered out altogether. However, the cold, if anything, seemed more intense, and despite thick clothing Les was visibly suffering, for his trips to toast himself before the fire became more and more frequent. Leeds had received more snow than anywhere else, since it lay a good 8 inches deep, and I looked forward to seeing some impressive drifts over the mountains. In this respect, though, I was to be disappointed, because no more than a thin layer covered anywhere north of Skipton; however, a brilliantly clear morning made the climb up to Ais Gill one of the most memorable with regard to scenic delight of the whole year.

By the time we retired to bed the winter sun was already sinking fast and, despite its day-long sojourn, the temperature had at no time even approached freezing point. After the cosy warmth of the lodge, stepping outside later that night was certainly a shock, for the air was bitterly cold and, although walking at a lively pace, by the time we arrived at the shed our teeth were beginning to chatter.

My second shock occurred when I mounted the footplate and found it knee-deep in stoker chips! It took the best part of 15 minutes shovelling before we could actually see the footboards and, realising the problem I was going to experience, I hunted around for some old firebars. The act of inserting these brought forth another avalanche, but this time it had to remain there, for the firebox already contained sufficient unburned coal.

Topping up at the water column produced yet another surprise. The tank lid was frozen solid, and it took several sharp clouts with the coalpick before I could gain access. Needless to say I left it open thereafter.

The fire burned up remarkably quickly, partly due to the small size of the coal and partly due to the fact that our engine was fitted with a rocking grate and the hopper ash-pan doors did not close securely. Despite leaving the firedoors wide open (an action much approved by Les), we proved to be a noisy nuisance until actually departing from Durran Hill.

Once under way I was able to fully appreciate the problems in dealing with this fuel. Under the action of a fairly substantial blast, it burned away almost immediately, giving off a fierce heat. This was grand as far as steaming was concerned, but with a standard firing shovel, even working continuously, I could barely keep pace with consumption. The action of firing was of course made doubly difficult by the river of coal flowing about one's ankles over the footplate and the necessity of keeping the footboards clear. Right up to Ais Gill I was kept working flat out, sweating profusely and cursing yet another of life's ironies.

At Skipton the coal ceased to fall from the tender on its own accord and, with the major hill-climbing behind us, life became a little easier. Even so, such was the rate of burning that I was using the original Saltley coal long before we reached Sheffield. One bonus accruing from these chips, though, was that it was only possible to retain the thinnest of fires. Consequently it remained exceptionally clean and on arrival at Washwood Heath even some of the bars were showing bare.

This miniature Ice Age that had descended upon Britain steadily intensified so that when we made our outward trip again two days later the air was noticeably colder. Once more we had a 'Black Five', and although Les arrived dressed more like an Eskimo than an engine driver, he suffered extreme hardship over the whole journey. For my part, working busily in front of the furnace and only looking out at odd times, I was comfortably warm, fully compensating for the agonies of heat endured in the hot summer months.

So cold was it in the mountains that it came as no surprise to find Garsdale water troughs completely frozen over. I did in fact drop the scoop on emerging from Rise Hill Tunnel, but only collected a few ice chippings for my trouble. It was obvious that obtaining water might prove something of a problem in these extreme conditions.

That night, as we walked from the lodge, the frost was indeed cruel. The air was so cold that the act of inhaling resulted in an acute pain at the top of one's nose, while ears and extremities soon felt decidedly frostbitten. We did not know it at the time, but the air temperature at Carlisle later fell to no less than 39°F of frost. That is just about as low as I have ever experienced in this country, while up in the mountains it was anyone's guess.

It was fortunate that our tender tank was full for, despite a brightly burning brazier nearby, the shed water column was solid. Again, we were well coaled with the 'steamboat' chips, but this time the Carlisle preparation crew had fortunately inserted three firebars beneath the tender doors, thus leaving only the minimum shovelling space and preventing the footplate from being swamped. Appreciatively glancing around the clean cab, I noticed a platelayer's shovel standing in the corner. This no doubt belonged to the shed steam-raiser who preferred it to a firing shovel. I was just about to pitch it off when the idea occurred to me that this might prove to be a much more effective implement for handling small chips. The blade area was double that of mine and it was less than half the weight. I tentatively tried a few swings and found that the firehole could just accommodate the full width. Furthermore it carried twice the quantity of coal with considerably less effort. It was of course impossible to obtain the accurate direction so easily achieved with the correct tool, but it was possible to dump a lot of coal into the firebox in a very short space of time, and I thereupon decided to take it along with me.

Les conducted a rather more hasty than usual inspection of the engine and, when all was ready, we shunted across the main line and backed into Durran Hill Sidings. Travelling tender-first, even for that short distance, provided an eye-watering experience I did not wish to indulge in too often.

During the 10-minute interval before departure I built up a substantial fire, using both shovels alternately. This restored my circulation nicely, but it did little for Les who was now looking somewhat blue. Unfortunately, an efficient anti-glare shield interposed betwixt driver's seat and firehole was just as efficient in blocking heat, so that he received very little warming radiation unless actually standing in the middle of the cab.

Immediately prior to leaving the sidings, I swilled down the footplate and filled the bucket with boiling water from the slaking pipe. Then, having seen our train of 32

'Black Five' No 44666 seen here at Crewe just after completion in 1949, and not yet fitted with a shed-plate. It was duly allocated to Saltley, where it proved a very popular locomotive. One of the last batch built at Crewe, it featured forward top-feed plus Ivatt modifications, rocking grate, hopper ashpan, self-cleaning smokebox and, although fitted with return-bend super-heater elements, it retained plain bearing axleboxes. This locomotive was still in excellent condition when I experienced a hectic run from Carlisle during an exceptionally cold spell in the winter of 1958-9.

vehicles nicely under way, I settled down to what I knew was going to be almost continual stoking. No 4666 steamed so well that I found it unnecessary to close the firedoors. This had the dual advantage of allowing the maximum amount of radiated heat to come out into the cab, while at the same time permitting me to fire without continually manipulating the firedoors.

Having built up the correct firebed shape, I found I could execute the bulk of my firing with the broad shovel merely by dumping chips just inside the mouthpiece, where the action of the blast completed distribution in a most satisfactory way. From time to time I did have to resort to the firing shovel in order to cover specific areas, mainly at the front and sides of the grate, but on the whole it was much easier than the previous run.

At precisely 12.45 am we arrived at Appleby for water and, so as to top up the boiler as quickly as possible, I attempted to use the live steam injector in addition to the exhaust steam one that I had been operating since Carlisle. We had tested both injectors before leaving the shed and knew it to be in good order, but now it was frozen solid. The water column, too, was in the same condition. We could neither pull the arm round nor turn on the water valve, despite the frost fire alongside belching forth a healthy flame.

Without wasting further time we set off with the 7 minutes watering time in hand. We

Appleby station looking north on a dreary August day in 1951. Thirty miles from Durran Hill, the Carlisle-Birmingham fitted freights were booked for a water stop here before tackling the formidable climb to Ais Gill. The water column, which on one winter's night we found frozen despite the roaring frost fire, was located at the end of the platform just behind the camera.

needed every second of it, for with Garsdale troughs frozen, the next column was Blea Moor and Les would now have to nurse our engine very carefully. This was not an easy task when faced with a ruling gradient of 1 in 100, but in such a situation Les Field's superb enginemanship came into its own and by judiciously 'losing' those 7 minutes we breasted Ais Gill dead on time, having used not a whisp more steam than was absolutely necessary.

Shovelling merrily away in front of that white-hot furnace for nearly two hours had left me, if not exactly done to a turn, certainly pleasantly warm. Not so poor Les, for when he drew his head in, I could see frost and little icicles hanging from his eyebrows, twinkling comically in the glare of the fire. Had he not wound a scarf around his head he would probably have lost his left ear through frostbite.

However, one of the best indications of how cold it was at these higher altitudes came to light when I tried to sweep the footplate. I often kept my handbrush in the bucket of water during cold weather. When sweeping up, this enabled me to lay the dust without making the floorboards as wet as when using the slaking pipe. The bucket had been left in its usual position standing at the back of the footplate alongside the cab doors. It was of course being subjected to the draught blowing under these doors, but at the same time it was little more than 6 feet from a white-hot fire radiating heat directly at it. I was therefore somewhat surprised when on grabbing the brush, the bucket came up with it. A quick jerk after a few seconds' examination in front of the fire pulled 2 gallons of ice out in one piece - like a jelly from a mould. Had I not seen it with my own eyes I would have found such an occurrence hard to believe.

At Blea Moor we received another nasty shock, for this column too was immovably frozen. Although our tank was very low on water and we still had 27 miles to travel until we reached Skipton, there was now no other choice but to proceed. Fortunately most of it was downhill and we could coast for the first 14 miles. With a clear road Les really let the train run down to Settle, faster in fact than I can recall on any previous occasion.

Having no firing to indulge in, it was now my turn to become cold, and subjected to icy draughts, seemingly blowing in from all directions, I soon came to appreciate the extreme discomfort Les must have been suffering.

We halted at the Skipton water column with no more than a couple of hundred gallons of water in the tender, and I must admit that I was fully prepared to drop the fire there and then. As luck would have it this column had been in frequent use, so although the bag was stiff with ice, I was able to swing the arm round and water actually flowed. While the train was being examined, Les and I lit a fire under our live steam injector with the aid of hot coals from the firebox and some oil-soaked waste, and just prior to departing managed to get it functioning once more. Thereafter I used both injectors alternately and experienced no further trouble.

The remainder of the journey through that icy night was straightforward enough, although Les was literally stiff with cold and I did a devil of a lot of shovelling, so that by the time we arrived at Saltley we were both very glad to get off.

It took some weeks for the coal supply position at Carlisle to revert to normal, and it is now past history that all three stoker '9s' were eventually converted back to standard engines.

The basic concept of mechanical stoking was sound enough, but on the journeys in this country it showed no particular advantage and was in fact wasteful on coal. With the correct fuel a fireman should have been relieved of much physical effort and should therefore have been able to devote more time to road learning. In the event I personally had been involved in a lot of extra effort, both with the stokers and afterwards when using up their special fuel on standard engines. It was an interesting experiment and, despite the various setbacks, I was very glad to have played a part in it.

We did not have the deep snows I had been led to anticipate that winter, but we did experience our share of heavy gales. The worst point invariably seemed to be Ribblehead Viaduct, and although we took the usual precautions to protect ourselves from the ravages of these hurricane-force blasts, the unexpected often happened.

On one particularly wild night we were pounding slowly over the viaduct on a 'Black Five', hauling no more than 30 vehicles, when Les resignedly pointed out that if it blew any harder we would come to a standstill. The engine was already fully extended and I was being kept very busy indeed. The cab doors were wedged with a fire iron to stop them blowing open, since the normal retaining spring was quite inadequate against the force of this particular gale.

I was in the middle of swinging yet another shovelful of coal into the fire when, due no doubt to constant vibration, the fire iron slipped out of position and the doors blew wide open. Instantly the cab was transformed into what felt like a wind tunnel. I clearly remember watching 20 lbs of cobbles disappear from the blade as if by magic, while the shovel itself was nearly torn from my grasp. My cap, which I had pulled down until painfully tight, was snatched from my head as I staggered to retain my balance. Unbelievable, you might think, yet it took the combined efforts of Les and myself to close and secure those doors again. Having these pressures to contend with over the whole length of the train, it was no wonder we could only manage about 10 mph flat out!

With the winds came also the rain. Rains that only mountain dwellers can appreciate. Rains that travelled horizontally and even upwards in continual sheets, driving into every corner of the cab until we were drenched to the skin. Every drop lashing in with such fury that it stung the face like an air gun pellet.

Despite the discomfort brought about by these extreme climatic conditions, battling with the elements only added more spice and sense of achievement to the Carlisle runs. Even on those rare tranquil nights there was always some excitement to stir the blood. For example, on departing from Carlisle at 11.45 pm we always made as much haste as possible in an effort to cover the greatest practical distance before being overtaken by the London-bound express sleeper.

Usually, if all went well, we were turned inside at Mallerstang and as soon as we had halted I knocked back our steam pressure to keep the engine quiet, then listened. Almost immediately in the prevailing silence one could hear a faint rumbling roar modulated by a fickle breeze. This roar gradually grew in intensity until it could be heard as a distinct pounding beat reverberating from the mountainside. Looking down the track we were then able to pick out the tiny twin dots of headlamps surmounted by a column of red sparks, shooting skywards like streams of tracer bullets. With individual beats only just distinguishable, the volume of sound quickly increased to an ear-splitting crescendo as a re-built 'Royal Scot' blasted by, while blazing particles of coal fell like rain for several seconds. A fleeting glimpse revealed in the brilliant white firelight a fireman toiling with his shovel and the regulator invariably right across. Just what cut-off they were using was anyone's guess, but I imagine that it was at lease 35 to 40 per cent.

What superb engines those re-built 'Scots' were, seemingly revelling in the terrific thrashing they received on that long climb. Watching them performing over this section was a most thrilling spectacle. How dear old Tommy Charles would have loved to work the 'Scots' up there, and I, too, for that matter.

Over the past year or two certain pressures both external and also of my own making had been building up. Pressure, I regret to say, arising from good sound reasons for departing from British Railways. . . Although at this time life for me was happy and exciting on the Carlisles, promotion was going ahead so rapidly that in all probability I would be called upon to take my driver's examination within a couple of years. While this might appear to be a highly desirable situation, it must be borne in mind that when once a driver, I would have to return to the bottom rung of the ladder again - the Shed link. The prospect of several years of shed work followed by a lengthy stay in the Control was not one to send a fellow doing cartwheels in ecstasy. Moreover, with dieselisation and electrification already going ahead apace, it was very much on the cards that by the time I came out into the road links again there would be no more steam engines left to drive. To me the fascination of railways began and ended with steam locomotives. Take away these and there was very little left. Only a few trips as a passenger on diesel railcars were quite sufficient to convince me that I did not want to become a mere 'tram driver'.

For many years there had been an atmosphere of growing discontent, particularly among the senior drivers. In their heyday the work of an engine driver had been surrounded by a certain glamour and had commanded the position of prestige now afforded to airline pilots. They were also paid a salary commensurate with the high regard in which they were held, and this took them comfortably above average earnings. Since the war both status and relative pay had slipped steadily down the national scale and this, coupled with deteriorating conditions and continual line closures, gave rise to an understandable disquiet.

Despite grandiose schemes for modernisation, many felt at that period that British Railways was a dying industry and the advice form the majority of older drivers was 'Get out, young man, while you still can'. Split shifts, long and uncertain hours, getting up when everyone else was going to bed and working during holidays was extremely onerous and a tremendous disruption to family life. I had no children then, but my wife, along with all other wives of railwayman, was forced to suffer hours of loneliness and only the barest minimum of social life.

When, therefore, the opportunity to 'make a break' arrived in March 1959 I was already in a suitable state of mind to make a decision. In keeping with my life-long interest in fast, exciting and noisy machinery, I had developed a great fondness for cars, especially vintage, sport and racing cars, and had, during the previous year, become quite friendly with the proprietor of a garage in Solihull specialising in such vehicles. To work with and be surrounded by the machines that were

now my principal hobby was a chance too good to be missed, so in April, just over nine years after signing on with British Railways, I handed in my notice.

However, as may be expected, I timed this so that my final week went out in a blaze of glory, so to speak, working the 4.45 pm Glasgow.

Looking back over those nine years one is bound to ask the inevitable question - was it all worthwhile? The tremendous physical strain, the acquisition of a vast amount of specialised knowledge, the dirt, the privations, the battle with the elements, being roasted, soaked or frozen and, above all else, the long hours of working all round the clock.

The answer always comes out the same. Yes, it most certainly was. The rapid demise of the steam locomotive only serves to emphasise this, for such an opportunity can never occur again. Few other occupations offered the same excitement, satisfaction and sense of achievement as that of operating a steam locomotive, and added to this was the wonderful spirit of comradeship that existed on the footplate. Furthermore, the work developed an iron self-discipline that, once acquired, stood one in good stead for the rest of one's life.

I must admit that, having once departed, I gave little thought to railways until 1968, when my brother sadly pointed out that steam traction for all practical purposes had ceased to exist in this country. The shock of this realisation was as sadly traumatic as losing an old and dear friend, since from my earliest memories there had always been steam engines and I tended to suppose that there always would be.

Fortunately, dedicated enthusiasts all over the country soon got together in an endeavour to rectify in some small part this tragedy and preserve an element of our great steam heritage. It is to these tireless and far-sighted individuals that I dedicate this book, and if they derive some small measure of pleasure and inspiration from these pages, then I consider the effort will have been well worthwhile.

INDEX